WORKING-CLASS
COMIC BOOK HEROES

WORKING-CLASS COMIC BOOK HEROES

Class Conflict and Populist Politics in Comics

Edited by
Marc DiPaolo

University Press of Mississippi / Jackson

www.upress.state.ms.us

The University Press of Mississippi is a member of
the Association of American University Presses.

First printing 2018
∞

Library of Congress Cataloging-in-Publication Data

Names: Di Paolo, Marc, editor.
Title: Working-class comic book heroes : class conflict and populist politics
  in comics / edited by Marc DiPaolo.
Description: Jackson : University Press of Mississippi, [2018] | Includes
  bibliographical references and index. |
Identifiers: LCCN 2017048412 (print) | LCCN 2017048858 (ebook) | ISBN
  9781496816658 (epub single) | ISBN 9781496816665 (epub institutional) |
  ISBN 9781496816672 (pdf single) | ISBN 9781496816689 (pdf institutional)
  | ISBN 9781496816641 (hardcover : alk. paper) | ISBN 9781496818188 (pbk. :
  alk. paper)
Subjects: LCSH: Comic books, strips, etc.—History and criticism. | Working
  class in literature. | Social conflict in literature. | Populism in
  literature. | Superheroes in literature. | Working class authors.
Classification: LCC PN6714 (ebook) | LCC PN6714 .W67 2018 (print) | DDC
  741.5/9—dc23
LC record available at https://lccn.loc.gov/2017048412

British Library Cataloging-in-Publication Data available

For Dad

CONTENTS

"It's Just Us Here"

Kevin Michael Scott

Jack Kirby

Andrew Alan Smith

Marvel's Shamrock

Christina M. Knopf

The Working-Class PI (AKA Jessica Jones)

Terrence R. Wandtke

ACKNOWLEDGMENTS

I would like to thank Steve Gooch for encouraging me to produce a follow-up to *War, Politics and Superheroes: Ethics and Propaganda in Comics and Film* (2011)—a monograph with a title that upsets him because it is missing an Oxford comma. This volume, which stands on its own, is a continuation of my work, nonetheless, and exists thanks to his prodding. In addition, I am grateful to Will Brooker, Tracy Floreani, and Karen Green for their help finding contributors for this anthology.

I am also in debt to Michele Fazio, an invaluable manuscript reviewer, who provided me with much-needed assistance, information, and encouragement.

Finally, I want to express my love and thanks to my family, including my wife, Stacey, my children, Keira and Quentin, my brother Brian, and my parents, Ted and Cathy.

WORKING-CLASS
COMIC BOOK HEROES

INTRODUCTION
Cultivating Empathy: The Subversive Potential of Populist Comic Books

Marc DiPaolo

"Working Class Hero" is a diagnosis song. [John] Lennon sits you down on one of those uncomfortable tables in the examining room and explains the lab reports. . . . The weariness in Lennon's voice is that of a doctor who's seen too many like you and has grown tired of giving the bad news. . . . For Lennon, the working class is a social conditioning that starts at birth and ends with the eternal promise we still cling to in adulthood and clutch as we die: the possibility of climbing the ladder, punching through the glass ceiling, achieving the American Dream and becoming "like the folks on the hill." If there's any doubt this is a relentless and exhausting promise, the song's repetitive structure and funereal pace make those qualities felt. If the drudgery doesn't kill you, the insanity will.
—ROBERT LOSS, "John Lennon's 'Working-Class Hero': Boundaries, Mobility, and Honesty" (2016)[1]

This anthology is about the working-class comic book heroes—some super-powered, some not—who populate serialized comic book narratives that have been adapted into recent, high-profile films and television shows. These figures are analyzed and deconstructed; their roles as fictional stand-ins for real-world blue-collar figures are considered within a broader cultural and historical context, as well as placed within the shifting conventions of genre fiction. The writers and artists who created these characters are also discussed, most notably Jack Kirby, the working-class Jewish artist who created several of the most recognizable "Everyman" comic book heroes, including steroid-enhanced Nazi-smasher Captain America and the cigar-chomping Golem Ben Grimm, a.k.a. the Thing.

Those who find it hard to believe that comic books, especially superhero comic books, could possibly treat class issues seriously are not necessarily wrong. Many comic book narratives take place in a heavily mythologized, escapist America free of social-class divisions, or in fantastical environments, such as the Justice League Watchtower orbiting the Earth like the Island of Laputa floating above Balnibarbi. However, some comic books are known for confronting issues of class and race frequently. Among the most notable of these are *Daredevil, Luke Cage,* and *Captain America*—all of which feature significantly in these pages—as well as Dwayne McDuffie's *Damage Control* and Gail Simone's short-lived tour de force *The Movement* (2014), which is a commentary on Occupy Wall Street that prophetically predicted many of the core conflicts and issues of Black Lives Matter. Those who read these comics probably assumed, with good reason, that they would never be adapted into films or television shows designed for mass consumption. Furthermore, fans probably assumed that, should such comics ever be adapted, they would be stripped of all their social import and turned into purely escapist fare. And yet, against all possible expectations, the Marvel Cinematic Universe adaptations of the comic books *Daredevil, Luke Cage,* and *Captain America*—as well as Damage Control's inclusion in *Spider-Man: Homecoming* (2017)—have been particularly adept at crystalizing the working-class themes found in the comic books instead of eliding them. In some cases the adaptations have even been more effective at depicting class issues than the comics, which is not something that veteran comic book scholars and fans would necessarily expect, since film adaptations of comic books have tended to be more politically simplistic and reactionary than their source material. Oddly, multimedia heroic narratives such as *Daredevil* and *Captain America* sometimes offer more-insightful cultural commentary than the so-called news analysis provided by the corporate-owned twenty-four-hour infotainment channels and tabloid newspapers. This book considers, in detail, how comic books offer sometimes surprisingly insightful cultural commentaries about class issues in the United States and Great Britain—and why their representations of working-class characters and their lives are important to study.

Thanks to the rise of the superhero in the multimedia landscape and its dominance of the motion picture industry since 2000—and of (web) television since 2015—the world of scholarly publishing has seen a notable uptick in monographs and anthologies centered around the study of superheroes, especially those that examine representations of the war on terror in heroic fiction and those that examine the treatment of identity politics in multimodal superhero adventures. And yet, while there have been many excellent scholarly works that have considered issues of race and gender in superhero narratives—including Adilifu Nama's *Super Black: American Pop Culture and Black Superheroes* (2011) and Carolyn Cocca's *Superwomen: Gender, Power, and Representation* (2016)—and while Ramzi Fawaz's *The New Mutants: Superheroes and the Radical Imagination of American Comics* (2016) addresses class issues, this is the first entire book to explore issues of socioeconomic class, cultural capital, and economics in comic book "heroic fiction."[2]

Careful readers will note, however, that this book is very pointedly *not* called *Working-Class Superheroes* but *Working-Class Comic Book Heroes*. That is because the term *superhero* is too narrowly defined to be of use in this conversation: keeping any analysis of "class" in comics confined to a discussion of super-powered characters takes too many important representations of working-class individuals off the table. Therefore, working-class heroes of both the super-powered and non-super-powered variety will be examined: in addition to the ubiquitous Marvel and DC superheroes, this book examines several of the most culturally significant cowboy and gangster heroes of mixed-genre heroic narratives, including the heroes found in comic book dystopian, post-apocalyptic, and steam-punk universes. Covering non-superhero comic book characters in these pages provides the opportunity to include race and gender more fully in the conversation about class, and to dissect the protagonists of popular narratives such as *The Walking Dead* and *Preacher* who would not be appropriate inclusions in a study of superhero figures alone. While many scholars and fans might object to a character such as Rick Grimes being examined in the same book as Ben Grimm, the two characters are spiritual cousins; studying the two together, in the same anthology, makes strategic sense, and readers will discover that the comparisons will bear unexpected intellectual fruit. This qualifier notwithstanding, traditional superheroes and supervillains are, indeed, those figures most often discussed in these pages.

Furthermore, while this anthology deals to one degree or another with the film and television adaptation of the comic books discussed, the focus of each of these essays is, first and foremost, the comic book source material. Indeed, some essays make only fleeting references to adaptations in the interest of giving the comic book originals their due. The adaptations are significant, however, because of the extent to which they have granted the characters examined in this book broader exposure to the general public than they had in their four-color incarnations alone. While many of the most recognizably working-class comic book heroes are not yet household names, several veterans of 1970s era Marvel comics have been tapped to spearhead Marvel's Netflix-exclusive multi-series contract. Daredevil, Jessica Jones, and Luke Cage have all been given their own shows and form a team of urban vigilantes called the Defenders in a series of the same name. Producers of the *Daredevil* show were correct to boast that it more closely resembles the gritty, class-aware HBO series *The Wire* than traditional superhero escapist fare. Meanwhile, Eric Powell has launched a Kickstarter campaign to raise the money for the filming of an R-rated *Goon* animated motion picture and is confident that the film will be completed and released in the coming years. Class issues *should* be central to all these comic adaptations, but one might well expect that some of the more subversive commentaries on economic injustice and systemic oppression of the workers will be left on the printed page and will not be translated to the screen in their more mainstream adaptations. Indeed, the recent *Constantine* television series loses most of its source material's incisive commentary on Thatcher-era Britain by shifting the action to contemporary America and giving Constantine's highly ordinary cabbie best friend the superpower of invulnerability, thereby defeating the very purpose of the character "Chas" Chandler.

As Tim Hayes wrote in "I Sing the Body Elastic: Lamenting the New Compliant Super-Flesh," "Market forces have led the slickest entertainment corporations in the world to bite down hard on the literature of American comic-book superheroes: a loose cannon of wish-fulfillment myths, social commentary, agitprop and soap opera, often created on a shoestring by urban leftists and the occasional rightist outlier. . . . [F]or the most part superheroes have been compelled to meet the mainstream's expectations. And mainstream culture remains wedded to the myth of redemptive violence, a fact for which someday, someway, we will be held to account."[3] It remains to be seen how faithful the upcoming adaptations of working-class hero narratives will be to their source material, and how subversive they will be. Whatever their relative quality as works of art, entertainment, and social commentary, they will likely bring greater public attention to the most blue-collar and urban superheroes in the Marvel and DC canon, and they have the potential to join the ranks of Katniss Everdeen as widely beloved populist icons. Consequently, the time is right to analyze the comic books that have inspired the launch of these films and television shows alongside other comic book narratives informed by class issues that depict clashes between the working and ruling classes.

Many sociologists would argue that the three main ways of understanding class include the Marxist, Weberian, and postmodern scholarly traditions. The Marxist tradition regards class as a fundamentally antagonistic, socially constructed relationship. Consider the iconic opening to *The Communist Manifesto*, which observes, "The history of all hitherto existing society is the history of class struggles. . . . Our epoch [possesses] . . . this distinct feature: it has simplified class antagonisms. Society as a whole is more and more splitting up into two great hostile camps, into two great classes directly facing each other—Bourgeoisie and Proletariat."[4] In contrast, the Weberian tradition adopts a historically contingent view that class is a social force that can be mobilized into political action and may be an instrument of change. Finally, postmodernist scholars are interested in how class is constructed in society rhetorically, especially representations of class in popular culture. Since most of the essays in this collection are from the interdisciplinary field of "cultural studies," and not the discipline of sociology, they fit the most comfortably in the postmodern tradition identified above. Also, since cultural studies critics are often concerned with exploring popular culture narratives, academic scholarship, and political rhetoric as potential vehicles for enlightening and reforming the individual, the academy, and society, they are, arguably, in greater sympathy with the Weberian than the Marxist tradition. However, it is not necessarily true that the essayists are likely to fall *firmly* into either the Marxist or Weberian camp. Definitions of class are notoriously fluid, and discussions of its social and historical context are notoriously difficult. However, it is fair to say that the scholarly contributors to this anthology are more concerned with raising difficult ethical questions than with coming to smug theoretical conclusions about how to "define" class and "solve" the class problem. What this text is most concerned with is having the latitude to meditate upon the various ways in which comic books have depicted the American class structure and dramatized conflicts between individual heroic and villainous characters who exist within real or imagined class structures—or in a post-apocalyptic world that may have abolished class division to an astonishing degree. The book is designed to examine case studies of fictional heroes as analogues of real-life working-class figures to encourage greater empathy between members of different classes. Doing so will help scholar, undergraduate, and fan readers understand the very contemporary context of Trump's America through the lens of fictional characters who are understandably resonant with a broad swath of the public during this politically divided time. This is the key aim of the book—aesthetically, politically, morally, and intellectually: the essays in this book contemplate the social anxieties that attend class conflict in the United States and Great Britain, and consider how fictional comic book narratives depict these cultural anxieties— and *anxiety* is, indeed, an appropriate word to use when considering class in the Western world of the early twenty-first century.

Interestingly, while "class" is a deeply important subject and worthy of great attention and study, it is also one that traditionally makes many Americans uncomfortable, especially since most of them like to think of themselves as belonging to one vast middle class. As Michael Zweig argues in *The Working-Class Majority: America's Best Kept Secret* (2000), "Class is one of America's best-kept secrets. Any serious discussion has been banished from polite company."[5] Furthermore, an awareness of class conflicts and divisions tends to blunt people's ability to feel empathy for members of what might be considered 'rival' classes. As cultural studies scholar Paul Fussell observed in *Class: A Guide through the American Status System* (1983), people often unintentionally reveal themselves to be a member of a given class based on just how emotionally charged the topic makes them.

> A tendency to get very anxious suggests that you are middle class and nervous about slipping down a rung or two. On the other hand, upper-class people love the topic to come up: the more attention paid to the matter the better off they seem to be. Proletarians generally don't mind discussions of the subject because they know they can do little to alter their class identity. Thus, the whole class matter is likely to seem like a joke to them—the upper classes fatuous in their empty aristocratic pretentiousness, the middles loathsome in their anxious gentility. It is the middle class that is highly class-sensitive and sometimes class-scared to death."[6]

Fussell also makes the provocative observation that members of the different classes tend to define "class" differently from one another: "At the bottom, people tend to believe that class is defined by the amount of money you have. In the middle, people grant that money has something to do with it, but think education and the kind of work you do almost equally important. Nearer the top, people perceive that taste, values, ideas, style, and behavior are indispensable criteria of class, regardless of money or occupation or education."[7] Interestingly, the middle classes take the greatest pride in their education and use it as justification to distinguish themselves morally and intellectually from the lower orders, because using that metric provides the greatest boost to their personal pride. In contrast, had they placed greater weight upon financial factors in their class analysis, they would feel far greater affinity for the working classes, whom they do not have much more money than, than they would for the wealthiest individuals, whose bank accounts, investments, material possessions, and real-estate and business holdings dwarf their financial assets. Also, even the most educated of the middle classes are not wealthy enough to begin to know what would constitute having good taste in food, clothing, and culture from an upper-class perspective—but they are just educated enough to think that they do.

Fussell's class breakdown above falls along traditional lines—the three classes he describes are the lower class, the middle class, and the upper class. This most common distinction is not necessarily universally embraced by class scholars. There have been several variants, some of which seem to provide primarily semantic differences from one another, and some which are provocatively different in their framing of class issues. In the two-volume, posthumously published *Economy and Society* (1922), Max Weber found it instructive to make distinctions between "class" and "status," noting that "class" standing was determined by how much money a person had and the power that money afforded them, and "status" was more of a mark of prestige and cultural capital. Weber also noted that social groupings were also determined by "party"—which, of course, indicates political allegiances—and by "caste," in which groups could congregate or be segregated on the basis of religion or ethnicity.[8]

(To illustrate this point about Weber's distinction between class and status: Miss Bates in Jane Austen's *Emma* is a poor, unmarried woman with an aristocratic lineage, so she boasts high "status" in the small town of Highbury and fraternizes with the wealthy and noble while occupying a lower-class financial position. The Weasley family in Harry Potter is much like Miss Bates: they are a venerable old wizard family that has fallen on hard financial times. The disconnect between their class standing and their status makes them objects of disgust in the minds of the Malfoy family members, wizard-world aristocrats who have maintained their wealth and privileged lifestyle over the centuries. Notably, J. K. Rowling's favorite novel is *Emma*, so it makes sense that she would revisit Miss Bates through Arthur Weasley and his family.)

In *The Theory of the Leisure Class* (1899), Thorstein Veblen condemned the culture of "conspicuous consumption" that characterized his society, which he regarded as part of "the higher stages of barbarian culture." According to Veblen, "The leisure class as a whole comprises the noble and priestly classes, together with much of their retinue. The occupations of the class are correspondingly diversified, but they have the common economic characteristic of being non-industrial. These non-industrial upper-class occupations may be roughly comprised under government, warfare, religious observances, and sports. . . . Manual labor, industry, whatever has to do with the everyday work of getting a livelihood, is the exclusive occupation of the inferior class. This inferior class includes slaves and other dependents, and ordinarily also all women." Those laborers whose work is the most altruistic in nature, such as those who teach, clean, produce food, or heal, are those deemed the most contemptible by the values of this society, while those lower-class members who contribute to warfare or the manufacture of weapons are accorded the greatest respect that members of the lower orders are allowed, as befitting a violent, late-barbarian culture.[9]

In an analysis of the American class system, Italian journalist and literary critic Giuseppe Antonio Borgese posited that there were once four strata: "the financial class, the political class, the Intelligentsia, the Common Man." But the period following the Gilded Age and the Great Depression saw the political class fall under the control of the financial class—effectively merging them into one group—reducing the strata to three and throwing off the balance of a once well-functioning social order. Borgese noted that the numbers of those counted among the Common Man were vast. In contrast, the Intelligentsia was comprised primarily of a few thousand East Coast writers. He wrote: "One should not judge by numbers alone. It is intellectually among the best equipped in the world. . . . [However,] its influence over the public realm is almost nil."[10] Borgese suggests that there is great potential for the Intelligentsia to exert more influence than it does, and for the Common Man to organize into a truly potent force for change, but—as Antonio Gramsci lamented—"the economic-corporate structure has so far always reacted effectively against them."[11]

It may already be apparent that each of these approaches to understanding class has its own value—and they are not necessarily mutually exclusive. However, it is difficult to pick one definition of class and embrace it as one that works for all cultures and all time periods. E. P. Thompson argued as much in the preface to *The Making of the English Working Class* (1963). For Thompson, changing economic realities, technologies, social conventions, demographics, and other factors consistently muddy the clarity of discussions of class. Also, making note of class distinctions is only so useful—the realities of class are best understood by interactions between the classes and by the individuals who constitute those classes, and within a specific historical and cultural context. Thompson explains that "class happens when some men, as a result of common experiences (inherited or shared), feel and articulate the identity of their interests as between themselves, and as against other men whose interests are different from (and usually opposed to) theirs. . . . Class-consciousness is the way in which these experiences are handled in cultural terms: embodied in traditions, value-systems, ideas, and institutional forms. . . . Consciousness of class arises in the same way in different times and places, but never in *just* the same way."[12] Given the importance of considering historical circumstance, of a study of relational behaviors within and between classes, and of the changing manifestations of class consciousness and class conflict, this anthology's approach—a series of thematically related case studies of representations of class in comic book heroic fiction—is intellectually justifiable in the tradition of working-class studies scholarship.

One of the mental and emotional roadblocks to studying class issues in the United States stems from the fact that, ideally, *there shouldn't be class division in America*. From the perspective of the mythic-folkloric view of American history promulgated by our K-12 education system, America is not supposed to have different social classes. Since the United States was founded upon the ideal that "all men are created equal" and its Founding Fathers saw to it that aristocratic titles and honors were illegal, the myth of classlessness in America is a long-cherished one. The myth has a stronger hold over the American consciousness during some periods than it does during others, and it has certainly stretched to the breaking point in recent years. And that is a good thing. As Zweig has aptly observed, "Because class is a question of power, understanding class can add to the power of working people."¹³

Members of both the left and right wings of the political spectrum are sometimes invested in the vision of America as being composed of one mono-lithic class. However, how these left- and right-wing cultural commentators would describe that one monolithic class would differ greatly, and the ideologi-cal motivations behind promoting a monolithic class concept are vastly differ-ent. The myth of classlessness has tended to come from primarily conservative forces extolling the opportunities for upward mobility afforded by free-market capitalism. However, more left-leaning forces have made arguments that have also blended social and cultural differences between the lower classes in the interest of fostering solidarity between the middle and working classes against the ruling classes. The notion "We are the 99 percent"—and, eventually, "We are all working-class"—rose to prominence during, and in the wake of, the Occupy Wall Street protest movement sparked in New York City's Zuccotti Park on September 17, 2011. The protests spread around the world but were eventually shut down by coordinated law-enforcement interventions. Notably, several of the protestors photographed and filmed participating in OWS gatherings wore Guy Fawkes masks in honor of the anarchist hero V, from the graphic novel *V for Vendetta* (1989) written by Alan Moore and illustrated by David Lloyd (see chapter 6). Since appearing in the 2005 film adaptation directed by James McTeigue and written by Lilly Wachowski and Lana Wachowski, the "V" mask has become closely associated with members of the activist hacker group Anonymous, which has aligned itself with several of the populist politi-cal aims of the Occupy Wall Street Movement. OWS's harshest critics have declared the movement a failure, though it did help inspire successor populist movements and organizations, and brought to national prominence issues of corporate overreach in the realms of politics and economics and the effects of globalism and the Great Recession upon the broader American populace. The 2016 US presidential election saw further evidence of a populist discon-tent with establishment politics, with Democratic primary candidate Bernie Sanders employing Occupy Wall Street rhetoric to mobilize his supporters in a political revolution against the top 1 percent, and with Republican Party nomi-nee Donald Trump exploiting nationalist and anti-immigrant sentiments to build his base of support while endorsing protectionist economic policies and criticizing the Democratic Party's embracing of the Trans-Pacific Partnership. Trump's ascendancy to the White House, facilitated in part by older, white, rural, non-college-educated voters nationwide, as well as by the discontent of residents of the Rust Belt that had once formed a part of a reliable "Democratic firewall" of midwestern "blue states," brought class issues back to into the national conversation with a renewed sense of urgency in the mass media. Indeed, the iconic "working-class Trump voter" has been a centerpiece of mass media election autopsies for nearly a year. Despite this iconic voter's omnipresence in national news, many working-class studies scholars—and critics such as Ta-Nehisi Coates—have argued that the working classes have been assigned too much of the credit and blame for Trump's victory, when a broad coalition of white voters of all class levels cast their votes for him, motivated primarily by an unacknowledged racism and threatened sense of white privilege. Whatever its merits or limitations, the myth of the unwavering working-class supporter of Donald Trump has brought intense, sustained media attention to class issues in contemporary America for the first time in recent memory.

Academic writing tends not to be as "topical" as journalistic writing, but this is a national conversation that scholarly texts should take part in. Some of the already-extant literature on the Rust Belt and deindustrialization includes *Boom, Bust, Exodus: The Rust Belt, the Maquilas, and a Tale of Two Cities* by Chad Broughton (revised and reissued in 2016 specifically because of the election), *Once in a Great City: A Detroit Story* by David Maraniss (2015), and *Nothin' but Blue Skies: The Heyday, Hard Times, and Hopes of America's Industrial Heartland* by Edward McClelland (2013). J. D. Vance's 2016 memoir *Hillbilly Elegy* and Philipp Meyer's 2009 debut novel *American Rust* are two more significant works on this theme. In addition, as of the writing of this introduction, Linkon is finishing work on *The Half-Life of Deindustrialization*, forthcoming in 2018 from the University of Michigan Press. More books on this topic are no doubt being written at this moment, with good reason. Since populist politics of the left- and right-wing varieties played a significant role in 2016, it is even more important that academia look more seriously at class issues in American, European, and world politics.

Of all the extant scholarly literature on comic books and graphic novels, the books that come closest to treating class and economic themes the most seriously are the industry histories and biographies of the writers and artists who have labored in the comics industry, most of whom were not properly paid for creating characters and storylines that became household names and transformed their once-modest publishers into multimedia corporate giants. For example, the tragic histories of how DC Comics did not adequately compensate Jerry Siegel and Joe Shuster for creating the Superman universe and how Marvel Comics underpaid Kirby for cocreating a sizable percentage of the most recognizable characters of the Marvel Universe—including the Hulk, the Fantastic Four, the X-Men, and a wide array of villains and supporting characters—are featured in Gerard Jones's *Men of Tomorrow: Geeks, Gangsters, and the Birth of the Comic Book* (2004) and Charles Hatfield's *Hand of Fire: The Comics Art of Jack Kirby* (2012).[14]

Focusing more on the other side of the economic spectrum and class divide is Dan Raviv's *Comic Wars: Marvel's Battle for Survival* (2004). That book's white-collar narrative concerns the 1996 bankruptcy of Marvel Comics, and its cast of characters includes the corporate players who regard comic book properties purely as arbitrage opportunities.[15] In addition to these works, my own monograph, *War, Politics and Superheroes: Ethics and Propaganda in Comics and Film* (2011), concerns representations of class in the comic books themselves. I examine the working-class superheroes Spider-Man, the Punisher, and John Constantine, offer close readings of class conflicts in *Batman* and other adventures, and analyze comic book depictions of former president Barack Obama as a thwarted champion of the disenfranchised.[16]

Outside of the realm of superhero comics, autobiographical comics by writers such as Harvey Pekar offer first-person accounts of working-class life. Pekar chronicles his formative years as the child of Polish Jewish immigrant shopkeepers in Cleveland in *The Quitter* (2005), and his later years working as a file clerk at Cleveland's Veterans Administration Hospital in *American Splendor* (1986).[17] He also adapted Studs Terkel's *Working* into a graphic novel in 2009. "Harvey Pekar Meets the Thing," a 2010 story about Pekar's encounter with the fictional character Ben Grimm, was the last story he wrote before his death. In the vignette, Grimm—a Hungarian Jew who went to the same Hebrew school as Pekar—asks his childhood friend to secure him a stress-free job with secure health benefits at the VA hospital. After all, Grimm tells Pekar, he's not as well paid as you'd think, is in enormous debt, and is expecting to lose his job with the Fantastic Four at any moment.[18] Notably, books and essays that examine Pekar and other working-class comics artists sometimes confront class issues directly but are often more concerned about psychoanalyzing the artists, dissecting the conventions of confessional autobiography, or discussing sexual trauma and identity politics. A book such as *Autobiographical Comics: Life Writing in Pictures* (2012) by Elisabeth El Refaie does all the above.[19]

At this juncture, it is important to offer a brief overview of the canon of published working-class studies scholarship. Unfortunately, despite yeoman work being done by scholars who are members of the Working-Class Studies Association, the Center for the Study of Working-Class Life at SUNY-Stony Brook, the Labor and Working-Class History Association, and related organizations, academia remains reluctant to engage in a discussion of class-based issues in popular culture and society. The academic presses most concerned with publishing working-class studies research include the University of Michigan (especially within its Class and Culture series), Cornell University

Press, and Routledge, the last of which will soon be issuing *The Routledge International Handbook of Working-Class Studies*, edited by Tim Strangleman, Christie Launius, and Michele Fazio. These presses aside, too many academic publishers seem content to avoid releasing works that explore class issues, instead leaving fielding such discussions to bloggers, underground presses, and columnists from *The Nation*, *Jacobin*, *In These Times*, and *Mother Jones*. Academia's reticence to engage with working-class issues is part of a long-standing tradition of ignoring the working class. While scholars are content to study middle- to elite-class culture and social mores all the time, working-class issues are another matter. As John Russo and Sherry Lee Linkon observe in "What's New about New Working-Class Studies?" (2005):

> Recently, a new version of multiculturalism has emerged that emphasizes the intersections among multiple categories of identity and culture. Yet most of these programs define their focus as the intersection among race, ethnicity, and gender, leaving class out of the equation, even though the people studied are often working-class. Students and scholars alike resist studying class, in part because class is a difficult concept to discuss, both personally and intellectually.... Others resist on a more political basis, fearing that working-class studies is too close to "whiteness studies," or that it is really a way of claiming space in the conversation for white, working-class, straight men. For others, talking about class may complicate discussions of the marginalization of people on the basis of race or gender; after all, looking at class differences reminds us that some people of color are in positions of privilege relative to others. For still others, lingering fears remain from earlier 'red scare' periods when leftist scholars who work focused on class were vulnerable to repression both in society [and in] ... the academy.[20]

According to Russo and Linkon, the foundation for contemporary working-class studies is labor history, which has traditionally been concerned with the lives of white, working-class men, and the consequence was that, in academia, "'working-class' came to be read as by definition white, male, racist, and sexist, while issues of gender and race eclipsed attention to class consciousness and class organizing."[21] Academia is not alone in keeping class awareness at arm's length. Even members of the working classes themselves have an undeveloped sense of their own class and their relationship to the broader class system. Some of the most helpful observations on this point may be found in the writings of activist and intellectual Theodore W. Allen, author of the two-volume academic study *The Invention of the White Race* (1994 and 1997). In formulating his response to David R. Roediger's *The Wages of Whiteness* (1991), Allen wrote:

According to the consensus, the relative absence of manifestations of class conscious American labor is to be ascribed to six peculiar factors of United States historical development: 1) the existence, from the very founding of the state, of the right to vote and other democratic liberties; 2) the heterogeneity of composition of the United States working class, a conglomeration of many tongues and kindreds; 3) the "safety valve" for social discontent provided by the availability of homesteading opportunities in the West; 4) the relatively greater access to social mobility in America; 5) the relative shortage of labor, resulting in a higher level of wages as compared with that prevailing in other countries; 6) the historic precedence of the trade union over the labor party in the United States, as contrasted to continental Europe, a condition facilitating the openly anti-socialist anti-labor party policies of the dominant corrupt "aristocracy of labor" within the working-class movement.[22]

Allen argues that these factors are all important to consider but fail to take into account the role that white supremacism plays in limiting the average American worker's class consciousness. A lack of awareness of the pernicious racism inherent in "American exceptionalism" continues to discourage political solidarity and true social awareness across the color line within the members of the working classes.

While there may not be adequate class awareness among average Americans, and there may not be "enough" regularly published working-class studies scholarship, there is, nevertheless, an excellent canon of literature on the topic waiting to be explored by interested parties. Among its significant foundational texts are those often designated as "classical sociological theory," including the writings of Karl Marx, Emile Durkheim, and Max Weber, as well as early works in the academic field of cultural studies, most notably the works of Thompson and Stuart Hall. Despite academia's reluctance to embrace working-class studies, a number of notable papers, journals, monographs, memoirs, and anthologies have been published by academic and trade presses and are milestone works in the field that build upon the foundations established by these early texts.[23] Some blend history and activism to make broad points about the potential reconstitution of society along a more egalitarian model, as does Gareth Stedman Jones's *An End to Poverty? A Historical Debate* (2004). Other books take a tighter-beam, individualistic focus, blending memoir and cultural commentary, including bell hooks's *Where We Stand: Class Matters* (2000) and Alfred Lubrano's *Limbo: Blue-Collar Roots, White-Collar Dreams* (2004).[24] Among the additional books that treat intersections of class, race, and ethnicity are *The Dignity of Working Men: Morality and the Boundaries of Race, Class, and Immigration* by Michèle Lamont (2002), *Unequal Childhoods: Class,*

Race, and Family Life, 2nd edition (2011) by Annette Lareau, and the anthology *Generation X Professors Speak* (2013) edited by Elwood Watson.[25]

Bringing labor and class issues to the forefront of literary studies, fighting to legitimize cultural studies in the academy, and expanding the curriculum taught in the classroom are the works of Paul Lauter and Janet Zandy. Further studies that blend working-class awareness, labor history, and literary studies include the scholarship of Michelle M. Tokarczyk and Laura Hapke. In the realm of film studies, Christopher Beach examines representations of the working classes in *Class, Language, and American Film Comedy* (2002), and Tom Zaniello wrote *Working Stiffs, Union Maids, Reds, and Riffraff: An Expanded Guide to Films about Labor* (2003) and *The Cinema of Globalization: A Guide to Films about the New Economic Order* (2007). Books on British kitchen-sink dramas, angry-young-man films, and comic-realistic directors such as Mike Leigh, Andrea Arnold, and Ken Loach by a variety of film scholars help illuminate class issues in Great Britain, including *Fires Were Started: British Cinema and Thatcherism* (2007) by Lester Friedman, and *Devised and Directed by Mike Leigh* (2013), which I coedited with Bryan Cardinale-Powell.[26]

Calls for class solidarity and organization against a global corporate elite are growing increasingly important to the field of working-class studies, and some of the most notable texts in this vein include Michael Zweig's *The Working-Class Majority: America's Best Kept Secret* (2000) and *What's Class Got to Do with It?: American Society in the Twenty-First Century* (2004), Lisa Dodson's *The Moral Underground: How Ordinary Americans Subvert an Unfair Economy* (2009), and Kim Scipes's *Building Global Labor Solidarity in a Time of Accelerating Globalization* (2016). [27] The works of progressive theologians are becoming more important to working-class studies as well. Joerg Rieger has written several books on intersections of religion and class, including one with his wife, grassroots organizer Rosemarie Henkel-Rieger. Jeremy Posadas, meanwhile, authored the significant essay "Theological Complicity in the Disappearing of the Working Class" for the theology journal *Dialog* in 2016.

While other studies of literary representations of the working classes exist, a study of comics and class is long overdue, as is a study of comic book heroes and class. *Working-Class Comic Book Heroes* therefore is designed to address the diverse concerns of working-class studies, comics studies, and media studies in the same anthology. The class discussions of this anthology take place within the framework provided by Russo and Linkon, who observe that new working-class studies

ask[s] questions about how class works for people at work, at home, and in the community. We explore how class both unites and divides working-class people, which highlights the importance of understanding how class shapes and is shaped by race, gender, ethnicity, and place. We reflect on the common interests as well as the divisions between the most commonly imagined version of the working class—industrial, blue-collar workers—and workers in the "new economy" whose work and personal lives seem, at first glance, to place them solidly in the middle class. In the twenty-first century . . . defining who is or is not working class is a slippery, complex task, and class as a concept carries multiple, contradictory, and complementary meanings. Understanding that class is a homograph (a word that has multiple, shifting, contested meanings), new working-class studies takes as its mission not the struggle among scholars and theorists to reach agreement about what class is but rather the exploration of how class works, as both an analytical tool and a basis for lived experience.[28]

The contributors featured in this volume include comics studies scholars, historians, literary scholars, communication and media studies scholars, professors of rhetoric and composition, women and gender studies, and comics bloggers and journalists. The diversity of disciplines in evidence provides a variety of voices and a narrative richness that helps ensure that class issues are treated from multiple angles. Throughout the book, scholars will discuss specific "working-class comic book heroes/anti-heroes/villains," what cultural values and anxieties they represent, and why their particular depictions of working-class figures are artistically and ideologically significant. In these times, when (super) hero stories cannot be more popular and issues of class and economics cannot be more pressing, the importance of such an anthology is apparent.

We Are All Working Class

In the 1990s, when the New Democrats and New Labour, under the leadership of self-described center-left leaders Bill Clinton and Tony Blair, embraced the neoliberal economic policies once associated primarily with Ronald Reagan and Margaret Thatcher, the interconnected American and British mass media began encouraging citizens of the Western countries to look upon themselves as members of one great middle class. While the idea that Americans might see themselves as belonging to one uniform class with equal access to the American Dream is nothing new, the notion that "we are all middle class" took hold with a vengeance in the years immediately preceding and following 9/11. Thanks to globalism and the economic opportunities afforded by the fledgling World Wide Web, the Clinton–Blair era promoted the idea that class division was a thing of the past, and if we are not all financially stable and successful yet, we all soon might be if we all commit to getting a college degree. One

consequence of this public relations campaign is that poorer and more working-class individuals whose very existence did not support the thesis that "we
are all middle class" were consistently caricatured and demonized in the press,
reality television, and popular culture as a whole, a phenomenon that Owen
Jones describes in his study of British culture, *Chavs: The Demonization of the
Working Class* (2011).[29]

Some of those who are most keenly aware of both the demonization of the
working classes and the sizable cultural gulf between the middle and working
classes are the working-class studies scholars in academia who grew up in blue-
collar backgrounds, were the first members of their family to attend college and
earn doctoral degrees, and now find themselves colleagues of faculty members from more privileged backgrounds. Dubbed class "Straddlers" by Alfred
Lubrano, these scholars find themselves too "elite" and "educated" to return
comfortably to the locales, friendships, and family gatherings of their formative
years but too rough around the edges and practical-minded to fit in properly
with the often bureaucratic, uber-philosophical, or merely snooty worldviews
of middle- and upper-class academics. Straddlers often have Facebook feeds
that include posts by both middle-class and working-class friends and family members, and the disparity between the tone and content of these posts is
often striking and troubling on several levels. In *Reading Classes: On Culture
and Classism in America* (2012), Straddler academic Barbara Jensen paints a
striking portrait of what it is like navigating such a Facebook feed:

> On one side of the class boundary, there are the real lives of working-class people
> ... that is all but completely invisible to anyone not of their class. And the disinterest
> goes both ways—they don't care what *people like that* think of them. The trouble is
> that the people they don't care about administer so many of the invisible particulars
> of their lives, deciding whether there are jobs or not, what they get paid at work,
> whether or not there are layoffs or forced overtime, the kind of education their chil-
> dren will receive in school, their ability to fact-check what crooked politicians and
> preachers holler at them, and much more.
>
>   On the other side of the class boundary, in my middle-class world, there are the
> ones who really believe they deserve so much more than the working classes.... [W]
> hile they may make anywhere from $20 to $1,500 an hour, they are the stockholders
> who vote to take away $2 an hour from people who make, and try to support a family
> on, $10 an hour. They ... routinely dismiss and denigrate working people, laughing at
> their language, making fun of their political views, and denigrating their religion.[30]

Jensen is using measured language to frame a tragic and frustrating scenario
while addressing an educated, middle-class academic reader. She is describing

a personal and cultural pain in an intellectual voice. Barbara Ehrenreich is the journalist and activist most known for reminding the American people that class differences exist in America with the publication of her landmark 2001 book, *Nickel and Dimed: On (Not) Getting By in America*. As someone who has, like Jensen, lived as a member of both the lower and middle classes, Ehrenreich uses her position as a journalist and author to write on behalf of the working poor, and to give eloquent public voice to their rage. She herself was poor growing up, experienced poverty again during the period following her marriage, and returned to low-wage jobs as an undercover journalist researching working-class culture for her nonfiction writing. As she explains:

> To be poor is to be treated like a criminal, under constant suspicion of drug use and theft. It means having no privacy, since the boss has the legal right to search your belongings for stolen items. It involves being jerked around unaccountably, like the time Wal-Mart suddenly changed my schedule, obliterating the second job I had lined up. It means being ordered to "work through" injuries and illness, like the debilitating rash I once acquired from industrial strength cleaning fluids.
>
> And what was most amazing to me: Being a low-wage worker means being robbed by the very employer who is monitoring *you* so insistently for theft. You can be forced to work overtime without pay or made to start working forty-five minutes before the time clock starts ticking. . . .
>
> [P]overty is not a culture or a character defect: it is a shortage of money. And that shortage arises from grievously inadequate pay, aggravated by constant humiliation and stress, as well as outright predation by employers, credit card companies, and even law enforcement agencies.[31]

Ehrenreich—like Linda Tirado, author of *Hand to Mouth: Living in Bootstrap America* (2014)—makes note of the assumptions that so many Americans from more privileged backgrounds have about the working classes. Typically, the financially well off moralize about poor people who "just need to get their act together," or go to college, or stop smoking or drinking or eating junk food, or stop having multiple children out of wedlock with different fathers. During the ten years she spent on a speaking tour of college campuses, conferences, and church gatherings, Ehrenreich encountered many fraternity-boy business majors who have been brainwashed by their Economics 101 professors into thinking that "the existing class structure is just, fair, and unchangeable."[32] After all, the American Dream promises that, with a little gumption and effort, all working-class people can class-jump the way that Jensen did. And yet, in a world of corporate globalism, crippled unions, government austerity budgets, wage theft, widespread hunger, and jobless economies, downward mobility seems more the norm than upward mobility. Indeed, many homeless PhDs probably began their career arcs convinced they could replicate Jensen's success in academia and, thanks to the dearth of tenure-track jobs, found that they could not.

Tirado has had an unstable life, going through alternating periods of financial stability and financial strife. She became an unintentional Internet sensation when in a 2013 online discussion she came to the eloquent defense of people on food stamps, reflecting upon the worst period of her life during a moment of relative financial stability. As her fame increased, her volatile financial standing evoked fierce debate from pundits, journalists, fans, and bloggers, as her "street cred" as a bona fide member of the working classes was discussed and debated. Anyone who searches for Tirado's name on Google will note that two of the first search engine results that will appear are the *RealClearPolitics* article from December 13, 2013, "Linda Tirado's Poverty Tale: Not Quite Fake, Far from Accurate," and a piece from *The Nation* published on December 11, 2013, "Linda Tirado Is Not a Hoax." This Internet controversy should surprise no one. Those who bring attention to a social issue of enormous import can expect to face a barrage of ad hominem arguments leveled at them by employees of the corporate media in response to their message. After all, why talk about a complex and emotionally and morally fraught issue when it is far easier to shoot the messenger instead? We see similar claims of "hypocrites unmasked" whenever a climate change activist is ridiculed for flying around the world trying to convince political and corporate leaders to develop renewable energy resources. Instead of being praised for their efforts, these activists are routinely mocked for the size of their carbon footprint by bloggers and reporters working for infotainment news sources. That specious argument stands ready to deploy, no matter which environmentalist steps forward to discuss the environmental crisis, and no matter how pure their actions and intentions are. The same kinds of personal attacks are always ready to be deployed against any "Marxist" or "phony" who tries to educate the American people about the lives of the working classes. Despite the "controversy" and "debate" over whether or not Tirado *has always been* and *will always be* working class, it is clear that Tirado's experiences temporarily living in poverty gave her an important perspective that she could share, especially on the issue of "downward mobility." Speaking from experience, Tirado observed that "downward mobility" is a reality for many:

> In fact, the Urban Institute found that half of Americans will experience poverty at some point before they're sixty-five. Most will come out of it after a relatively short time, 75 percent in four years. But that still leaves 25 percent who don't get out quickly, and the study also finds that the longer you stay in poverty, the less likely it becomes that you will ever get out.

Most people who live near the bottom go through cycles of being in poverty and being just above it—sometimes they're okay and sometimes they're underwater. It depends on the year, the job, how healthy you are. What I can say for sure is that downward mobility is like quicksand. Once it grabs you, it keeps constraining your options until it's got you completely.

I slid to the bottom through a mix of my own decisions and some seriously bad luck. I think that's true of most people. While it can seem like upward mobility is blocked by a lead ceiling, the layer between lower-middle class and poor is horrifyingly porous from above. A lot of us live in that spongy divide.[33]

As it turns out, many comic book heroes live in the same spongy divide. Although many of us do not allow ourselves to feel much empathy for real-world figures such as Tirado, perhaps we are willing to extend more sympathy to our favorite comic book characters when they find themselves in the kinds of dire financial and social straits that Tirado had to face in her life. In this way, contemplating the pain suffered by comic book characters can be a useful exercise in cultivating greater empathy for real-world working-class heroes who deserve greater respect, support, solidarity, and kindness than they often receive from the rest of society. Tirado and Ehrenreich are engaged in a campaign to undermine Establishment-led efforts to stereotype and marginalize members of the working classes in the manner described by Owen Jones in *Chavs: The Demonization of the Working Class*. Some of the most socially aware comic books are engaged in a similar project of subversion of anti-working-class sentiment, though they are disguised as harmlessly apolitical entertainment for the classic "fifteen- to thirty-five-year-old male" target demographic. As a case in point, one of the comic books that is most skilled at exploding the myth that all members of the working classes are demons is a comic book *about a demon*.

The title character of the comic book *Hellboy* is a demon who protects humanity from a variety of supernatural threats, including other demons and interdimensional invaders that resemble classic H. P. Lovecraft–style tentacled monsters. The heroic Hellboy is a celebration of Old World, blue-collar machismo—a Jack Kirby–style breed of manhood that has arguably vanished since the dwindling of the World War II generation and the fall of organized labor. Indeed, *Hellboy* creator Mike Mignola revealed (on the special features for the home video release of the 2006 *Hellboy: Sword of Storms*) that the inspiration for his character was his cabinetmaker father, who was injured daily and merely shrugged off his array of wounds to press on and get the job done. Guillermo del Toro, who directed two *Hellboy* films and produced two *Hellboy* animated movies, called Mignola a "genius" and praised the comic

As the tagline of the poster to the 2008 film *Hellboy: The Golden Army* indicates, working-class comic book heroes carry the stigma of "monstrousness" often borne by their real-world counterparts. This means it is invariably surprising when working-class characters are depicted as heroic instead of villainous. Pictured here are Ron Perlman as Hellboy, Selma Blair as Liz Sherman, and Doug Jones as Abe Sapien. The film, directed by Guillermo del Toro, is an adaptation of the Mike Mignola comic series. Photo courtesy of Universal Pictures.

creator for celebrating a working-class male character. In del Toro's *Hellboy II: The Golden Army* (2008), the American public discovers Hellboy's existence and is terrified of his crimson skin, massive stone hand, and sawed-off demon's horns. Unimpressed that Hellboy has stood between Earth and the apocalypse on a multitude of occasions, everyday Americans are too prejudiced against demons to accept the notion that one of their number could be redeemable and "one of the good guys." Therefore, the public shuns Hellboy, making him doubt whether he was right to choose to live his life serving a populace that hates and fears him. The prejudice that Hellboy faces works well as a commentary on racism. It is also a very effective metaphor for classism.

A similar subversion of reader expectations may be found in *The Goon*. Eric Powell's comic book series is a horror-comedy about two mob extortionists who protect a small town from being overrun by an encroaching, ever-expanding zombie horde. The title character is a tight-lipped, hard-drinking, muscle-bound figure with a heavily scarred face, who would be a villain in a comic like *Dick Tracy* but is the hero of his own comic. Powell's retro artistic style, gleeful enthusiasm for violence, and strain of anti-intellectualism earmark the comic book as conservative and nostalgic, but its anarchic, pseudo–Marx Brothers-style humor makes it a favorite of many liberal comics readers. In its earliest issues, the comic book's humor is broad, but it grows more complex, serious, and poignant as it proceeds, surprising readers with its many plot twists and the unexpected emotional depths of the seemingly apish protagonist. This narrative and thematic arc is a mix of the deliberate, intuitive, and accidental on Powell's part. In an interview Powell describes how he created *The Goon* to be a pastiche of Depression-era crime fiction as well as the Universal monster films of the 1930s and 1940s. New to the craft of writing his own comics, Powell did not have a master plan for the narrative but allowed the story to unfold organically. While this explanation suggests that Powell never *planned* to make *The Goon* unexpectedly deep and cleverly anti-elitist, he later reveals that part of his intent from the beginning was to break down the walls between the genres and challenge reader expectations.

> I wanted to be able to tell tragic stories, humor and horror and anything that interested me and I had the idea that . . . the Goon got his scars in Chinatown. . . . I wanted it to be a sad story that wasn't funny at all. Because I wanted it to twist the readers' idea of what the comic should be. I wanted to surprise readers, to keep them guessing what I was trying to go for with the comic. It's important for me that the characters, whether they're goofy or cartoony, should still have emotional depth. . . . You're limiting yourself to what you can do with the character if you yourself see the character as one-dimensional. Some of the funniest people on the planet are the most tragic. You hear all the time about comedians and these tragic sad lives that

they had, but through their comedy they found an escape or release from that. I want to have characters that show some depth and have a little more meaning than just something out there for a laugh.[34]

This quote is from an interview, and Powell is speaking extemporaneously, but he is describing a process by which he frustrates reader expectations about how comic books, genre storytelling, heroic fiction, humor, and blue-collar manhood should be perceived. Powell clearly feels that comic book readers have an overly simplified view of all the above, and one of his goals in creating *Goon* stories is challenging these narrow-minded perspectives.

Indeed, the medium of comic books is fascinating and troublingly well suited to both reinforcing and exploding stereotypes, as both the infamous yellow-peril racial stereotypes of World War II era comic books and the stereotype-exploding contemporary graphic novel work of Asian American auteur Gene Luen Yang demonstrate. In an essay from the scholarly anthology *Multicultural Comics* (2010)—which examines Yang's comics, and those of his contemporaries Adrian Tomine and Derek Kirk Kim—Jared Gardner crafts a history of the comic book medium that traces its evolution from racist, single-panel political cartoons published in "yellow journalism" tabloids of the nineteenth century to a sequential art medium co-opted by a newly minted population of immigrant journalists in the early twentieth century. According to Gardner, these "newer immigrants or the children of recent immigrants" proved themselves adept at subversively undermining ubiquitous racist stereotypes through the very medium that so effectively perpetuated them in the first place. However, Gardner contends that it is important to be aware that

> the formal properties of the medium itself [played] a significant role in the beginnings of a shift away from cartoon racism toward what we might call "graphic alterity." . . . A single-panel cartoon gag of an ethnic or racial stereotype is contained by its frame; it does the work of stereotyping as the term originally was defined: printing from a fixed mold. It is static and resists ambiguity, directing the reader to very specific ways of reading. . . . But if the single-panel comic can put the gap between word and image in the service of racist stereotype, this gap—once combined with the space between the panels and the vital role of individual readers in making up the difference—is precisely what makes the sequential comic so resistant to racialized work.[35]

Here again, it takes only a simple thought experiment to translate Gardner's observations about the comic medium's ability to both reinforce and explode *racial* stereotypes into an awareness of how the medium can be equally adept at both reinforcing and exploding *classist* stereotypes. Consciously or

Promotional art for *The Goon* comic book series, created by artist and writer Eric Powell. The title character is a muscular, horribly scarred antihero who protects a small town from regular attacks by supernatural beings. This picture is unusual, because it depicts a moment of political solidarity between the working-class Goon and his bitter enemies, the hordes of "great unwashed" zombies. Art by Eric Powell.

subconsciously, Powell and Mignola are both engaged in an effort to use the medium of comic book heroic fiction to turn in on themselves widespread public assumptions that members of the working classes are monsters. Their artistic representations of the "blue-collar" Hellboy as a giant red demon with shorn-off horns as well as the scarred face and exaggerated musculature of the Goon would seem to go a long way toward validating the notion that members of the working class are "monsters." If Hellboy and the Goon are represented in only one static image—one comic book panel or cover, for example—then they do, indeed, risk reinforcing such a stereotype. However, posters, action figures, and promotional materials aside, Hellboy and the Goon live in multipanel narratives that aid in their creators' efforts to shame audience members for their latent tendencies to underestimate or misjudge members of the working classes. Indeed, the substance of the *Goon* and *Hellboy* comic narratives—a combination of the words and thoughts and actions of these characters, the way they are treated by other characters, and the very nature of the Scott McCloud–dubbed "gutters" described above by Gardner—contributes to Powell's and Mignola's efforts to unmask the stereotypes for the lies that they are.

The comic book medium is not the only place where the working classes are ironically depicted as monstrous. Tony Williams reveals in *The Cinema of George A. Romero: Knight of the Living Dead* (2015) that the multimedia series of *Living Dead* zombie movies and comic books by Romero, starting with the classic independent film *Night of the Living Dead* (1968) and ending with the 2014 Marvel Comics miniseries *Empire of the Dead*, depicts zombies as shifting metaphors that, alternatively and simultaneously, represent masses of "othered" figures—from the homeless, to members of racial and ethnic minorities, to members of the working classes.[36] When they are not serving as a metaphor for an apocalyptic event, the zombies are stand-ins for "the great unwashed." Romero tends to begin his horror films casting the zombies as frightening masses of cannibals eager to swarm respectable middle-class suburban communities and rip apart and devour the citizenry, but he usually ends his narratives by suggesting that the civilized, middle-class people are the real monsters, and the zombies are only what they have been made by society. Keeping this tradition in mind, it is particularly evocative in *The Goon* comic book when the title character is pitted against hordes of zombies and does what he can to behead them all in the service of protecting a small American town. It is equally—if not *more*—evocative, when Powell draws the Goon standing in solidarity with his fellow proles, the zombies, in a picket line protesting low wages, the gentrification of society, and corporate rule. At moments such as that, the Goon can look past the external differences between himself and the zombies and see what they have in common. Yes, he is alive and they are undead, but *they are all working-class*. This notion is ridiculous in the context of a zombie apocalypse story but profound in its moral and social implications in the real world.

Like the title character of *The Incredible Hulk*, who is one part werewolf and one part Frankenstein monster, the Thing of the Fantastic Four seems to be a horror movie monster who has wandered into a superhero comic book by mistake. The Thing is a golem. He is monstrous, Jewish, and working-class. He is also one of the most lovable characters in the history of Marvel Comics. This stereotype-affirming/challenging juxtaposition of character traits found in a 1960s character anticipates those of Hellboy, who first appeared in 1993, and the Goon, who debuted in 1995. The Thing is an ugly, angry rock man who explores the universe and defends the Earth alongside the more glamorous and traditionally "superheroic" members of his adoptive family, the married Reed and Sue Richards, and Sue's brother, Johnny Storm. Externally, he is monstrous. His speech patterns are classically blue-collar and might suggest, to the unenlightened, that he is uneducated. His manners are unpolished and his

Michael Chiklis played the iconic working-class comic book hero Ben Grimm (a.k.a. the Thing) in director Tim Story's 2005 film adaptation of Marvel's *The Fantastic Four*. Chiklis also appeared as the Thing in *4: Rise of the Silver Surfer* (2007), and Jamie Bell inherited the role in the 2015 *F4NTASTIC*. Promotional art courtesy of 20th Century Fox.

demeanor occasionally fierce. However, the Thing has the most beautiful blue eyes imaginable, and the eyes are the windows into the soul.

The members of the Fantastic Four all have elemental powers. The elastic Reed has a free-flowing body that evokes the element of water. Sue, the Invisible Woman, is symbolically an air elemental. Johnny Storm, the Human Torch, is (obviously) the fire elemental. The Thing, with his rock-hard body, is Earth. In the medieval cosmology found in Dante's *Paradiso* and *The Cosmopraphia* of Bernardus Silvestris, the Earth elemental would carry the least moral weight. In the very different moral cosmology laid out by *Fantastic Four* writer Roberto Aguirre-Sacasa in *Fantastic Four: Season One* (2011), the elementals are balanced out in a way that would seem counterintuitive to everyone except those who read the comics and know these characters well. Aguirre-Sacasa identifies Sue as the "heart" of the team, Johnny the "body," Reed the "brain," and the Thing the "soul" of the Fantastic Four. The Thing's eyes are beautiful, and his soul is beautiful, and, therefore, the soul of the Fantastic Four is beautiful.

Considering all the above information together, we can observe something about the Thing, a.k.a. Ben Grimm of Yancy Street in Brooklyn, that is true of many working-class comic book heroes, and many members of the working classes in the real world.

The Thing is a monster.

He is a hero.

He is working-class.

He is beautiful *despite* being working-class.

He is beautiful *because* he is working-class.

Who are the Working-Class Comic Book Heroes?

Throughout their history, superheroes have appeared in comic books, films, and television narratives depicted as secularized demigod figures, multibillionaire gentlemen heroes, and members of the military industrial complex. Recent multimedia Batman, Iron Man, and Thor adventures have underscored the idea that superheroes often act as fictionalized stand-ins for, and commentaries on, members of our real-world ruling classes. While it is unclear precisely how wealthy and politically influential some of these figures are, several journalists and bloggers have made striking estimations of their financial worth. As a case in point, Buddy Loans published an infographic by Jon Emge that identified the Marvel hero the Black Panther (a.k.a. King T'Challa of the fictional, resource-rich African nation of Wakanda) as the wealthiest superhero and "worth" an estimated $500 billion.[37] Emge gave second place to Tony Stark, who he calculated spent an estimated $1.5 billion developing his Iron Man suits while being worth $100 billion overall. Bruce Wayne, who owns Wayne Manor, Wayne Enterprises, and one-third of the land that Gotham City is built upon, boasts an estimated $80 billion portfolio, and Lex Luthor, a corporate villain, mad scientist, and former president of the United States in the *Superman* universe, is worth $75 billion. Doctor Doom, evil technomage and totalitarian ruler of the Eastern European nation of Latveria in Marvel Comics, is worth $35 billion. Oliver Queen, the central character of the *Green Arrow* comic books and the television series *Arrow*, is the $7 billion man and the Robin Hood–like owner of Queen Industries.[38] Emge's estimates are notably higher than those unveiled by Jacob Davidson of *Time* magazine on July 9, 2015; Davidson posited that T'Challa was the wealthiest superhero at $90 billion, Stark second at $12.4 billion, and Wayne third at $9.2 billion.[39] Whether Emge's or Davidson's figures are more accurate, both sets of figures contribute to the public perception that superheroes represent the ruling classes, not the working classes, and that superhero narratives promote conservative, establishment, patriarchal values.

And yet, while Stark, Wayne, and T'Challa are among the most famous and recognizable superheroes, there are other superheroes who are decidedly impoverished, and those whose class and economic statuses are complicated by the distinction between the lives they live as superheroes and the lives they live as civilians. Indeed, many other superheroes may boast exceptional physical strength and supernatural powers, but their enhanced physical abilities do not necessarily translate to a stable income or high class status in American culture. A number of what might be colloquially called B- and C-list superheroes come from humble roots, pose as impoverished Everymen in their civilian alter egos in a *My Man Godfrey* (1936) manner, or may be considered legitimately working-class heroes in both their secret and superhero identities.

Complementing the above charts of the wealthiest superheroes are recently released articles that identify the poorest comic book characters. Goliath blogger Wes Walcott's list of "The 12 Poorest Marvel Superheroes," published on February 25, 2016, named Spider-Man and the heroes Luke Cage and Jessica Jones—both of whom made their move from comic books to the Netflix web series *Jessica Jones* in 2015—as three of the most-broke superhumans.[40] Of Spider-Man, the seventh-poorest character listed, Walcott wrote: "It should come as no surprise that Marvel's flagship character is among the poorest superheroes. Peter Parker's job as a freelance photographer could earn him about $40,000 a year. Typically, newspaper photographers are only paid $65 per photo assignment. When you consider that photographers are usually required to submit five to ten photos for the client to choose from, that would mean that the value of each photo is about $10."[41]

The romantically linked private detectives Luke Cage and Jessica Jones were positioned just below Spider-Man. As Walcott observed, "Generally speaking, American small business owners make about $60,000 to $70,000 a year, yet, according to a study by American Express, close to 15% of those small business owners need to work a second job just to make ends meet. Which probably explains why Luke Cage decided to open up that bar."[42] One might infer that the expenses incurred running the small business possibly account for their positioning under Spider-Man, when his salary appears lower on the surface, and Spider-Man's access to a measure of white male privilege—even despite his working-class status—may give him certain social advantages over the female Jones and African American Cage.

Another notable catalogue of impoverished heroes, this one by Rob Cramer for *The Richest* website, identifies the heroes who live outside the margins of society as the poorest, including the Incredible Hulk, Spawn, Swamp Thing,

Krysten Ritter and Mike Colter bring the working-class Marvel superheroes Jessica Jones and Luke Cage to life in the Netflix series *Jessica Jones* (2015), created by Melissa Rosenberg and based upon comic books written by Brian Michael Bendis. The actors reprised their roles in the follow-up Netflix shows *Luke Cage* (2016) and *The Defenders* (2017). Photo courtesy of Netflix.

Man-Thing, the Maxx, and the Teenage Mutant Ninja Turtles. Cramer matches Walcott's estimate of Peter Parker's photographer salary as being approximately $40,000 or $41,000 and notes that Parker got a minor income boost when he became a high school science teacher for the New York City public school system in the early 2000s: $55,000.[43] Cramer's observation that private investigators earn approximately $46,000 a year would offer an idea of what both Cage and Jones would earn, though he notes that the shared expenses and divided salaries of Cage with his partner Danny Rand (a.k.a. Iron Fist) suggests that each earns $37,000. Meanwhile, Cramer observes, Kick-Ass's minimum-wage job as a comic book store clerk likely nets him a mere $19,000 per annum. Yet Cramer's most provocative observations concern Superman:

> He may have a secret hideout in the arctic that's filled with rare artifacts and creatures from around the universe, but to keep his secret identity hidden he works a day job as a mild-mannered reporter. Print journalism is a dying medium and reporters tend to earn very little—that's probably why Clark Kent lives in a small apartment. Journalists earn an average salary of just under $37,000 in the United States. Clark Kent spent his childhood growing up on a small, struggling farm, so he is accustomed to financial hardship. He's much more concerned about protecting the human race than he is with his finances.[44]

Cramer's argument about Superman's class allegiances is worth discussing on several levels, because it is filled with controversial-yet-legitimate assertions. The first, and easiest to discuss, is the idea that Superman's civilian salary makes it difficult for him, or any of the other reporters working for the *Daily Planet*, to afford an apartment in Metropolis, one of the DC Universe's two stand-ins for New York City (the other being Gotham)—despite its occasional positioning in western Kansas in certain iterations of the Superman saga. On March 12, 2015, *Business Insider*'s Drake Baer revealed that the "average monthly rent in February for a studio apartment in Manhattan is $2,351. The average rent for a one-bedroom is $3,400. The numbers—both of which are the highest in seven years of record-keeping—come from a report by real estate appraiser Miller Samuel Inc. and broker Douglas Elliman Real Estate."[45] In a related article, Baer revealed that Brooklyn was the most expensive place to buy a home in America, noting that internationally wealthy figures have bought up 30 percent of condo sales in Manhattan, pushing the slightly less wealthy to purchase homes in Brooklyn, and driving up property values there, frustrating the middle class and creating a desperate housing crisis for the poor.[46]

While one might balk at the New York–centric quality of this information, it is important to note that, according to recent studies, the superhero Kick-Ass couldn't afford to live *anywhere* in America on his minimum-wage salary alone. Kevin Matthews reported for the left-leaning web page *TruthOut* on June 13, 2016:

> According to data compiled by the National Low Income Housing Coalition, there's not a state or county in the country where the average price of housing is affordable to a person working full-time for minimum wage.... In most states, people earning minimum wage would need to work 60–80 hours per week to afford a one-bedroom apartment. In some states—Maryland, Virginia, New Jersey and New York—minimum wage employees would have to work over 100 hours each week.... Moreover, 88 percent of people on minimum wage are over the age of 20. These aren't just teenagers who still live at home—these are adults working full-time who ought to be able to afford housing."[47]

Superman is worth considering in greater detail here to help us consider how difficult it is for superhero comic books to treat class issues in a serious and realistic manner. Casual consumers of *Superman* adventures might understandably glean the impression that the reporters and editors of the *Daily Planet* are middle-class professionals living in nice apartments and working in a bustling, well-equipped office. However, since the 1980s, their class status has been on a decline, and the comic books and film and television adaptations released during the past twenty years have increasingly depicted the newspaper as being understaffed, filled with broken equipment, and under constant threat of being purchased by a Rupert Murdoch–style mogul who dictates that progressive reporters such as Lois Lane be prevented from writing exposés on white-collar crime and corporate malfeasance. In fact, there have been notable storylines in comic books by Jeph Loeb and Grant Morrison—and in the grotesque-but-not-meritless film *Superman IV: The Quest for Peace* (1987)— in which Murdoch-figures such as Lex Luthor, Glen Glenmorgan, and David Warfield purchase the paper and transform it from a respectable, center-left source of news into a far-right-wing tabloid. At the conclusion of some of these storylines, efforts led by editor-in-chief Perry White to buy back control of the paper are successful, and a well-timed heroic feat of Superman's sometimes gives it the circulation boost it needs to survive just when it is on the brink of going under without the support of corporate money. In other extended storylines, such efforts at achieving autonomy fail, and the reporters do the best they can to maintain their personal integrity working for a newspaper that is usually a propaganda sheet but occasionally reports the news, as in the Zach Snyder films *Man of Steel* (2013) and *Batman v Superman: Dawn of Justice* (2016).

There have been many versions of the central characters seen over the years in various media, but Lois Lane has alternatively been depicted as an army brat, an autodidact who is brilliant but cannot spell, a chain smoker who drinks fresh orange juice, a compulsive swearer, a Pulitzer Prize–winning reporter who writes about climate change, and someone who is bitter over the various ways in which Perry appears to censor her edgiest news stories. While Superman may be problematic as a working-class figure because he has a Fortress of Solitude he can retreat to and superhuman powers that make him nigh invincible, Lane is often depicted as a fascinating example of a working-class female professional—or a lower-middle-class one. Geoff Johns, the comic book writer who explored Wally West as a working-class superhero in *The Flash* from 2000 to 2001, emphasized the rough-around-the-edges qualities of the *Planet* staff in his stories *Secret Origin* (2009–2010) and "Brainiac" (2008).[48] According to Johns, photographer Jimmy Olsen began his career as an unpaid intern who relied upon family money to follow his career as a photojournalist. Only his friendship with Superman saved his career, but even after years of working at the paper and becoming a staff photographer, his day-to-day tasks often included fetching coffee and donuts and performing other menial tasks for the reporters normally in the purview of absent temp workers—absent, presumably, because their positions had been eliminated to keep down the costs of running the paper. These facts aside, Olsen has been the most financially secure of all the *Planet* staff members; he inherited billions of dollars from his white-collar criminal parents when they faked their own deaths to avoid a string of lawsuits. In the Johns-written *The Men of Tomorrow* (2015), Olsen is so moved by the plight of a number of the poorest, most desperate residents of Metropolis that he encounters while covering a breaking news story that he chooses to help them by redistributing his massive inheritance among them to give them a new start. Olsen's Frank Capra–style, *Mr. Deeds Goes to Town* (1936) show of generosity is made in the spirit of his populist hero, Superman. Olsen observes: "I gave away every cent! It's what Superman would do."[49] The other *Planet* staff reporters would share Olsen's populist sentiments but would not have the money to make such a grand gesture.

Sports editor Steve Lombard briefly played professional football before being sidelined by an injury. In Johns's comics, Lombard wears tight fluorescent T-shirts to show off his six-pack abs, has a '70s pornstache, sexually harasses the female reporters, and picks fights with intellectual African American reporter Ron Troupe for being overeducated, activist, and black. Johns depicts gossip columnist Cat Grant as an aging beauty who has had breast augmentation surgery, dresses provocatively, and flirts with the male reporters. In Johns's stories, Lois finds Cat and Steve too grotesque to stomach and respects Ron Troupe, but Clark sees the "good" in all of the reporters—even the sexist and racist Lombard—and promotes solidarity and harmony among the diverse yet uniformly working-class staff. Clark's perspective is that they are "all in this together," and the *Planet* staff members need to put aside their personal differences to do what they can to protect the citizens of Metropolis from the corporate rule of Lex Luthor by writing the best news stories they can. Clark developed his egalitarian views when he was raised by poor, kind-hearted Methodists on a farm in Smallville, Kansas, and he has brought Jonathan and Martha Kent's "Main Street U.S.A." liberalism to Metropolis, which is often too cut-throat, corporate, and cynical to see his liberalism as anything more than an outmoded, apple-pie worldview.

If one is inclined to regard Superman as an elite figure of alien royalty masquerading as working-class, he has nevertheless made the not-insignificant decision to betray his class and ally himself with the less fortunate of Metropolis. In *Superman: Earth One* (2010) by writer J. Michael Straczynski and artist Shane Davis, Clark Kent first arrives in Metropolis interested in being a chemist, engineer, baseball player, football player, or investment banker. At each job interview, he so impresses his would-be bosses that they all offer him whatever salary he wants if he would only accept the job. In the end, he turns down all of his various blank-check job offers and decides to work at the *Daily Planet* because he is so impressed with the bravery and integrity demonstrated by Lois and Jimmy in their efforts to fight for truth and justice . . . and to boldly confront an army of alien invaders instead of fleeing a battlefield. When he chooses a career with such a modest salary, he elects to stay in the humble apartment he had chosen as a temporary base upon moving into the city and becomes romantically involved with his next-door neighbor, Lisa Lasalle, an only partially successful model who sometimes works as a prostitute to earn enough money to survive in Metropolis.[50] Also, in the pilot episode of *Lois & Clark: The New Adventures of Superman* (1993), Clark is seen living in squalor in the world's smallest one-room apartment, calling his parents in Kansas and thanking them for wiring him money so that he can make his rent.

It is instructive comparing the depictions of issues of social class, status, labor history, and economics in Superman adventures with how they are dealt with in Batman and Wonder Woman adventures, which are also published by DC Comics or produced by Warner Bros. as comic adaptations for film and television. Batman, the aristocratic vigilante hero of Gotham City, is often seen protecting black-tie parties from attack by proletarian gangsters and terrorists, or defending private and museum-display jewelry collections from theft by gifted working-class thieves. The members of the Gotham City police department, like the staff of the *Daily Planet*, are mostly working-class. The officers who are depicted as being more "moral" and "upstanding," such as James Gordon, Renee Montoya, and Crispus Allen, are coded as better dressed and spoken than those who operate in a morally grey manner and may be accepting bribes from Don Carmine Falcone, such as the slovenly, profane, and overweight Harvey Bullock, whose "overt" working-class cultural signification is a sign of his moral corruption. Like Superman, Wonder Woman is a royal illegal immigrant on American soil who advocates for New Deal–style (if not outright socialist) political reforms while championing the rights of women and children. During her more than seventy-five years of multimedia adventures, Wonder Woman has worked as a secretary, in the fast-food industry, as a military attaché and a U.N. diplomat. She, like Superman, is sometimes presented as occupying dual, conflicting class standings. As a civilian, she is often working-class. As a superhero, she is royalty. The same argument may be made for Superman: Clark Kent is working-class; Superman, the son of the greatest scientist on Krypton, the head of New Krypton's military, and the overlord of the Fortress of Solitude, is not.

When the Marvel superheroes began to appear in the 1960s, the distinctions between the working-class civilian identities and the more aristocratic superhero identities began to blur more significantly, as characters such as the Thing retained their working-class colloquialisms and mannerisms in their superhero guise, and characters such as the comic, malcontent, borderline libertarian Spider-Man never fully outgrew the need to work for a living to pay the rent. The increased realism in handling of class issues is, essentially, the reason why Marvel characters are often regarded as more "realistic" and "relatable" than DC heroes. "Realistic" and "relatable" are sometimes comic-book-fan code words for a discussion of power levels. Batman has no superpowers, so he is more "relatable" than Wolverine, who does—even though Batman's extreme wealth might make him harder to relate to than Wolverine, who sometimes lives in a trailer, SUV, or cabin in the Canadian wilderness. On the other hand, "realistic" and "relatable" are also frequently employed comic-book-fan code words for "working-class"—though few comic book fans are aware that they are making class-based arguments when they employ this terminology. It is precisely because Marvel heroes have, traditionally, been more "realistically" rendered in terms of their class status that Marvel heroes dominate this anthology, and DC superheroes are less well represented. Nevertheless, even in the cases of Marvel heroes, a healthy willingness to suspend disbelief is often required of any consumer of superhero narratives interested in their "realistic" depictions of class in order for the stories to make any measure of sense.

The disconnect between superhero and civilian identities creates a massive cognitive dissonance that makes a discussion of class issues in superhero comics quite difficult. Nevertheless, in order for the working-class superhero to have any chance at all to be a "hero" and defeat the forces of the top 1 percent, that hero needs enough resources to mount a populist offensive. Those resources almost always amount to a wish-fulfillment magic bag of weapons that are not available to working-class people in the real world. The question remains: once a working-class superhero gains access to a superpower, an ultimate weapon, a cache of money, or guaranteed shelter, do they cease being working-class? In a very real way, they do. On the other hand, many such characters retain their working-class values, wardrobes, mannerisms, and cultural ties, and try to remain permanently working-class, even after they become rich. In this respect they walk the kind of cultural and economic tightrope that Bruce Springsteen has for years.

Consider as a case in point Lisbeth Salander, the populist heroine of Stieg Larsson's *Millennium* book series, a.k.a. *The Dragon Tattoo Trilogy* or the *Men Who Hate Women* series. Salander was the illegitimate daughter of a prostitute, grew up a ward of the state, spent years in a mental institution, played for the riot grrrl band Evil Fingers, trained in boxing under Swedish champion Paolo Roberto, educated herself to become one of the world's most powerful computer hackers (with the avatar Wasp, after Janet van Dyne), allied herself with the leadership of a private security firm and Sweden's most respected progressive periodical, and downloaded an entire fortune from the secret bank account of a corporate criminal. Once Lisbeth acquires enough wealth to buy herself an expensive apartment, she is, ostensibly, no longer working-class. However, she continues to wear an assemblage of punk and Goth outfits, pointedly leaves her apartment largely unfurnished, avoids all social contact, and continues to wage a single-minded hacker war against the male-chauvinist forces of the corporate patriarchy. The question here is, does the so-called Girl with the Dragon Tattoo cease to be a working-class figure when she steals Hans-Erik Wennerström's fortune? Or does his fortune merely serve as a MacGuffin, Ring of Gyges, or similar form of plot device, needed to make her working-class campaign against the upper classes dramatically credible? Is it a mistake to get to caught up in her secret lair, just as it is a mistake to become too obsessed with Superman's Fortress of Solitude or the Thing's residence in the Baxter Building? Are such bases of operations distractions, or are they too significant signifiers of wealth to ignore? These questions will arise repeatedly in these pages, and different scholars come to different conclusions when wrestling with such contested and fascinating issues.

The Essays in This Volume: An Overview

The essays in this book are organized into two sections. The first is "Representations of Class and Populism in Horror and Science Fiction Comics," which is principally concerned with some of the most well-respected and recognizable genre comics released by DC's Vertigo imprint and other, independent presses. The comics covered in this section are written by industry stalwarts Alan Moore, Grant Morrison, Garth Ennis, and Robert Kirkman, and the essay on the science-fiction elements of the Superman universe is the only one that deals overtly with superhero figures. The characters discussed in the other essays in this first half of the book are all working-class comic book heroes without traditionally understood superhero powers.

The Marvel superheroes come to the fore in the essays featured in the second half of this book, in the grouping of essays called "Marvel Comics, Netflix, and the Working-Class Superhero." The essays collected in this section examine the classic working-class superhero known as "the Thing," the more obscure female superhero Shamrock, and the recently famous stars of the Netflix television shows *Jessica Jones, Luke Cage,* and *Daredevil.*

This book—and part 1 on class in genre comics—begins with "Past Lives: Memory and the Meaning of Work in *The Walking Dead*" by Michele Fazio. As Fazio observes, the popularity of AMC's *The Walking Dead* is a case in point in which zombies are more than just a form of entertainment; they are socially significant. From the ghastly flesh-eaters of horror films and apocalyptic prophecies to a symbol as a form of protest during Buy Nothing Day and the Occupy Movement, the zombie figure is a ubiquitous presence in American society and culture pointing to the inevitability of humanity's impending doom. In Robert Kirkman's graphic narrative, the zombie apocalypse acts an equalizing force, bringing together disparate groups of survivors from all walks of life, who join forces to combat the living dead. Yet Kirkman's emphasis on each character's work history sheds light on the divisive class and economic power that continues to haunt protagonist Rick Grimes and a host of minor characters who display a profound sense of disillusionment and worker alienation in attempting to achieve the American Dream. Kirkman's anticapitalist slant as demonstrated by many of the characters' relief in having escaped the endless cycle of commerce, consumerism, and capitalism that consumed their lives before the zombie invasion occurred becomes a useful tool to discuss how labor impacts lived experience. Fazio's essay provides an overview of major themes and conflicts related to class antagonism and explores its significance in the creation of a new kind of working-class hero.

"You Can Be Whatever the Hell You Want: Heroism and the Female Working Class in *Preacher*" is by Kelly Kanayama. She examines the ways in which the Vertigo series *Preacher* subverts gender norms regarding constructions of heroism and criticizes patriarchal expectations surrounding women's labor. As a revisionist Western comic following in the tradition of revisionist Western films, *Preacher* continually questions certain boundaries and conventions of its genre while adhering strongly to others. This tension is best embodied in the character of Tulip O'Hare, the series' female lead. In Tulip we see the traits of the typically male classic Western hero and superhero; a repudiation of the gendering of recreational pursuits; and the obligation of ongoing labor placed upon women in a male-dominated society, which in her case plays out against a staunchly working-class socioeconomic background. Comparing Tulip's story to those of *Preacher*'s other female characters reveals a broader link between class-based oppression and oppressive gender norms, which in turn highlights and reproaches the restriction of women—regardless of socioeconomic privilege—to roles of perpetual unrewarded labor.

Scholars James Gifford and Orion Ussner Kidder collaborated on the third essay, "Alan Moore and Anarchist Praxis in Form: Bibliography, Remediation, and Aesthetic Form in *V for Vendetta* and *Black Dossier*." By privileging anarchism as a movement, a philosophy, and a methodology, these scholars extend its operation as an organizational concept across Moore's oeuvre, particularly to his later works, which often do not contain explicit anarchist content or for which critical consensus has been elusive. Moving from *V for Vendetta* to *League of Extraordinary Gentlemen: The Black Dossier* both demonstrates the continuity of anarchist thought in Moore's work and emphasizes a shift from explicit thematic contents to implicit formal and stylistic traits.

"Truth, Justice, and the Socialist Way? The Politics of Grant Morrison's Superman" by Phil Bevin returns to the theme of Superman's class allegiances, as outlined in this introduction. Bevin argues that Grant Morrison's contribution to DC's New 52 presents readers with a Superman who starts his career as a partisan social activist fighting for the rights of the most vulnerable in society but who transitions to a superhero who defends "everyone" as his story progresses. Bevin places his analysis in the context of Morrison's earlier work to argue that his tenure on *Action Comics* follows his well-established thematic preoccupations and that Superman's development throughout mirrors the writer's own political evolution from a critic of Margaret Thatcher's right-wing United Kingdom government to a popular philosopher suspicious of any strict political dogma, conservative, liberal, or otherwise. Bevin also applies the theories offered by cultural materialist Alan Sinfield in *Faultlines* (1992) to suggest that, as a result of his political development, Morrison is now suspicious of moral absolutes and clear binary divisions. In his work for the New 52, Morrison presents his audience with a variety of alternate Supermen against whom the hero from the main DC Universe might be examined and interrogated. This interrelationship between multiple Supermen indicates that Morrison believes Superman's value and his ability to represent "everyone" stem from his status as a mosaic whose meaning and identity are shaped by a great number of different interpretations, and who can be reworked to serve any agenda.

The first essay in Part II is "From the Streets to the Swamp: Luke Cage, Man-Thing, and the 1970s Class Issues of Marvel Comics" by Blair Davis. As Davis observes, Marvel Comics regularly embedded a concern for working-class politics within stories about two of their less-well-known characters from the 1970s: Luke Cage and Man-Thing. Luke Cage positions himself as a "Hero for Hire," often helping out working-class citizens of New York City from his squalid Times Square office. Unlike other superheroes, however, Cage charges for his services in order to support himself financially (which often proves difficult). Man-Thing also emerges as a defender of the weak and lower-class, albeit as a largely inadvertent hero. The character is an empath who can sense the emotions of others but possesses no rational consciousness himself. He has no need for nourishment or material goods, and hence is altogether a classless being. The two characters demonstrate varying degrees of subtle and overt commentary on issues of class in 1970s America, albeit using a narrative split between urban and rural settings. Luke Cage frequently battles with mobsters and struggles to pay the bills, while Man-Thing regularly crosses paths with ruthless construction magnate F. A. Schist, who tries to develop a new airport on swampland. Cage later teams up with wealthy industrialist Danny "Iron Fist" Rand, adding an additional dynamic to how class issues are depicted when the comic's title was changed to *Power Man and Iron Fist*.

The next essay is "'It's Just Us Here': Daredevil and the Trauma of Big Power," by Kevin Michael Scott. As Scott explains, Daredevil is regularly depicted as belonging, uncomfortably, in two worlds. He is a superhero and a high-powered lawyer, capable of earning wealth-creating fees, but one who regularly sacrifices those opportunities to defend gang members because he can literally hear their heartbeats reveal the truth of their testimony. His arch-nemesis, Kingpin, is a parody of the popular image of wealth, with his white suit and ascot and his penchant for abusing the innocent. Scott examines Daredevil's positioning in the Marvel Universe as belonging to the super-powered 1 percent but simultaneously representing both the non-super-powered and the economically disadvantaged. Moreover, the figure of Daredevil crystalizes the tensions inherent in the fascination with (and vicarious thrills experienced through) superheroes as special and "different," a complex relationship mirrored by our social love/hate relationship with the wealthy. Famous for his guilt-ridden moodiness and Hamlet-like uncertainty, Daredevil enacts our own discomfort with feeling less than special in a culture that both resents and hallows those that are.

In "Jack Kirby: The Not-So-Secret Identity of the Thing," Andrew Alan Smith observes that Ben "The Thing" Grimm of the Fantastic Four is portrayed as a working-class "guy." His language, speech pattern, and lifestyle all indicate his blue-collar background, despite the vast amount of money at his disposal as a principal in Fantastic Four, Inc. However, his origins go back further than his first appearance in 1961, to the childhood of his cocreator and original artist, Jack Kirby. Kirby, a working-class Jew from the slums of Lower East Side New York City in the early part of the twentieth century, patterned Grimm after himself. Even after both Kirby and cocreator Stan Lee left *Fantastic Four*, successive writers and artists would include new pieces of background information about the character cementing the direct correlation between the fictional Thing and his real-world creator and alter ego, Jack Kirby. A journalist, Smith crafts his contribution to this volume as an appreciation of Kirby as an artist, and as a tribute to the Thing, the elder statesman of working-class superheroes.

Christina M. Knopf's essay about the obscure Marvel superhero Shamrock is "Haunted Heroine, Working Woman, Guardian of the Galaxy." Knopf argues that Molly "Shamrock" Fitzgerald is one of the most fascinating superheroines to appear in the Marvel Universe. Psychically connected to a war she disavows, she stays modestly in the background when possible and takes up a feminine stance against fighting and a maternal role of educating. Her character was not based on an earlier male character, and both her super and ordinary identities often succeed without the assistance or companionship of a man. The interplay of Shamrock's gender, nationality, powers, and vocations is intricately revealing about the place of woman in history, modern society, and international affairs. Though Molly does not want her powers, she accepts the responsibility of them and uses them to speak on behalf of those who have no voice: women, laborers, children, and the dead.

Terrence R. Wandtke wrote the final chapter, "The Working-Class PI (AKA Jessica Jones): *Alias* as a Narrative of Quiet Desperation." Starting with the development of workers' movements, superhero comics, and hard-boiled detective fiction in the twentieth century, the essay focuses on the comic series *Alias* as an examination of those historical cross-currents. Through its portrayal of the ex-superhero private investigator Jessica Jones, the series uses her female perspective to revise traditional narratives of the blue-collar worker, the superhero, and the hard-boiled detective. Ultimately, it demonstrates how the comic book's carefully crafted depiction of "quiet desperation" is lost in its television adaptation as the Netflix series *Jessica Jones*.

Final Thoughts (or, a few words on *The Movement: Class Warfare*)

While the tragically short-lived comic *The Movement* does not have its own essay in this book, the abortive narrative is worth considering for a moment as this introduction comes to a close. The back-cover blurb of the trade paperback edition of the series' first and only volume, *Class Warfare* (2014) provides a plot summary that more than adequately prepares readers for the comic book's content and tone:

> The sprawling streets of Coral City are home to two kinds of people: have and have nots. The haves have it all. The have-nots have nothing.
>
> But that's about to change.
>
> A new power is rising in the 'Tweens, the section of the city where the rich and the powerful never dare to tread. Tired of being preyed upon by corrupt cops, bought out by heartless corporations, and sold out by ruthless politicians, the citizens wear masks to disguise their identities, even as they use the tools of technology to turn surveillance back on their oppressors.
>
> No longer outcasts. No longer misfits. They are The Movement. They're a revolution in the making. And they're going to change the world . . . or die trying![51]

Promotional materials that were disseminated before this comic's release made it clear to fandom writ large that this was a radical artifact of mass culture on the order of Sam Greenlee's 1969 black power novel *The Spook Who Sat by the Door* and its mysteriously suppressed 1973 film adaptation. Consequently, a minor culture war erupted on Twitter over *The Movement*. Naturally, right-wing comic book fans decried its imminent release, and left-wing comics fans expressed anticipation for the first issue. Gail Simone tried to defuse some of this political polarization evident on Twitter by downplaying the extent to which the comic book could be enjoyed only by readers of her progressive political stripe. In interviews given on the eve of the release of the first issue, Simone asked her readers to consider her story's iconic and apolitical power to move readers to sympathy for the downtrodden:

> [T]he best adventure fiction is based on the idea of standing up for the little guy against oppressive forces. If you go back and look at Zorro, or the Shadow, or the Lone Ranger, you can see that that idea of a masked protector pre-dates comics entirely. There's something very powerful about that, and it's completely non-partisan. The idea of someone laying their life on the line for others is a big part of why I read superhero comics, and yet, even in some really popular books, I feel like that

theme has been lost a little—there's a bloodthirstiness to a lot of books and you can't always see why these characters are heroes, or even admirable anymore.

This book isn't about the Occupy movement, it's a superhero adventure story. But at its heart it's about young, poor people, who normally would be without power in society, who manage to fight back, not for themselves, but for others who are powerless.

They mess up. They lack experience and wisdom. But they're trying.[52]

They're *trying.*

As are we all.

Read together, the essays in this book offer a wide-ranging study of multi-modal manifestations of heroic and villainous working-class figures in super-hero and comic book narratives. The essayists approach these figures from a variety of methodological and disciplinary perspectives. Superheroes offer us a unique opportunity to consider such emotionally charged issues in a border-line safe space. After all, it is, in some ways, easier to contemplate class issues when we are discussing our old friends the Thing and Rick Grimes than it is diving right into a fraught Facebook discussion of class in the real world. Naturally, it would behoove us all to think more lucidly and compassionately about class issues in our own reality. The contributors to this volume hope that, by discussing fictional working-class superheroes in both an intellectual and entertaining manner, they will help all of us consider more fruitful, enlight-ened, and empathetic ways of discussing issues of economics, class conflict, and class identity in the real world.

Notes

1. Robert Loss, "John Lennon's 'Working-Class Hero': Boundaries, Mobility, and Honesty." *Pop Matters.* January 12, 2016. http://www.popmatters.com/column/john-lennons-working-class-hero-boundaries-mobility-and-honesty/. Accessed May 21, 2017.

2. See also Jill Lepore, *The Secret History of Wonder Woman* (New York: Alfred A. Knopf, 2014); Adilifu Nama, *Super Black: American Pop Culture and Black Superheroes* (Austin: University of Texas Press, 2011).

3. *Sight & Sound* online exclusive, January 29, 2015.

4. David McLellan, *Karl Marx: Selected Writings* (Oxford: Oxford University Press, 1977), 222.

5. Michael Zweig, *The Working-Class Majority: America's Best Kept Secret* (New York: Cornell University Press, 2000), 4.

6. Paul Fussell, *Class: A Guide through the American Status System* (New York: Simon and Schuster, 1983), 16.

7. Ibid.

8. H. H. Gerth and C. Wright Mills, *From Max Weber: Essays in Sociology* (London: Routledge, 1991), 180–195.

9. Thorstein Veblen, *The Theory of the Leisure Class* (New York: Dover, 1994), 1–2.

10. Quoted in Antonio Gramsci, *The Antonio Gramsci Reader: Selected Writings 1916–1935,* ed. David Forgacs. New York: New York University Press, 2000, 298.

11. Quoted in ibid., 299.

12. E. P. Thompson, *The Making of the English Working Class* (New York: Vintage, 1966,) 9–10.

13. Zweig, *Working-Class Majority*, 6.

14. Charles Hatfield, *Hand of Fire: The Comics Art of Jack Kirby* (Jackson: University Press of Mississippi, 2012);Gerard Jones, *Men of Tomorrow: Geeks, Gangsters, and the Birth of the Comic Book* (New York: Basic Books, 2004).

15. Dan Raviv, *Comic Wars: Marvel's Battle for Survival* (New York: Marvel Comics, 2004).

16. Marc DiPaolo, *War, Politics and Superheroes: Ethics and Propaganda in Comics and Film* (Jefferson, NC: McFarland, 2011).

17. Harvey Pekar and Dean Haspiel, *The Quitter* (New York: DC Comics, 2005); Harvey Pekar, *American Splendor* (New York: Ballantine Books, 2003).

18. Harvey Pekar and Ty Templeton, "Harvey Pekar Meets the Thing," *Strange Tales II* (New York: Marvel Comics, 2011).

19. Elisabeth El Refaie, *Autobiographical Comics: Life Writing in Pictures.* Jackson: (University Press of Mississippi), 2012.

20. John Russo and Sherry Lee Linkon, "What's New about New Working-Class Studies?" *New Working-Class Studies*, ed. John Russo and Sherry Lee Linkon (Ithaca: Cornell University Press, 2005), 5.

21. Ibid., 3.

22. Theodore W. Allen, "On Roediger's *Wages of Whiteness*," *Cultural Logic: An Electronic Journal of Marxist Theory and Practice* 4, no. 2 (Spring 2001). http://clogic.eserver.org/4-2/allen.html. Accessed: August 9, 2016.

23. Linda Tirado, *Hand to Mouth: Living in Bootstrap America* (New York: Berkley Books, 2014).

24. bell hooks, *Where We Stand: Class Matters* (New York: Routledge, 2000); Alfred Lubrano, *Limbo: Blue-Collar Roots, White-Collar Dreams* (London: Wiley), 2004; Barbara Jensen, *Reading Classes: On Culture and Classism in America* (Ithaca: Cornell University Press, 2012).

25. Michèle Lamont, *The Dignity of Working Men: Morality and the Boundaries of Race, Class, and Immigration* (Cambridge: Harvard University Press, 2002); Annette Lareau, *Unequal Childhoods: Class, Race, and Family Life*, 2nd ed. (Oakland: University of California Press), 2011; Elwood Watson, ed., *Generation X Professors Speak* (Toronto: Scarecrow, 2013).

26. Christopher Beach, *Class, Language, and American Film Comedy* (Cambridge: Cambridge University Press), 2002; Lester Friedman, *Fires Were Started: British Cinema and Thatcherism* (New York: Wallflower Press, 2007); Bryan Cardinale-Powell and Marc DiPaolo, *Devised and Directed by Mike Leigh* (New York: Bloomsbury, 2013).

27. Zweig, *Working-Class Majority*; Lisa Dodson, *The Moral Underground: How Ordinary Americans Subvert an Unfair Economy* (New York, London: New Press, 2009); Kim Scipes, *Building Global Labor Solidarity in a Time of Accelerating Globalization* (Chicago: Haymarket Books. 2016).

28. Russo and Linkon, "What's New?," 10–11.

29. Owen Jones, *Chavs: The Demonization of the Working Class* (London, New York: Verso, 2011).

30. Jensen, *Reading Classes*, 25.

31. Barbara Ehrenreich, "Foreword," in Tirado, *Hand to Mouth*, xi–xii.

32. Ibid., xii.

33. Tirado, *Hand to Mouth*, xxi–xxii.

34. Shathley Q., "Legacy v. Statement: Talking with Goon Creator Eric Powell," *Pop Matters*, January 30, 2015, http://www.popmatters.com/feature/190092-legacy-v-statement-talking-with-goon-creator-eric-powell/. Accessed May 2, 2017.

35. Jared Gardner, "Same Difference: Graphic Alterity in the Work of Gene Luen Yang, Adrian Tomine, and Derek Kirk Kim," *Multicultural Comics: From Zap to Blue Beetle* (Austin: University of Texas Press, 2010), 135–38.

36. Tony Williams, *The Cinema of George A. Romero: Knight of the Living Dead* (New York: Wallflower Press, 2015).

37. Jon Emge, "The World's Richest Superheroes," *Buddy Loans*, May 7, 2014, https://www.buddyloans.com/blog/the-worlds-richest-superheroes/. Accessed: June 18, 2016.

38. Ibid.

39. Jacob Davidson, "These Are the 5 Richest Superheroes." *Time*. July 9, 2015, http://time.com/money/3950362/richest-superheroes-comic-con/. Accessed: June 18, 2016.

40. Wes Walcott, "The 12 Poorest Marvel Superheroes," *Goliath*. February 25, 2016, http://www.goliath.com/comics/the-12-poorest-marvel-superheroes/12/. Accessed: June 18, 2016.

41. Ibid.

42. Ibid.

43. Rob Cramer, "The 10 Poorest Superheroes," *The Richest*. September 4, 2014, http://www.therichest.com/rich-list/poorest-list/the-10-poorest-superheroes/. Accessed: June 18, 2016.

44. Ibid.

45. Drake Baer, "The Average Rent for a Studio Apartment in Manhattan Just Hit a New Record," *Business Insider*, March 12, 2015, http://www.businessinsider.com/manhattan-studio-rent-breaks-records-2015-3. Accessed: June 18, 2016.

46. Drake Baer, "Brooklyn Is Officially the Most Unaffordable Housing Market in America," *Business Insider*, January 30, 2015, http://www.businessinsider.com/brooklyn-is-officially-the-most-unaffordable-housing-market-in-america-2015-1. Accessed: June 18, 2016.

47. Kevin Matthews, "Minimum Wage Workers Can't Afford to Live Anywhere in the US." *Truth Out*, June 13, 2016, http://www.truth-out.org/opinion/item/36404-minimum-wage-workers-can-t-afford-to-live-anywhere-in-the-us. Accessed: June 18, 2016.

48. Geoff Johns and Gary Frank, *Superman: Secret Origin* (New York: DC Comics, 2010); Geoff Johns and Gary Frank, "Brainiac," *Superman: Last Son of Krypton* (New York: DC Comics, 2013).

49. Geoff Johns and John Romita, Jr. *Superman: The Men of Tomorrow* (New York: DC Comics, 2015).

50. J. Michael Straczynski and Shane Davis, *Superman: Earth One* (New York: DC Comics, 2010).

51. Gail Simone (writer) and Freddie Williams III (artist), *The Movement, Volume 1: Class Warfare* (New York: DC Comics, 2014).

52. Josie Campbell, "Simone Rallies the 99% for 'The Movement.'" *CBR*. April 5, 2013, http://www.cbr.com/simone-rallies-the-99-for-the-movement/. Accessed: April 30, 2017.

PART I

REPRESENTATIONS OF CLASS AND POPULISM IN HORROR AND SCIENCE FICTION COMICS

PAST LIVES
Memory and the Meaning of Work
in *The Walking Dead*

Michele Fazio

Zombies, as a popular cultural art form, seem impossible to escape these days. Since George Romero's landmark film *Night of the Living Dead* (1968), they have remained a pervasive presence in the mainstream. No longer relegated to a costume or a celebrated film genre during Halloween, the zombie has taken center stage year-round, with zombie-themed party supplies and cookbooks to calendars and action figures, entertaining and satisfying the excessive appetites of the modern consumer and, subsequently, generating high profits.

Take, for example, the success of survival video games like *Resident Evil* (1996–) or blockbuster films such as *28 Days Later* (2002), *Zombieland* (2009), and *World War Z* (2013). Best-selling novels, too, such as Seth Grahame-Greene's *Pride and Prejudice and Zombies* (2009) and Colson Whitehead's *Zone One* (2011) have transformed the contemporary literary marketplace, proving that the zombie craze continues to spread at an alarming rate. Even the US government, in response to the ever-increasing popularity of Robert Kirkman's *The Walking Dead* (2003), has joined in on the action by using the zombie figure to promote disaster preparedness for the Centers for Disease Control and Prevention's website: "Don't be a zombie! Be prepared!"[1]

The resurgence of the dead—particularly since 2007—has coincided with the United States' recent struggles to overcome the devastating effects of an economic downturn that marked the beginning of the mortgage crisis and record high unemployment rates, spurring what many have deemed the Great Recession.[2] In contrast, the cultural currency and profitability of the "'zombie industry,'" as Murali Balaji reports, "is now generating upward of $5 billion a year" (ix). He further explains that AMC's "re-versioning" of Kirkman's comic has created a "formidable television brand" and a "lucrative multimedia franchise" (228, 227).[3] Who knew that reanimated corpses as a result of a pandemic supervirus could breathe such life into America's lagging economy?

Despite the present marketability of zombies, scholars remind us that the "zombie renaissance" has everything to do with the evolution of social, political, and economic tensions that define contemporary life.[4] Kyle Bishop attributes the proliferation of zombie cinema to real-life apocalyptic "after-effects of war, terrorism, and natural disasters" since the 1950s through the 2000s, noting how the 9/11 terrorist attacks "caused perhaps the largest wave of paranoia for Americans since the McCarthy era" ("Dead Man Still Walking" 18). Shawn McIntosh adds that the fear and terror produced by a zombie apocalypse also has its roots in "reflecting a general popular distrust with big government and big business" (9) as can be seen in Romero's *Dawn of the Dead* (1978)—a critique of capitalism where survivors hold out in a shopping mall while the dead roam the earth. No matter the form taken (slow, fast, flesh-eating, mad, comical, or romantic), zombies "speak for the cultural moment—expressing paranoia, alienation, and a sense of ever-present threat" (Badley 49).[5] As these critics argue, zombie narratives embody social anxieties that range from health epidemics and biological warfare to the preservation of social order in the face of widespread panic and unrest.

Kirkman's *The Walking Dead* plays into the fascination and fear over the potential consequences of a zombie apocalypse. Since its television debut in 2010, the series has consistently attracted record viewers during its first five seasons, and, with the premiere of season 6 in October 2015 drawing nearly twenty million viewers, its popularity makes clear that zombies are here to stay.[6] However, if we consider Kirkman's representation of the human condition and ignore the impending threat of zombies for the moment, a continuous narrative thread emerges in the comic (and later in the television series) that can be summed up in a single word: labor—both the work performed in the past and the work necessary to survive the zombie apocalypse in the present. According to Kirkman, "Good zombie movies show us how messed up we are, they make us question our station in society . . . and our society's station in the world."[7] Nowhere is this "question" about "station" more prominently displayed in *The Walking Dead* than in the comic's condensed work histories each character reveals about themselves as they integrate into the larger group of survivors. The discussion of jobs, usually occurring just before or directly following a zombie attack, creates a space in the narrative for individuals to reflect upon their past lives, and these stories illustrate a shared lack of power and dissatisfaction over their former occupations before the zombie apocalypse occurred. More than just a way to introduce central characters and establish solidarity among those still living, these worker vignettes reveal apocalyptic-economic anxieties, providing detailed commentary about contemporary American labor relations.

The Walking Dead's character-driven storyline goes beyond simply preserving the human race in a fantastic and frightful new world order.[8] Each volume (twenty-seven to date) explores the complexities of human nature—individual desires, emotions, and motivations—amidst the trauma of witnessing mass carnage at home and on the road. Rather than focus on the reasons behind the zombie outbreak and the inevitable breakdown of society on all levels, the comic considers the social and ethical consequences inherent in daily threats of contact with the dead as well as with the living.[9] *The Walking Dead* is ultimately a story of migration in which a group of displaced survivors, thrust together in the most extreme situations, continuously need to relocate to ensure their existence. The distinctly familiar trope of a father/sons's journey and coming-of-age as well as the transformation of each character and their developing relationships with one another significantly advance a plot that features work in all its forms—skilled and unskilled, wage, and unpaid labor—all of which differentiate class positions among the characters. As the great equalizer, the zombie apocalypse eradicates social distinctions in one fell swoop, becoming, as one critic argues, "the ultimate meritocracy" (Steiger 107). The goal to stay alive in a post-apocalyptic setting thus creates a unique opportunity to establish community among individuals from all walks of life who, prior to the end of the world, would otherwise have remained socially and culturally divided.

While scholars have examined many important cultural aspects in *The Walking Dead* such as the perpetuation of white privilege and patriarchal power as well as racial and gender conflict, work as a signifier of class identity has been limited to day-to-day survival strategies such as procuring food, shelter, and security. Undoubtedly, these survival efforts constitute a full-time job—one that rarely allows for getting ahead as supplies and safe zones dwindle. To illustrate this point, the comic features countless panels of ravaged landscapes, abandoned streets, and deserted towns, depicting a world that is no longer beholden to needless material objects. In fact, conspicuously absent from the text are any scenes portraying individuals looting worthless commodities formerly associated with wealth. Instead, only the basic essential items necessary for survival are collected and preserved—that is, weapons (namely, guns) and food products, which replace bankrolls as the new source of power and prestige among survivors.[10]

Despite the end of capitalism and all recognizable social systems, the memory of work still lingers. Several characters remain haunted by the hard times and become restless over a need to be useful—to do actual work—while others utilize their former skills or learn new ones to stay alive. Without a time clock to punch, deadlines to meet, or coworkers to complain about, survivors struggle through a social malaise and forge ahead, redefining family and community ties. The questions Kirkman raises on each volume's back cover—"When is the last time any of us REALLY worked to get something we wanted? How long has it been since any of us really needed something that we wanted?"—matter most.[11] As a subject underscoring lived experience, work is the common denominator that unites the living, providing proof of consciousness in a world teeming with the dead. But work also takes on new meaning in a post-apocalyptic setting, providing a profound sense of satisfaction and self-worth compared to the relentlessly unrewarding and oftentimes alienating working lives that characters held prior to the onset of the zombie virus. As Bishop contends, "long-term and detailed character development . . . shifts focus away from grisly monsters and onto the besieged human survivors" ("Pathos" 8). In doing so, the recurring theme of work in *The Walking Dead* encourages a reading of its potential to empower survivors—one that calls into question the exploitation of the working class in a pre-zombie world. To this end, the depiction of work in this "blood-soaked masterpiece" serves not only as a catalyst for self-development and reinvention but, more importantly, as a means to humanize both the living and the dead (Lowder xvii).

Barely Alive: Working for a Living

From the professional middle class to those in the service industry, members of America's workforce—scientists, lawyers, mechanics, army personnel, teachers, truck drivers, the clergy, politicians, and administrative assistants alike— are featured prominently in *The Walking Dead*. One need only to look upon the opening pages in the first volume, *Days Gone Bye*, which begins with the action-packed panel sequence of a police shootout with an armed criminal on the run, to see how class division functions prominently in the comic. This initial scene introduces readers to Officer Rick Grimes, who, after recovering from a bullet wound, wakes up alone and disoriented in a hospital to discover the world has become overrun by zombies. Kirkman draws upon the familiar occupations of law enforcement and health care to establish plot and setting, noting at once the decline of two governing systems that once protected and preserved life. The story moves quickly as Rick acclimates to a world filled with fear, uncertainty, and death: after several run-ins with zombies and seeking shelter with a stranger, he "borrows" a squad car and a bag of guns from his own police station and sets off on a solitary journey from Harrison County,

Rick pays a visit to the police station where he worked and procures guns, ammo, and a squad car to head into Atlanta. This image shows Rick's commanding presence as an officer of the law. (Robert Kirkman, Tony Moore, and Cliff Rathburn, *The Walking Dead, Volume 1: Days Gone Bye*)

Kentucky to Atlanta, Georgia, to search for his family. Rick's remarkable recovery in a matter of a few days from coma patient to urban cowboy (he eventually runs out of gas and procures a horse to ride into the city) establishes early on his role as a working-class hero in the story.[12]

Working-class is a necessary adjective to use in describing Rick's character, because of what the comic reveals about his life. As a family man driven by integrity, his character embodies a strong work ethic throughout the story. He dons his uniform like armor "both as personal identification and as symbol of authority" (Nurse 71). He reports to duty to "protect and serve," explaining to Morgan and his son, Duane, the first human survivors he meets, that he is "just doing [his] job."[13] For Rick, the vestiges of his officer's uniform, including

After running out of gas, Rick discovers a horse at a farmer's stable and rides into the city, only to greeted by a swarming mass of zombies. (Robert Kirkman, Tony Moore, and Cliff Rathburn, *The Walking Dead, Volume 1: Days Gone Bye*)

his hat, cowboy boots, and holster, create order and normalcy in this new law-less and chaotic world, but these items also serve as formal relics of the past—ones that starkly contrast with the tattered clothing of the dead. His wife, Lori, and their son, Carl, meanwhile, have been living in a camp on the outskirts of Atlanta, and once reunited with his family, Rick, who describes himself as a "small town cop" and a "regular Barney Fife," assumes a leadership role.[14] His background in law enforcement earns him immediate respect among these remaining survivors; likewise, assuming his place as head of his family estab-lishes stability and hope for a future.

Rick's arrival, however, also provides one of the most compelling moments in *The Walking Dead* that reinforces the significant meaning work carries in shaping identity among the living. As the group sits together to eat dinner in front of a campfire, Rick prompts a discussion about the past, admitting, "That reminds me . . . I still don't know what most of you were doing for a living before all this *shit* started happening."[15] The three-page panel sequence that fol-lows slows down the narrative to allow each character to introduce themselves (all by first name only), offering just enough information to reveal similar sto-ries of class struggle. Here, we meet Dale, a retired salesman of forty years, who states, "I spent most of my life behind a desk on the phone."[16] He was driv-ing a camper with his wife, having "set out to see America" when the attacks began, and along the way rescued sisters Andrea, a clerk at a law firm, and Amy, a college junior majoring in physical education, who were stranded on the highway.[17] We also meet Alan, a shoe salesman, and Donna, his wife, who both complain about barely breaking even every month. Carol explains, too, that she used to sell Tupperware to help with household expenses and that her dead husband, "the breadwinner," was a car salesman.[18] Jim, perhaps the most stereotypical working-class male character among the group, offers up a single word to describe himself to Rick: "mechanic."[19]

But it is Glenn, the self-proclaimed pizza delivery boy, who arguably sums up the economic malaise plaguing most Americans before the apocalypse; he admits, "I was swimming in debt and would've given anything to get out of it. . . . I was in bad shape. About to lose my apartment . . . my car . . . I was going to have to bite the bullet and go crawling back to my parents for help."[20] College educated and chronically underemployed, Glenn's character speaks to the precarity of the millennial generation, who saw the national unemployment rate for all workers peak at 10 percent in 2009, 16 percent for those in their mid-twenties, and close to 7 percent for recent college graduates in 2010.[21] His confession to Rick that he sometimes had to steal cars "to make rent" reveals a self-consciousness about ethics as well as the reality about his dire financial situation.[22] As the boy-next-door-turned-car-thief, Glenn becomes the group's

These three panels serve as character introductions, showing both working-class individuals and families surviving before, during, and after the zombie apocalypse. (Robert Kirkman, Tony Moore, and Cliff Rathburn, *The Walking Dead, Volume 1: Days Gone Bye*)

saving grace in this new world—a redemptive "honorable" figure who single-handedly keeps them alive by making solo trips into Atlanta to collect food supplies.[23] Despite his humble admission "I was just doing my part," this new role provides Glenn with a sense of purpose, replacing his earlier hopelessness with a sense of pride.[24] As Stephen Brett Greely writes, "Indeed, Glenn is noted for his daring and his compassion. These powerful traits are not realized in the mundane jobs of a civilized society. Only when the fetters have been released and the walls crushed can the hero rise" (174). Whereas Glenn's life before the zombie apocalypse hit left him emotionally bereft and financially bankrupt (a failure in society's eyes), his present existence saving lives is by far a more personally rewarding and fulfilling experience. Recognized for his usefulness to the group, Glenn becomes a living embodiment of the ideal he could not achieve before the world ended: a self-respecting working-class hero.[25] In the face of total societal collapse, each character, representing the social stratification of contemporary society, is reminded of their humanity by talking about work. Even though their words relay an acute awareness about increasing anxiety over debt and class antagonism, bonds are forged through this shared experience, and what emerges is a collective identity among this seemingly disparate group of survivors.

Kirkman continues to use the subject of work in later volumes to illustrate characters' relief in having escaped the endless cycle of commerce and capitalism that consumed their lives prior to the zombie plague. He introduces other central characters such as Hershel, a veterinarian who turned to farming after his practice closed due to financial mismanagement. Contrary to his economic failure, Hershel's formal medical training and homestead become an indispensable asset to the group; yet his motivation is not self-serving. Instead, he values the "honest work" of being a self-sufficient farmer, claiming, "There's nothing quite like living off the land . . . providing for yourself . . . knowing exactly where every piece of food you eat comes from."[26] Hershel's words hark back to a simpler time—a rather utopian reclamation of preindustrial agrarian life; to be sure, his "pastoral farm" provides Rick's group with a much-needed alternative to life on the run (Keetley 13). In contrast to Hershel's story, Tyreese, a former NFL player who played for the Atlanta Falcons for two years, is the epitome of a twentieth-century self-made man, whose career-ending injury led to his downward mobility from making several hundred thousand dollars a year to working as a bouncer and at other "odd jobs" until eventually settling to become a car salesman.[27]

Kirkman's representation of contemporary society also incorporates those that exist outside the parameters of America's workforce, such as four inmates holed up at a prison: Dexter, convicted of murdering his wife and her boyfriend;

This panel, signaling the end of the introductions, conveys a particularly somber mood. The absence of dialogue suggests the group's contemplation of a future that bears little resemblance to the earlier pressures of maintaining the status quo. It's worth mentioning that immediately following this scene a horde of zombies attacks the camp, resulting in Amy's death, which underscores how silence and the natural setting provide a rare moment of reflection and reprieve in a plot propelled by gruesome violence. Interestingly, though this scene appears in the television series, the dialogue about work and debt is replaced with a story told by Dale about his watch and the passage of time, which also produces a thoughtful and humorous interruption that allows the group to strengthen ties with one another. (Robert Kirkman, Tony Moore, and Cliff Rathburn, *The Walking Dead, Volume 1: Days Gone Bye*)

Andrew, who is in for drug trafficking; Thomas, who pled guilty for committing tax fraud; and Axel, convicted of armed robbery, who, as the only one who lives long enough to join Rick's group, remains troubled by the existence of zombies. While plowing an area inside the prison grounds to create a vegetable garden, Axel gives voice to what the other survivors try their best to avoid, telling Hershel, "I think about them all the time, who they were—what they did before they died— . . . I think about what jobs they had, or if they had any family, and if so, where they went or what happened to them. . . . I mean those things all used to be people. Every single one of them had lives."[28] Axel's personal identification with zombies reinforces Kirkman's portrayal of the scope of society in *The Walking Dead* in which all—whether young or old, poor or wealthy, working or unemployed—are affected. Work becomes the bridge that unifies differences among survivors, serving as a painful reminder over the loss of humanity. Alternatively, the television series has Rick ponder this point over Wayne's body, the zombie corpse whose blood and guts are used by the group to impersonate the dead as they escape from a building in downtown Atlanta. As Rick searches Wayne's wallet, he performs a quick eulogy to acknowledge how the dead were once human, exclaiming, "He used to be worried about bills, about rent . . . he used to be like us."[29] Critics Marty McKendry and Michael Da

Silva argue, "The utter respect with which Rick and the survivors treat Wayne's body changes an apparent desecration into an act of heroism. The more grue-some the act, the nobler the sacrifice," and this honoring of the dead—of a fel-low worker—reveals both Rick's humanity and class consciousness (64).

In a zombie apocalypse, daily survival becomes a full-time job, and, as the focus on Wayne's corpse shows, every moment could be the last in a world where the preservation of human life has replaced the accumulation of capital. A focus on labor—that is, what it takes each day to survive (securing food, set-ting up camp, warding off attacks by the dead *and* the living, and strategizing future plans)—is critical to understanding how, as Andrew Tripp argues, "apoc-alyptic narratives create spaces for the disenchanted within the larger society." Take, for example, Andrea's character. In the comic, her dead-end career as a law firm clerk left her feeling powerless and unfulfilled. By contrast, she becomes a skilled shooter and an integral member of the group, exhibiting more satisfac-tion in the present than she had experienced thus far in her life. Consequently, Andrea does not mourn the loss of the past when she states, "That job is one of the few things I don't miss."[30] Instead, she appears, as do many of her coun-terparts throughout the narrative, relieved that this aspect of life is over. Even Philip Blake, the leader of Woodbury who goes by the moniker "the Governor," recalls the difficulty in living up to the expectations of the American Dream. He admits to Andrea in the television series, "Pay off the car, work fifty hours a week, get married, and buy a house. That was survival for me."[31] That he assumes greater responsibility now calls attention to the immense powerless-ness he experienced before zombies ruled the world—a point he makes clear to Rick during their meeting to negotiate terms over ownership of the prison, "I was at work . . . taking shit from a boss half my age and an IQ even lower."[32] The Governor's relentless drive to dominate, which includes killing the innocent, lying to his people to advance his own agenda, and taking whatever stands in his way (including other people's property and supplies), originates out of his previous inability to achieve the same level of satisfaction and self-worth in his life, and however distorted and disturbing his vision of reality may be, the zombie apocalypse allows him to exercise agency and control over the future more than ever before.

While the television show focuses on Rick and the Governor as two leaders in a perpetual epic battle over good and evil—one that eventually culminates in the latter's barbaric murder of Hershel and the forced displacement of Rick's group after blowing up the prison—the comic continues to develop the theme of working-class angst when Nicholas, one of Alexandria's residents, attempts to take a stand against Rick soon after he and the others arrive. After realizing his mistake for wrongly believing that Rick was going to kill people in order to assume leadership over the community, he apologizes to Rick, admitting, "I was a failure in the world before . . . I was lucky to get a job digging ditches. And this . . . what's happened to all of us, this was supposed to be an opportunity to do better, to make something better of myself . . . and I felt like you were keeping me from that."[33] Aptly named *We Find Ourselves*, this volume signals a turning point, as the group solidifies their collective power as threats from outside the walls loom large. The end of economic worry and job dissatisfaction makes way for reinvention, offering survivors the opportunity to explore alternative forms of self-expression and to experience positions of authority as they continuously adapt to the struggles of surviving in this new world. According to Torie Bosch, "In *The Walking Dead*, the strongest survivors come from blue-collar backgrounds—cops, hunters, mechanics . . . we see a social order upended." The dramatic shift from mainstream mediocrity to extreme self-reliance illustrates how the parameters of work have irrevocably changed, redefining power relations among survivors and creating new opportunities to express their individuality in meaningful ways.

The television series also contains pivotal moments where several characters overcome feelings of inadequacy by utilizing previous job skills to resolve a crisis, proving their usefulness to the group.[34] For instance, in "Guts," Jackie's knowledge of drainage tunnels from working in the city zoning office provides the group with a potential escape route out of the department building in Atlanta where they are trapped; however, when Glenn questions her, she simply states, "It's my job. Was."[35] Similarly, Glenn later devises an elaborate plan to retrieve the bag of guns Rick was forced to leave behind on the city streets. Impressed, Daryl Dixon, the southern rebel known best for his tracking skills, asks, "Hey kid, what'd you do before all this?" to which Glenn off-handedly replies, "Delivered pizzas."[36] Lilly, the Governor's soon-to-be love interest after the fall of Woodbury, also finds the return to work a welcome distraction. When ministering to a gash in his head, she implores, "Let me be a nurse again. . . . It feels good to have something to do. No one ever mentioned how boring the end of the world was going to be."[37] Though humorous to some degree, these responses point to a reliance of the past in the present, indicating how deeply ingrained the memory of work remains in the lives of Kirkman's characters. These moments also reveal how maintaining a work ethic becomes an important coping mechanism to preserve order and stability. In the episode "Vatos," Guillermo, a custodian, and Felipe, a nurse, provide yet another example by remaining behind at the nursing home to care for the elderly when all other staff members have left. Guillermo's crew, the Latino gang that attempts to confiscate Rick's stockpile of guns, "keeps busy" caring for the sick, fixing cars, and scavenging for supplies in the hopes of leaving Atlanta.[38] Once again, the power shift from service worker to group leader earns Guillermo respect and control in which he protects and cares for society's most vulnerable community.[39] Dr. Edmund Jenner, a scientist at the Centers for Disease Control and Prevention, also demonstrates a strong pull toward upholding the routine of daily work, opting to continue conducting experiments while many of his coworkers abandoned their posts in order to join their families. After a "rash of suicides" by those who remained inside, he tells Rick, "I'm all that's left. . . . I just kept working. Trying to do some good."[40]

As these examples show, one's work ethic takes on new meaning after the collapse of capitalism; it signifies a moral and humanist drive to do what is socially deemed right. Each character measures his or her self-worth against the capacity to be of use, to do something to ensure human survival and, in the case of Guillermo and Jenner, do so against the stigma of shame. If zombie narratives "manifest the predominant cultural anxieties of their times, anxieties usually repressed or ignored by the mainstream media," as Bishop claims (*American Zombie Gothic* 26), the recurring theme of work to develop characterization in *The Walking Dead* signals a profound awareness of class conflict—a too-often overlooked or misunderstood subject that privileges the false notion of America as classless or mainly middle-class.[41] As Kirkman makes clear, the majority of his characters lived fragmented lives, barely making it before the world became inundated by flesh-eating monsters. They were consumed by fear of debt and failure, and now with no government, media, or material items to distract them, these individuals' actions deflect the realities of contemporary class struggle that once seemed impossible to escape.[42] Each story paints a picture of America's diverse workforce, revealing how the American Dream remained out of reach for so many, yet, in the end, previous efforts no longer matter. The bygone days of work are over, and in writing about working-class people's struggles, Kirkman makes heroes of them all.

"We All Got Jobs to Do": Killing Zombies and the New Labor Economy

The collective experience of work plays an even greater role, beyond defining identity by creating new systems that ensure human survival. Whether it's Hershel's farm, the prison, Woodbury, Terminus, Grady Hospital, or the gated community of Alexandria, each locale serves as a work site for characters to perform jobs in *The Walking Dead*.[43] Season 5 of the television series presents two important examples of systemized labor to consider the functionality of work in a post-apocalyptic setting: first, the human slaughterhouse located in Terminus, replete with a butcher who, even when under attack, remains unfazed and reprimands his coworker for attempting to abandon his position ("We have a job to do . . . you blew protocol . . . security ain't our job");[44] and second, Grady Hospital, which operates with the utmost efficiency under the leadership of Officer Dawn Lerner, the head of law enforcement, who chastises Beth, Hershel's daughter, about the value in preserving life no matter the sacrifice ("In here, you are part of a system").[45] While many individuals take turns making supply runs to stockpile inventory and guard the perimeters of these locations, others learn new skill sets: Glenn, for instance, is mentored by Dale on vehicle maintenance, and Carol receives training by Hershel to treat medical conditions. In fact, the phrase "We all got jobs to do" becomes a mantra of sorts for the Greene family in the television series.[46] This line, uttered first by Beth to assuage Maggie's worry about the flu epidemic sweeping through the prison, refers to their father's philosophy—that service to aid others in need trumps individual concerns. Hershel's holistic approach to community building applies to parenting, schooling, gardening, and health care—any endeavor that in the long run saves lives. As such, he puts himself at risk by volunteering to gather elderberry in the woods outside the prison to administer tea and other breathing treatments to those in quarantine. Hershel later repeats this phrase to Lizzie, one of the younger children he encounters on his way to treat a patient, when he advises her to finish reading the novel *Tom Sawyer* in an effort to distract her from the rising death toll.[47] Maggie, too, draws strength in using her father's words during the Governor's attack on the prison. For example, after he brutally beheads Hershel in front of Rick's group, Maggie orders her sister, Beth, to drive the bus that will lead the larger group to safety, even if it means leaving her and Glenn behind, "We all have jobs to do."[48] Glenn, now married to Maggie, also adheres to Hershel's code when, a few seasons later, he tells Michonne of his plan to divert the "herd" away from their small group so they can return safely to Alexandria: "We all have a job to do."[49] The repetition of this phrase illustrates a profound level of self-sacrifice in the face of extreme danger to ensure life—once again proving how survivors maintain a work ethic that is no longer measured by a now-defunct capitalist framework: their compensation lies in living to see another day.

No one is exempt from having to pitch in to maintain their existence, but, as the comic reveals, life in a zombie apocalypse is not ideal, and with the creation of new jobs comes the danger of upholding gender and class division typical of the pre-zombie world. As early as the first volume, the comic contains several pivotal scenes that illustrate a clear division of labor among the group once they set up camp in the outskirts of Atlanta. Women take on domestic duties such as washing clothes and tending to the children, while the men hunt to secure food and patrol the area for imposing threats, and the reinstatement of these traditional gender roles complicates group dynamics. For example, when Donna complains that doing laundry "is such bullshit," Lori fires back, "This isn't about women's rights. . . . It's about being realistic and doing what needs to be done."[50]

Kirkman's depiction of this scene onscreen (and the representation of women's work in general) has sparked considerable debate among critics. Whereas Ashley Barkman contends Donna's "complaint is unmerited . . . and ironic," considering the safety and privilege that domestic chores afford her compared to the men who risk their lives outside the camp (101), Kay Steiger suggests that the communal act of doing "menial domestic work" creates "a sisterhood saloon that allows a sanctuary in the midst of what has suddenly become for them a very hard life" (108). The comic, alternatively, features a scene at the prison where Andrea happily volunteers to be the group's seamstress, converting prison jumpsuits into seasonal clothing, and serves as a case in point of Kirkman's uneven portrayal of female agency: "I can sew pretty good and I enjoy it, and it is important."[51] In contrast to the earlier scene with Donna—whose concerns are dismissed—Andrea asserts her leadership by calling a meeting with the entire group not only to instruct them about her plans, but also to let them know she expects their cooperation and assistance. No one questions Andrea's directives or interrupts her during the ten panels it takes to explain her process—a rather remarkable domestic scene sequence in an otherwise male-driven, violent narrative. Steiger further argues that scenes in the television series of women using washing machines at the prison "is unsettling, perhaps even distastefully retro" (108). Clearly, both mediums show how the roles men and women adopt or get assigned are determined by gender and power, and as Martina Baldwin and Mark McCarthy note, *The Walking Dead* "perpetuates the pre-feminist idea that feminism is not truly necessary since at the end of the day—or during an apocalypse—the only way to survive is with the support of and protection by a (preferably white) male" (86).[52] Evidence of this can be seen when Rick initiates target practice so that the women and children can learn to defend themselves, and, of course, practice gun safety—a decision that seems more practical than ideologically based.[53]

Men too wrestle with gender and class antagonism in the comic. The group's arrival in Alexandria, for instance, provides Sergeant Abraham Ford with a glimpse of how little class difference among owners and workers has changed in the new world. When he begins working on the construction crew to "earn [his] place," he learns from his coworker, Bruce, how community leader Douglas Monroe assigns jobs based on his interview process: "It's bullshit. I don't know how all the pretty girls somehow end up qualified for jobs where he'll see them frequently. . . . But the most screwed up thing is us. You think

The comic regularly features scenes with commentary such as this to develop characterization and perspective. This panel, which occurs shortly after Rick's arrival, illustrates the tensions inherent in domestic life in a zombie apocalypse. The disagreement about women's rights creates discord among the married women in the camp, who also happen to be mothers—that is, noticeably absent from the conversation are the sisters Andrea and Beth, who are both single. (Robert Kirkman, Tony Moore, and Cliff Rathburn, *The Walking Dead, Volume 1: Days Gone Bye*)

we're the strongest, or the fastest, sent out to build this wall. But you saw all those guys—they're just the dumbest. We're the dumbest. The most expendable."[54] This conversation between two working-class guys on a job site reveals a clear articulation of class consciousness and solidarity—a Marxian analysis of collective labor, its demand and value.[55]

As with Romero before him, Kirkman's use of the zombie is political, and the images of reanimated corpses in the comic function to establish the story's focus on class and power relations. As Dawn Keetley explains, "The distinct 'humanity' of the zombie horde is clearly in service to its function as allegory of the underclass; indeed, the film [Romero's *Land of the Dead* (2005)] is at pains to align the zombies with the poor, oppressed, and racially marginalized among the human survivors" (5). Kirkman (and artists Tony Moore, Charlie Adlard, and Cliff Rathburn), however, do more than reduce zombies to an indistinguishable mass of masticating monsters to use as props; instead, a fair amount of detail is presented throughout the comic series and, most notably, on its covers to reveal the former identities of individuals before they "turned." Even though zombies in *The Walking Dead* become, as Dave Beisecker claims, "*just the situation, not the metaphor*" (emphasis his, 207), adding that their "increasingly marginalized role" operates as "mere distractions" (209), the comic depicts zombies from nearly every social group, from the average citizen to the professional elite. While the majority of zombies remain a gory, ghoulish group bent on consuming flesh, countless close-ups of exercise instructors, young school children, college students, priests, gas station attendants, computer geeks, farmers, administrative personnel, and punk rockers appear in panels, sporting a variety of clothing such as uniforms, jewelry, and other accessories.

Their physicality creates a cross-class portrait of individuals from urban, suburban, and rural backgrounds, highlighting gender and age as well as ethnic and racial differences. On the one hand, these adornments serve to differentiate the dead, providing a glimpse of their working lives; on the other hand, they reflect the values and livelihoods of the survivors—a reminder of their former selves. Simon Pegg writes, "More subtly, the zombie represents a number of our deeper insecurities. The fear that deep down, we may be little more than animals, concerned only with appetite. Zombies can represent the threat of collectivism against individuality. The notion that we might be swallowed up and forgotten, our special-ness devoured by the crowd."[56] While the zombie figure in *The Walking Dead* symbolizes the "fear" of becoming nothing—a thing—the particular details about zombie identities add another layer to understanding how class functions as a humanizing element among the dead.

Arguably, one of the strongest examples of the importance of work in the apocalypse rests in the creation of a new form of labor: the physically violent and

Stylistically, the effective use of panel sequencing in these images, from the zombie sporting a bolo necktie (where he literally falls off the page) to the distinctive close-up of a woman adorned with a pearl necklace to the gamer geek, provide a glimpse of their former human selves. The quick succession of death blows accented by the use of onomatopoeia "Spak" and "Splagg," as well as the spattering of zombie blood and brains, does much to advance the adeptness with which Rick and his group can thwart off an attack, but the details with which each zombie is identified emphasize that those being killed (again) could be lawyers, bankers, health care professionals, teachers, security guards, farmers, truck drivers, etc. The specific details of their dress raise questions about who they were as well as what they were doing at the time of the zombie uprising. (Robert Kirkman, Charlie Adlard, and Cliff Rathburn, *The Walking Dead, Volume 4: The Heart's Desire*; *Volume 15: We Find Ourselves*; *Volume 9: Here We Remain*; and *Volume 5: The Best Defense*)

messy work of killing zombies. It's a dirty and dangerous job, to be sure, but as one character puts it, "I gotta do something to help out."[57] The ever-present threat of zombies is imminent and, at times, predictable, yet the conflict resolution is swift: one either survives the attack or dies trying. Perhaps the most remarkable aspect of this new job, however repulsive, rests on its reliance on physical strength and prowess. This shift towards "meaningful work" and "self-reliance," according to Matthew B. Crawford, "brings certain experiences into sharper focus" (7). A number of scenes in the television series depict various characters who engage in killing zombies, and this return to manual labor becomes far "more engaging intellectually" and "tangible" work than the unrewarding careers corporate America produced for them in the past (5). Take Michonne, for example, a former lawyer and fencer extraordinaire who resents being forced to remain at Woodbury among residents that seem too comfortably removed from the dangers outside their protected community. To prove her selfhood, she sets loose a number of zombies that have been locked in a cage on the Governor's order, only to slaughter them all in a matter of seconds, immediately breathing a long sigh of relief upon completing her task.[58] In a similar fashion, Andrea takes matters into her own hands and jumps over Woodbury's wall to knock over and stab a stray zombie in the head. Her reaction afterward is even more pronounced than Michonne's: she smiles broadly and proudly, exclaiming to Haley, the expert archer whose arrows fail to stop the zombie from approaching, "That is how it's done."[59] In both instances, killing become an outlet for these two former legal professionals in which they relish the power and satisfaction their physical labor provides. But their actions also signify a resistance to the idea of teamwork and building cohesiveness among coworkers (or, in the case of Woodbury, among its residents) (128, 148). Both Michonne and Andrea act individually, illustrating how their will to survive and show of physical strength surpass any desire to assimilate or perpetuate the middle-class fantasy life Woodbury creates. As Bosch explains, "[t]he zombie apocalypse is a white-collar nightmare: a world with no need for the skills we have developed. Lawyers, journalists, investment bankers—they are liabilities, not leaders in the zombie-infested world." That both characters are women further suggests how representations of female labor are continually being redefined as Kirkman's story develops.

The immediate effects of killing zombies also impact blue-collar characters such as Abraham and Daryl, who, later in the television series, are accused of drawing pleasure from the act, "smiling" and toying with the dead moments before crushing their skulls.[60] Beth admonishes Daryl, telling him, "Killing isn't supposed to be fun."[61] Zombies, however, as McIntosh asserts, "symbolize a monster that can be killed guilt-free" (13). They are, in a sense, satisfying to kill precisely because it fills the void of idleness that a post-apocalyptic world creates. As a result, the act of killing zombies reaffirms life without fear of moral consequence. Michonne, Andrea, Abraham, and Daryl each achieve a sense of fulfillment and empowerment greater than a paycheck or a career could produce. The resulting action provides these individuals with a sense of purpose—a show of dominance over the dead—as well as a deeper connection to the end product (human life) compared to previous forms of labor (a living death). No longer rendered invisible or replaceable by the machine of capitalism, these survivors/members of a new workforce against the backdrop of a zombie apocalypse become human.

Although slaughtering zombies may be far less alienating work, killing for a living—literally to stay alive and to make a living—also becomes tedious work. Safely ensconced in the prison, members of Rick's group systematically thin out the herd of zombies that form alongside the fence. This task becomes a rote exercise in which the characters view the job as a nuisance rather than a serious threat. Even so, this new form of labor offers characters a way to release bottled-up frustrations, exacting revenge on a known enemy and, in the process, escaping mind-numbing mediocrity; more importantly, the ability to fight zombies (and win) is a powerful life-affirming act, illustrating a shared camaraderie among survivors that remained beyond their reach in the past but is now instantly recoverable on a daily basis.

The New Status Quo

Perhaps the greatest class irony of all in *The Walking Dead* is that Alexandria—the eco-sustainable planning development with homes starting at $800,000—becomes the epicenter for survival in season 5 of the television series. After Rick's group escapes certain death in Terminus and finds themselves traveling on the open road in search of shelter, food, and water, Aaron, Alexandria's recruiter, appears suddenly at their makeshift camp to offer assistance. He tells Rick about his community and, after admitting to tracking their movements to ensure they are trustworthy people, informs him, "My job is to convince you to come back with me."[62] Though reluctant, Rick eventually agrees to follow Aaron, and what the group discovers at Alexandria astounds them. Not only does the community contain hardworking families who are raising their children, but the middle-class American Dream lifestyle that remained unobtainable for so many before the zombie apocalypse has now become a safe zone—an inclusive modern-day "resort" containing electricity, running water, sewerage, food pantry, home furnishings, technology, and other material comforts. Deanna, the Ohio congresswoman who manages the community, conducts video interviews with the new arrivals—a process she undergoes to learn more about the world outside Alexandria's walls and each person's character. Her meeting with Rick reveals a philosophical debate between her belief that what individuals did in the past matters still and his position on abandoning the old ways to survive the present: "It's all about survival now. At any cost. People out there are always looking for an angle to play on your weakness. They measure you from what they can take from you. By how they could use you to live."[63] Deanna measures their words and actions and assigns each person a job (based on their prior work history and what they hope to offer to ensure the community's survival). Whereas Rick resumes a role in law enforcement as Alexandria's new constable and, like the others, begins to acclimate to life on the inside, Daryl balks at his new surroundings, refusing to take a shower and insisting on carrying his crossbow and the possum he killed for dinner during his "job interview" with Deanna. His resistance stems partly out of distrust of these other survivors and also from his profound discomfort with middle-class life. When Deanna asks him if he desires to stay, he simply replies, "The boy and the baby [Rick's two children] deserve a roof, I guess."[64] His persistent aloofness allows him to maintain his independence without conforming, and while there have been instances where Daryl has let his guard down (notably with Carol after her daughter's disappearance), he remains a loner who follows his own set of rules—a social enigma that Deanna struggles "to figure . . . out."[65]

More than any other character in *The Walking Dead*, Daryl is class-conscious; this fact is particularly noteworthy, given that his role was created solely for the television series. Referring to himself as a "redneck asshole," Daryl admits to having spent most of his life "drifting around" as a "nobody."[66] Yet the struggle to assimilate with other survivors in his group illustrates how he remains conflicted by class difference. Evidence of Daryl's discomfort with middle-class mediocrity can be seen in his interaction with Beth, whose suicide attempt while still living at her father's farm in his view reveals her privileged upbringing. After escaping Terminus, the two find themselves separated from the rest of the group and wander through the woods until they emerge onto a golf course. While exploring the clubhouse to satisfy Beth's whim to drink alcohol for the first time, Daryl's anger becomes full-blown. The display of wealth, as seen by well-dressed zombies wearing blazers, polo shirts, and pearls, along with a female corpse bearing the sign "Rich Bitch" fastened to her chest, triggers a strong reaction in Daryl, so much so that he opts to "play golf" during a threatening zombie attack (presumably made up of club members who survived hidden within the clubhouse for as long as possible). Despite the fact that he knows a direct hit to the head would end the imposing threat immediately,

Daryl instead prolongs the killing, repeatedly clubbing one dead man until the final swing (the fifteenth) knocks a portion of its head off, splattering Beth's newly donned white cardigan with blood and brains. That he later shoots darts at framed photographs of the club presidents' heads (all white men) in the lounge further shows the impact Daryl's transgression—of crossing over class boundaries and entering a space previously off limits—has on him, as he begins to exact his own kind of retaliation against the wealthy.[67] Another instance of class angst occurs later in the series when Daryl and Carol go searching for Beth in Atlanta; she has been taken to Grady Hospital against her will by two men. Taking refuge in a high-rise office building to find supplies, Daryl pauses in one of the offices to view the opulent decor, and he remarks on the brush-strokes of an abstract painting: "I bet this cost some rich prick a lot of money. It looks like a dog sat in paint and wiped his ass all over the place."[68] While Carol disagrees with Daryl's assessment, his gruff response shows utter disdain for anyone who aligns themselves with rich, elitist culture—a point he consistently reminds folks of by making class-based comments throughout the series, such as the time he discovers a kitchen stocked with food items at an abandoned funeral home: "Peanut butter and jelly, diet soda, and pigs' feet. That's a white-trash brunch right there."[69]

Daryl's old-school ways—tracking, shooting a crossbow, and hunting wild game—become an asset in this new world, and a highly valued commodity that Aaron recognizes is worth cultivating, especially in aiding him to seek out potential new recruits for Alexandria. Over a spaghetti dinner that shows Daryl slurping through his meal and wiping his mouth on his sleeve, Aaron offers him a job because he "know[s] the difference between a good person and a bad person."[70] This scene illustrates a powerful moment of bonding between two men in which class differences disappear, similar to the kind of brotherhood that develops between Daryl and Rick because of their shared experiences surviving on the road. Daryl undergoes a transformation, experiencing what critic Chris Boehm calls an "'un-burdening' quality to losing the old way of life" (126). When he accepts the scouting job, stating tersely, "I got nothing else to do," Daryl's character begins to evolve from white-trash southern good old boy to that of a working man. He experiences class mobility for the first time, as well as a sense of belonging in Aaron's and, on a larger scale, Alexandria's middle-class subur-bia.[71] The example of Daryl is but one of many survivors who, as the series pro-gresses toward the second half of its sixth season, experience the value of work (farming and other skill-related labor) in order to create a sustainable future.

With no solution to the rise of crippling debt and contingent labor in con-temporary society, Kirkman's references to real-world economic issues in his comic should not be discounted, especially if reflecting on how zombies, as

Cory James Rushton and Christopher M. Moreman argue, "force us to reconsider the nature of the meanings that we currently attach to self and society" (7). In the context of *The Walking Dead*, the apocalypse becomes a turning point—an endgame moment—for survivors to reclaim power and control over their lives. While some of the characters consider this a possibility to recreate a more just world, others exploit it for their own advantage. Among other reasons for Kirkman's creating the comic was a desire "to explore how people deal with extreme situations and how these events CHANGE them."[72] The appearance of Negan, the narcissistic gang leader of the Saviors, in the final episode of season 6, is the strongest example to date of Kirkman's testing the limits of humanity. Demanding supplies from neighboring communities in exchange for protection, Negan governs by fear, taking ownership of everything in his path and exacting human life as payment for resistance. In fact, he refers to the cat-and-mouse game he implemented to round up Rick and other members of his group as "career day," informing them that their new "job" is to "work" for him.[73] Negan takes perverse pleasure in dethroning Rick as one who once "ruled the roost" to impart his code of "rules," telling him, "You answer to me. You provide for me. You belong to me."[74] Negan puts additional strain on an already untenable situation for Rick and his group in which he demands payment in the form of half of any available and newly acquired resources, or what one Alexandrian resident sums up as "taxes."[75] His point-based system—of "earn[ing] what you take"—is reinforced by the austerity of his well-guarded feudal complex. Likewise, the force of his mandate draws an explicit correlation between the product of one's labor and class position—that is, the ability to work and to produce serves as a bargaining chip for individuals to stay alive.[76]

The survivors in *The Walking Dead*—average citizens who suddenly find themselves thrust into a life of extreme, endless violence—reveal not only the facade of the world they left behind, but the pointlessness of having lived a past that focused solely on mindless materialism. *The Walking Dead* tackles many aspects of working-class culture, suggesting that the world's ending does not erase class difference entirely; on the contrary, social conflicts among survivors reveal how attached to their identity the meaning of work remains. Labor itself undergoes a transformation, allowing characters to express themselves in more creative, equitable, collective, and practical ways—the ideals of self-reliance and individual agency Crawford proposes are tied to autonomy in the workplace (7, 201, 207–208). Power struggles between men and women, leaders and their followers, and existing groups continuously emerge; and, in a world of perpetual psychological torment and never knowing if the present moment is the last, Kirkman reminds us of the fact that work functions as a humanizing and stabilizing force in an unknown future—an aspect of everyday life that inspires hope, pride, and purpose.[77] The fight to believe in a future beyond day-to-day survival is predicated on contributing to and combating an endless cycle of work, and the radical shift in labor from earning a livable wage to staying alive is a compelling topic to examine how survival strategies—in all their forms—continue to shape identity and community in a world plagued by the living dead both in fiction and in reality.

Notes

1. The CDC's Office of Public Health Preparedness and Response runs a website, complete with a blog and novella of its own, inviting *Walking Dead* fans to participate in emergency preparedness.

2. More recently, the zombie has been used as performance art worldwide to stage political and social protests against Wall Street (the Occupy Movement) and corporate power (Monsanto) in organized walks and flash mobs, raising awareness about food justice, environmental rights, and class inequity. Andrew Tripp explains, "Apocalyptic and post-apocalyptic narratives provide space for those who feel a lack of agency in a larger society, or who feel deadened by the quotidian demands of mundane existence." He further points out, "Zombie marches as performance of apocalyptic narratives produce specific social spaces that move through the decline of social order, which at best would perhaps invert the social order in a carnivalesque fashion." The image of large crowds of crazed consumers battling one another to purchase goods the day after Thanksgiving, which closely resembles a swarming mass of "zombies," is not lost on protestors who participate in "Buy Nothing Day" to boycott Black Friday.

3. His essay "Eating the Dead: AMC's Use of Synergy to Cultivate Zombie Consumption" in *Thinking Dead: What the Zombie Apocalypse Means* details the corporate branding and marketing strategies used to generate revenue since the show's creation.

4. For an overview of the rise in zombie narratives, see Kyle Bishop's essay "Dead Man Still Walking: Explaining the Zombie Renaissance." See also the introduction to his book-length study, *American Zombie Gothic*, as well as Todd K. Platts's "Locating Zombies in the Sociology of Popular Culture," which explores the history of zombies as a popular cultural phenomenon.

5. Many scholars have examined the historical and cultural significance of zombie cinema. For a fuller discussion of the origins of the zombie as deriving from Haitian folklore and as racially colonized subjects represented in film, see McIntosh's essay "The Evolution of the Zombie: The Monster That Keeps Coming Back."

6. See Patten's essay "'*Walking Dead*' Ratings Hit Almost 20M Viewers for Season 6 Debut in Live + 3" for a comparison of season openers over the years: http://deadline.com/2015/10/walking-dead-ratings-season-6-debut-live-3-amc-1201585196/.

7. Volume 1: *Days Gone Bye*, Introduction.

8. As Bishop contends, "*The Walking Dead* isn't about the zombies at all; it's about human character" (*American Zombie Gothic* 206); consequently, the story focuses on "a human underground fighting to retain its humanity" (Bonansinga 63). This human dimension amid a world of reanimated corpses underscores the story's focus on producing emotionally driven rather than high-impact action scenes; as Bonansinga claims, "The characters of *The Walking Dead* are not mere characters; they are people. They are terrified, and they are morally sickened, and they long for deliverance, and they love their children, and they will do anything to protect their families" (57).

9. Kirkman's new series, *Fear the Walking Dead*, explores the emerging zombie outbreak and collapse of society. Set in Los Angeles, the show premiered in August 2015.

10. The significance of these items is revealed during a conversation between Rick and Paul Monroe (a.k.a. Jesus) as they negotiate a trade agreement between their respective communities in Volume 6, "A Larger World."

11. Robert Kirkman, Tony Moore, and Cliff Rathburn, Volume 1: "Days Gone Bye."

12. P. Ivan Young reads Rick's character as a "mythic cowboy" (60)—a Western hero who "struggles to maintain the illusion of 'righteous power'" (56). His essay offers an analysis of Western motifs in *The Walking Dead* that underscore the prevalence of violence in redefining the self.

13. Kirkman, Moore, and Rathburn, *The Walking Dead, Volume 1: Days Gone Bye*.

14. Robert Kirkman, Charlie Adlard, and Cliff Rathburn, *The Walking Dead, Volume 2: Miles Behind Us*.

15. Kirkman, Moore, and Rathburn, *Days Gone Bye*.

16. Ibid.

17. Ibid.

18. Ibid.

19. Ibid.

20. Ibid.

21. According to the Department of Labor, unemployment rates jumped from 5 percent in January 2008 to 10 percent in October 2009; see http://data.bls.gov/timeseries/LNS14000000 for a complete list of figures. Jaison R. Abel, Richard Deitz, and Yaqin Su reported even more dire statistics for college graduates in "Are Recent College Graduates Finding Good Jobs?" claiming those able to secure work did so by finding low-paying positions that did not require a college degree. Glenn's character embodies the toll job loss and underemployment cause to human life and national consciousness, suggesting, too, that a college education is not an investment that pays off in the long run.

22. Robert Kirkman, Charlie Adlard, and Cliff Rathburn, *The Walking Dead, Volume 5: The Best Defense*.

23. Kirkman, Adlard, and Rathburn, *Miles Behind Us*.

24. Ibid.

25. Dave Beisecker reads Glenn's heroism differently, identifying his character as the "stereotypical geek who now has the opportunity to ride out the ultimate geek-fantasy. He gets to take revenge upon (and denounce as "geeks") all those who once would have strung him up by his underwear in the locker-room but have preceded him to the other side. Plus, . . . he gets the girl, too" (211).

26. Kirkman, Adlard, and Rathburn, *Miles Behind Us*.

27. Ibid.

28. Robert Kirkman, Charlie Adlard, and Cliff Rathburn, *The Walking Dead, Volume 4: The Heart's Desire*.

29. *The Walking Dead*, Season 1: Episode 5, "Wildfire," written by Glenn Mazzara and directed by Ernest Dickerson.

30. Kirkman, Moore, and Rathburn, *Days Gone Bye*.

31. *The Walking Dead*, Season 3: Episode 4, "Killer Within," written by Sang Kyu Kim and directed by Guy Ferland.

32. *The Walking Dead*, Season 3: Episode 13, "Arrow on the Doorpost," written by Ryan C. Coleman and directed by David Boyd.

33. Robert Kirkman, Tony Moore, and Cliff Rathburn, *The Walking Dead, Volume 15: We Find Ourselves*.

34. In some cases, one's previous work experience is also used against them, as in the case of the episode "Judge, Jury, Executioner" from season 2, when Dale and Andrea, who in the television series is identified as a former civil rights lawyer, debate whether or not to kill Randall, an outsider, to protect the group from being attacked by a group of marauding men. As mediator, Dale's plea to save the young man's life becomes the ultimate sales pitch for Rick's group to consider: "You fight with words. The power of ideas. . . . That's what a civilized society does. . . . The world we know is gone, but keeping our humanity . . . that's a choice." The philosophical quandary causes the group to define a new code of ethics; equally important, then, is recognizing how Andrea's former career provides the basis for maintaining morality in the new world.

35. *The Walking Dead*, Season 1: Episode 2, "Guts," written by Frank Darabont and directed by Michelle MacLaren.

36. *The Walking Dead*, Season 1: Episode 4, "Vatos," written by Robert Kirkman and directed by Johan Renck.

37. *The Walking Dead*, Season 4: Episode 6, "Live Bait," written by Nichole Beattie and directed by Michael Uppendahl.

38. "Vatos."

39. Danee Pye and Peter Padraic O'Sullivan read Guillermo's and Felipe's characters in terms of masculinity, arguing, "While there's a certain amount of gender-role reinforcement with their protector statuses, these two play much deeper roles as both caretakers and caregivers. There is almost a sense, after the revelation of their true roles, that they're both vaguely uncomfortable with the hyper-masculine, or *vato* persona they have to adopt" (112).

40. *The Walking Dead*, Season 1: Episode 4, "TS-19," written by Adam Fierro & Frank Darabont and directed by Guy Ferland.

41. This statement is informed by Michael Zweig's definition of class as being rooted in power rather than income and lifestyle (4). See his edited collection *What's Class Got to Do With It? American Society in the Twenty-First Century*, especially his introduction as to how the subject of class is an understudied concept in American society. As new characters are introduced in Kirkman's comic, the terms "boss" and "job" consistently appear, reminding readers of the ways in which economic power shapes everyday life.

42. Like the rotting corpses, appearances of Texaco, McDonald's, and Walmart litter the deserted landscape in the comic, symbolizing the end of corporate America. These iconic relics of the past also emphasize the need for self-reliance. None of the characters mentions them or even desires the products they once offered, which suggests these abandoned structures serve merely as a haunting reminder of the dissatisfaction consumerism bred in their previous lives—a fact that is becoming more irrelevant as each day passes. Kirkman also reinforces this message on the comic's back cover: "The world of commerce and frivolous necessity has been replaced by a world of survival and responsibility. . . . In a world ruled by the dead, we are forced to finally start living."

43. Each of these settings provides opportunities to reinvent (or, in some cases, to reinstate) systems of labor. According to Balaji, "In *The Walking Dead*, property rights—a pillar of capitalism—become embedded in the storyline" (xi). These communities symbolize the power of ownership and commodities; they also represent sites of resistance where major battles are fought to protect the living from the threat of zombie attacks and other groups of survivors.

44. *The Walking Dead*, Season 5: Episode 1, "No Sanctuary," written by Scott M. Gimple and directed by Greg Nicotero.

45. *The Walking Dead*, Season 5: Episode 3, "Four Walls and a Roof," written by Angela Kang and Corey Reed and directed by Jeffrey F. January.

46. *The Walking Dead*, Season 4: Episode 3, "Isolation," written by Robert Kirkman and directed by Daniel Sackheim.

47. *The Walking Dead*, Season 4: Episode 5, "Internment," written by Channing Powell and directed by David Boyd.

48. *The Walking Dead*, Season 4: Episode 8, "Too Far Gone," written by Seth Hoffman and directed by Ernest Dickerson. Other variations of this work ethic appear when people ignore their responsibilities, such as when Maggie sharply reprimands the priest, Gabriel, for not opening the doors of his church to save parishioners: "You had a job. You were there to save your flock, but you didn't. You hid. Don't act like that didn't happen" (Season 5: Episode 10, "Them," written by Heather Bellson and directed by Julius Ramsay).

49. *The Walking Dead*, Season 6: Episode 3, "Thank You." Written by Angela Kang and directed by Michael Slovis.

50. Kirkman, Moore, and Rathburn, *Days Gone Bye*.

51. Kirkman, Adlard, and Rathburn, *Heart's Desire*.

52. Kirkman incorporates this narrative thread in the television series as well. In "18 Miles Out," Andrea dismisses Lori's belief that women "are providing stability" and accuses Lori of "playing house" (*The Walking Dead*, Season 2: Episode 10, "18 Miles Out," written by Scott M. Gimple and Glenn Mazzara and directed by Ernest Dickerson). This battle of wills between the two women, what Baldwin and McCarthy refer to as "backlash post-feminism" rhetoric, has much to do with Andrea's desire to contribute significantly to the group's defense—that is, to learn how to clean and shoot a gun to defend herself, instead of just washing clothes (85). The argument, which takes place in Hershel's kitchen, marks a schism between traditional and more unorthodox gender norms and breaks open the meaning of the domestic sphere in the apocalypse. While Kirkman missed an opportunity to develop Andrea's strong female character more fully by having her enter into a romantic relationship with the Governor—a decision that ultimately leads to her death—he does offset this representation of women by having Carol undergo a transformation from a meek, battered housewife to an instrumental, heroic figure responsible for ensuring the group's safety on several occasions. Once the group settles in the suburbs of Alexandria, she enacts the role of an "invisible" housewife, admitting sarcastically to Daryl that it's "time to punch the clock and cook the casseroles" in order to carry out her ruse as "den mother" to find out more information about its residents ("18 Miles Out").

53. As the series develops, the focus on the separation of domestic labor and equal opportunity among female characters, which originally served to establish characterization, decreases significantly as danger from both the living and the dead escalates.

54. Kirkman, Adlard, and Rathburn, *The Walking Dead, Volume 13: Too Far Gone.*

55. Kirkman develops the common bond of work much earlier in the television series between Rick's and the Governor's inner circles. While the two leaders meet privately to discuss the fate of the prison, "henchmen" Daryl and Martinez engage in a verbal sparring match, prompting Hershel to warn, "We don't need this. If all goes south in there, we'll be at each other's throats soon enough" ("Arrow on the Doorpost"). Later in the episode, the two men find common ground discussing the inevitability of having to fight one another, while Hershel and Milton, the Governor's resident scientist, use the time to share information about medicine and healing practices. This exchange among potential enemies results in each character knowing their limitations, and the ensuing dialogue reveals a clear delineation between those in charge and those who take orders. A more humorous example of work camaraderie occurs between Daryl and Rick, who head out for a supply run. Comfortably settled within Alexandria's walls, they act as if it is just another day on the job—two working stiffs listening to music, sharing a candy bar, and engaging in playful banter with each other to pass the time. After losing a truck full of goods and enduring an intensely physical altercation with a newcomer he captures and brings home, Rick asks Michonne, "You want to tell me about your day?"—a corny but familiar throwback to typical end-of-the-day banter of the past (Season 6: Episode 10, "The Next World," written by Angela Kang and Corey Reed and directed by Kari Skogland).

56. Kirkman, Adlard, and Rathburn, "Afterword," *Miles Behind Us.*

57. Kirkman, Adlard, and Rathburn, *Heart's Desire.*

58. *The Walking Dead*, Season 3: Episode 5, "Say the Word," written by Angela Kang and directed by Greg Nicotero.

59. *The Walking Dead*, Season 3: Episode 6, "Hounded," written by Scott M. Gimple and directed by Daniel Attias.

60. *The Walking Dead*, Season 4: Episode 11, "Claimed," written by Nichole Beattie and Seth Hoffman and directed by Seith Mann; Season 4: Episode 12, "Still" written by Angela Kang and directed by Julius Ramsay.

61. "Still."

62. *The Walking Dead*, Season 5: Episode 11, "The Distance," written by Seth Hoffman and directed by Larysa Kondracki.

63. *The Walking Dead*, Season 5: Episode 12, "Remember," written by Channing Powell and directed by Greg Nicotero.

64. Ibid.

65. Ibid.

66. "Still."

67. As Daryl proudly gives Beth "her first real drink" from the stash of moonshine housed at a shack deep in the woods, he reveals how he was raised in a similar home, where his father drank, chewed chaw, and played target practice in the living room. Beth's playful "I've never" drinking game, however, quickly turns ugly when Daryl gets drunk and rages against their class differences: "I've never been out of Georgia. I've never been on vacation. I've never had frozen yogurt. I've never had a pet pony. I've never gotten nothing from Santa Claus. I've never relied on anyone for protection before. Hell, I've never relied on anyone for anything." As Daryl's tirade makes clear, his life was not a "big game," but much like the "ugly" day-to-day survival he finds himself living through now. The scene results in a stunning power play against Beth's youth and gender (Daryl calls her a "girl" and a "dumb college bitch") after forcing her to play target practice with his crossbow to kill a zombie. In the end, he breaks down, blaming himself for the Governor's attack on the prison, which resulted in Hershel's death. The image of his hardened character defeated and slumped forward as Beth clings to his frame from behind mirrors the dead male zombie Daryl's arrow pins to the tree, suggesting simultaneously the fragility of life in general and, more specifically, the vulnerability of working-class masculinity. In a symbolic gesture meant to purge this chapter of their past, Beth and Daryl burn the house, lighting the fire with a wad of $100 bills he had taken from the golf clubhouse—an ultimate sign that the reliance on materiality has ended and that with this action comes the promise of remaking oneself in the present (ibid.)

68. *The Walking Dead*, Season 5: Episode 6, "Consumed," written by Matthew Negrete and Corey Reed and directed by Seith Mann.

69. *The Walking Dead*, Season 4: Episode 13, "Alone," written by Curtis Gwinn and directed by Ernest Dickerson.

70. *The Walking Dead*, Season 5: Episode 13, "Forget," written by Corey Reed and directed by David Boyd.

71. Ibid.

72. Kirkman, Moore, and Rathburn, "Introduction," *Days Gone Bye.*

73. *The Walking Dead*, Season 6: Episode 16, "Last Day on Earth," written by Scott Gimple and Matt Negrete and directed by Greg Nicotero.

74. *The Walking Dead*, Season 7: Episode 1, "The Day Will Come When You Won't Be," written by Scott Gimple and directed by Greg Nicotero.

75. *The Walking Dead*, Season 7: Episode 7, "Sing Me a Song," written by Angela Kang and Corey Reed and directed by Rosemary Rodriguez.

76. *The Walking Dead*, Season 7: Episode 3, "The Cell" written by Angela Kang and directed by Alrick Riley.

77. Applicable here is Bishop's Hegelian analysis of Romero's *Dawn of the Dead* (1978), in which he contends that "by losing their productive labor, the feckless individuals living in Romero's mall ultimately lose that which makes them essentially "human," and they regress to a more primitive, animal state" ("Idle Proletariat" 235).

Bibliography

Abel, Jaison R., Richard Deitz, and Yaqin Su. "Are Recent College Graduates Finding Good Jobs?" *Current Issues in Economics and Finance* 20.1 (2014). Web.

Badley, Linda. "Zombie Splatter Comedy from *Dawn* to *Shaun*: Cannibal Carnivalesque." *Zombie Culture: Autopsies of the Living Dead*. Ed. Shawn McIntosh and Marc Leverette. Lanham: Scarecrow Press. 35–53. Print.

Balaji, Murali. "Thinking Dead: Our Obsession with the Undead and Its Implications." *Thinking Dead: What the Zombie Apocalypse Means*. Ed. Murali Balaji. Lanham: Lexington Books, 2013. ix–xviii. Print.

Baldwin, Martina, and Mark McCarthy. "Same as It Ever Was: Savior Narratives and the Logics of Survival." *Thinking Dead: What the Zombie Apocalypse Means*. Ed. Murali Balaji. Lanham: Lexington Books, 2013. 75–87. Print.

Barkman, Ashley. "Women in a Zombie Apocalypse." *The Walking Dead and Philosophy: Zombie Apocalypse Now*. Ed. Wayne Yuen. Chicago: Open Court, 2012. 97–106. Print.

Beisecker, Dave. "Afterword: Bye-Gone Days: Reflections on Romero, Kirkman, and What We Become." *'We're All Infected': Essays on AMC's The Walking Dead and the Fate of the Human*. Ed. Dawn Keetley. Jefferson, NC: McFarland, 2015. 201–214. Print.

Bishop, Kyle William. *American Zombie Gothic*. Jefferson, NC: McFarland, 2010. Print.

———. "Dead Man Still Walking: Explaining the Zombie Renaissance." *Journal of Popular Film and Television* 37.1 (2009): 16–25. Print.

———. "The Idle Proletariat: *Dawn of the Dead*, Consumer Ideology, and the Loss of Productive Labor." *Journal of Popular Culture* 43.2 (2010): 234–248. Print.

———. "The Pathos of *The Walking Dead*: Bringing Terror Back to Zombie Cinema." *Triumph of the Walking Dead: Robert Kirkman's Zombie Epic on Page and Screen*. Ed. James Lowder. Dallas: BenBella Books, 2011. 1–14. Print.

Boehm, Chris. "The Zombie and the (r)Evolution of Subjectivity." In *"We're All Infected": Essays on AMC's The Walking Dead and the Fate of the Human*. Ed. Dawn Keetley. Jefferson, NC: McFarland, 2015. 126–141. Print.

Bonansinga, Jay. "A Novelist and a Zombie Walk into a Bar: Translating *The Walking Dead* to Prose." In *Triumph of the Walking Dead: Robert Kirkman's Zombie Epic on Page and Screen*. Ed. James Lowder. Dallas: BenBella Books, 2011. 53–65. Print.

Bosch, Torie. "First, Eat All the Lawyers: Why the Zombie Boom Is Really about the Economic Fears of White-Collar Workers." *Slate* 25 October 2011. Web. 4 November 2015.

Crawford, Matthew B. *Shop Class as Soulcraft: An Inquiry into the Value of Work*. New York: Penguin Press, 2009.

Greely, Stephen Brett. "Monsters of Modernity." In *The Walking Dead and Philosophy: Zombie Apocalypse Now*. Ed. Wayne Yuen. Chicago: Open Court, 2012. 167–176. Print.

Keetley, Dawn. "Introduction." In *"We're All Infected": Essays on AMC's The Walking Dead and the Fate of the Human*. Ed. Dawn Keetley. Jefferson, NC: McFarland, 2015. Print.

Kirkman, Robert. "Introduction." *The Walking Dead*. Vol. 1. Image Comics, 2010. Print.

Lowder, James. "Introduction." *Triumph of the Walking Dead: Robert Kirkman's Epic on Page and Screen*. Ed. James Lowder. Dallas: BenBella Books, 2011. xiii–xvii. Print.

McIntosh, Shawn. "The Evolution of the Zombie: The Monster That Keeps Coming Back." *Zombie Culture: Autopsies of the Living Dead*, edited by Shawn McIntosh and Marc Leverette. Lanham: Scarecrow Press. 1–17. Print.

McKendry, Marty, and Michael Da Silva. "I'm Gonna Tell Them about Wayne." *The Walking Dead and Philosophy: Zombie Apocalypse Now*. Ed. Wayne Yuen. Chicago: Open Court, 2012. 53–64. Print.

Nurse, Angus. "Asserting Law and Order over the Mindless." In *"We're All Infected": Essays on AMC's The Walking Dead and the Fate of the Human*. Ed. Dawn Keetley. Jefferson, NC: McFarland, 2015. 68–79. Print.

Patten, Dominic. "'*Walking Dead*' Ratings Hit Almost 20M Viewers for Season 6 Debut in Live + 3." *Deadline* 16 October 2015. Web. 16 October 2015.

Pegg, Simon. "Afterword." *The Walking Dead: Miles behind Us*. 2004. By Robert Kirkman, Charlie Adlard, and Cliff Rathburn. Berkeley: Image Comics, 2010.

Platts, Todd K. "Locating Zombies in the Sociology of Popular Culture." *Sociology Compass 7* (2013): 547–60. Web. 8 May 2015.

Pye, Danee, and Peter Padraic O'Sullivan, "Dead Man's Party." *The Walking Dead and Philosophy: Zombie Apocalypse Now*. Ed. Wayne Yuen. Chicago: Open Court, 2012. 107–116. Print.

Rushton, Cory James, and Christopher M. Moreman. "Introduction." *Zombies Are Us: Essays on the Humanity of the Walking Dead*. Jefferson, NC: McFarland, 2011. 1–7. Print.

Steiger, Kay. "No Clean Slate: Unshakable Race and Gender Politics in *The Walking Dead*." *Triumph of the Walking Dead: Robert Kirkman's Zombie Epic on Page and Screen*. Ed. James Lowder. Dallas: BenBella Books, 2011. 100–113. Print.

Tripp, Andrew. "Zombie Marches and the Limits of Apocalyptic Space." *Nomos Journal* 7 August 2013. Web. 25 November 2015.

Young, P. Ivan. "Walking Tall or Walking Dead? The American Cowboy in the Zombie Apocalypse." *"We're All Infected": Essays on AMC's The Walking Dead and the Fate of the Human*. Ed. Dawn Keetley. Jefferson, NC: McFarland, 2015. 56–67. Print.

"Zombie Preparedness." Office of Public Health Preparedness. Centers for Disease Control and Prevention. n.d. Web. 1 August 2015.

Zweig, Michael. "Introduction: The Challenge of Working Class Studies." *What's Class Got to Do with It? American Society in the Twenty-First Century*. Ed. Michael Zweig. Ithaca: Cornell University Press, 2004. 1–17.

YOU CAN BE WHATEVER THE HELL YOU WANT
Heroism and the Female Working Class in *Preacher*

Kelly Kanayama

Created by Northern Irish author Garth Ennis and English artist Steve Dillon, the Vertigo comic series *Preacher* (1995–2000) relates the exploits of Texan preacher Jesse Custer, his lover Tulip O'Hare, and his vampiric best friend Cassidy as they battle God and a religious paramilitary organization bent on controlling the world. As a reworking of the American Western, *Preacher* combines traditional elements of the genre with subversive exploration of the larger constructs underlying these elements. More precisely, through the character of Tulip, the series interrogates generic tropes regarding the relationships between gender dynamics, socioeconomic status and labor obligations, and the perception and demonstration of heroism.

Revisiting the Revisionist Western

Although *Preacher* is often classified as a Western, it incorporates characteristics of various genres into its narrative, including Gothic horror, southern fiction, action film and comics, and fantasy.[1] This revisionist approach to the Western, though, is by no means atypical for the period. At the point when Ennis (who was born in 1971) wrote and published *Preacher*, the Westerns of the early 1990s, such as *Dances with Wolves* (1991) and *Unforgiven* (1992), were attempting to critique the colonialist, sexist violence of the myth of the West perpetuated in earlier films; this followed on from a reappraisal begun in the 1960s that saw John Wayne satirize his previous characters through the role of Rooster Cogburn in *True Grit* (1969) and the introduction of Italian-made

A resurrected Tulip affirms her identity (in the face of being called a "cooze" earlier),
about to take revenge for her own murder and the sexist slur. From *Preacher* #12.
Writer: Garth Ennis. Artist: Steve Dillon, 1996.

spaghetti Westerns to American/Anglophone cinema, starting with Sergio
Leone's *A Fistful of Dollars* (1967).[2] In an interview with Christopher Frayling,
Leone describes his masterpiece *Once Upon a Time in the West* (1968) as featuring "the most stereotypical characters from the American Western—on loan!"[3]
Although the phrase "on loan" suggests a lack of ownership, Leone's comment
here draws attention to the process whereby Western films in general relied
on archetypes to perpetuate a simulated version of the American West, meaning that the characters and settings from the cinematic repertoire that inspired
him were similarly "on loan" from a collective set of myths. Further, *A Fistful of
Dollars* is a remake of the Japanese samurai film *Yojimbo* (1961), itself an adaptation of Dashiell Hammett's noir novel *Red Harvest* (1929): a transnational,
transmedia mélange of genres and historical periods leading to what is considered one of the foremost examples of the Western film—a quintessentially
"American" genre.

   This legacy of revisionism and categorical elision is highly evident in
Preacher, which works within this male-dominated framing genre to critique
the gendered constructs underlying the conventions not only of the Western
but of the socioeconomic marginalization of women in a patriarchal society.

Westerns tend to prioritize the struggles and experiences of men over those of women, often to the extent that female perspectives are nearly erased from the classic Western.[4] As Wright notes, these male heroes are cast as "decent citizens" who provide a morally upstanding counterpoint to "the selfish, money values of the villains"—a dichotomy apparent in *Preacher*, where villains tend to be very wealthy (Grail leaders D'Aronique and Starr, the l'Angelle family) or at least perpetuators of capitalist systems (meatpacking plant owner Odin Quincannon).[5] Jesse's malevolent grandmother Marie l'Angelle, described by Labarre as "a fallen belle in a crumbling plantation manor," is descended from French Huguenots who settled in the American South "around the time of Napoleon [and] converted the local Indians to corpses"; in other words, her legacy is that of landed gentry who established their presence on the land by eradicating the presence of others.[6] D'Aronique and Starr, the successive leaders of paramilitary religious organization the Grail, seem to enjoy access to unlimited financial resources and operate in physical structures that appear to have been built at great expense. D'Aronique also exhibits characteristics associated with older models of wealth, such as extreme obesity and consuming food to the point of vomiting, and is the nephew of member of the southern gentry Marie l'Angelle. Although less wealthy than Marie or the Grail leaders, Odin Quincannon nevertheless displays a "money values"-oriented attitude as a corrupt business owner whose meatpacking plant is the primary source of revenue for the Texas town of Salvation.

This foregrounding of wealth and its effects is linked with an adherence to traditional gender roles that reduce women to objectified bodies whose sole purpose is to serve as vessels for reproduction and enactments of male sexuality. Much of Starr's sexual activity, for instance, involves the degradation (paid for, of course) of a female sex worker. As Jesse notes, Marie and the l'Angelle women "were meant for nothin' more 'n' breeding the next generation, which they took to real well."[7] Likewise, Quincannon's use of the term "split-tails" for women implicitly equates women with animals while focusing on their genitalia rather than their personhood.[8] He also commits the ultimate act of objectification by building a giant woman-shaped structure out of meat from his own meatpacking plant, which he treats as an oversized sex doll. The meat-woman is the only female-appearing entity in the comic with which Quincannon has an intimate relationship; it is no coincidence that she/it, as an inanimate creation, lacks agency and is made of consumable products under his ownership. In this patriarchal narrative genre, a commodification-focused worldview incorporates not only material wealth but control over women—the marginalized gender.

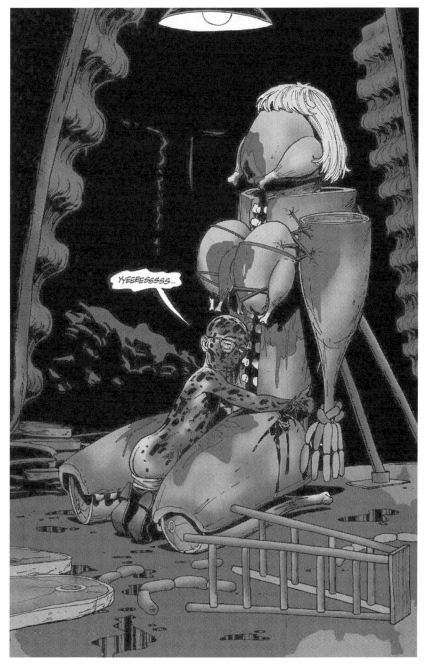

Odin Quincannon and his sex doll made of meat. From *Preacher* #48. Writer: Garth Ennis. Artist: Steve Dillon, 1999

"You Can Be Whatever the Hell You Want"

Like the superhero, the hero of the Western is typically viewed as a manifestation of the American myth of individualism, set apart from the ordinary
masses by virtue of his outstanding ability and great achievements.[9] Wright's
model of the Western hero sets out a division between the hero and the society
with which he interacts, stipulating that "the society recognizes a difference
between themselves and the hero" and "does not completely accept the hero."[10]
Given the gender conventions of the Western, heroes who follow this model are
almost always male. In *Preacher*, this hero is ostensibly embodied in the title
character: Jesse Custer, a former minister who abandons his faith in God and
abusive family home to seek the truth regarding his encounter with Genesis,
the illicit offspring of an angel and a demon. However, Jesse has grown up in
an atmosphere of socioeconomic privilege, due to being raised by the affluent
l'Angelles, and is a man who clings to preexisting codes of masculine behavior
in a male-dominated society; in fact, he idolizes John Wayne to the point where
he receives visitations from a phantomlike manifestation of the archetypal
cowboy characters Wayne portrays on film (although it must be noted that the
source of this idolization is *True Grit*, wherein Wayne's character serves as a
satire of his work in earlier Western films).[11] Applying Wright's criteria that the
hero is the character who succeeds in fighting and defeating the antagonist(s)
of the narrative further disqualifies Jesse from fully claiming the title of the
Western hero, as he is too occupied with fighting his ex-best-friend to kill Starr,
the leader of the organization orchestrating the majority of the conflict that the
protagonists experience.[12]

Instead, the traits of the Western hero converge in another of *Preacher*'s
lead characters: the indomitable ex-hitwoman Tulip O'Hare. As a working-
class woman who is remarkably capable with a gun and has a history of not
conforming to norms of gendered behavior, she demonstrates sharpshooting
ability far beyond average levels and is often met with incomprehension or
attempts at oppression from the patriarchal, economically privileged structures
governing the society of the narrative. She is also the one to ultimately succeed
in fighting and defeating the villain when she shoots Starr (while the male protagonists are busy exchanging blows) in the culmination of a one-on-one face-
off that places a contemporary gloss on the traditional Western showdown.

If Tulip can thus be read as a Western hero, can she by extension be read
as a superhero? While the specifics of exactly what constitutes a superhero are
mutable, Judge Learned Hand's 1952 ruling—which describes the superhero
as possessing, among other characteristics, "extraordinary abilities," "a code-
name and iconic costume," and "distinguish[ability] from characters of related

genres"—provides a working legal definition that can be applied to many super-heroes, such as Superman, Batman, Doctor Strange, Kate Bishop/Hawkeye, and so on.[13] As a mortal human woman with an ordinary wardrobe who is a lead character in a revisionist Western narrative, Tulip fulfills none of these criteria. Her divergence from the usual definition of a superhero is made particularly apparent by the contrast between her and the male leads in *Preacher*, who do possess superhuman abilities and easily distinguishable modes of dress. Unlike Jesse, who wears an iconic black shirt and minister's collar for most of *Preacher*, Tulip is depicted wearing different outfits and styles throughout the series, including cocktail dresses, jeans, tank tops, and T-shirts in a variety of colors. Jesse and Cassidy also display what could be classified as super-powers, with Jesse's ability to force people to do whatever he orders them to through the power of Genesis, and Cassidy's superhuman strength and relative invulner-ability (the advantages of being a vampire). Tulip is an expert markswoman but does not display extreme physical or mental powers on this scale.

Yet she is far from an everyday human being. In issues #10 and #11 of *Preacher*, she experiences a firsthand brush with the divine when she is killed by a bullet to the head and is then resurrected by God. Moreover, she dem-onstrates the desire and ability to defend the innocent and punish the guilty; during a group of men's attempted sexual assault of her friend Amy at a col-lege party, she drives a truck into the house where the party is held, threatens the men with a shotgun, and enables Amy to escape to safety. The climactic battle that concludes *Preacher* involves Tulip singlehandedly killing a garrison of enemy soldiers and the series' primary antagonist, while Jesse and Cassidy are too engaged in their fistfight with each other to take an active role in saving their own or anyone else's lives. These acts demonstrate a capacity to succeed in extraordinary circumstances, which is a major hallmark of the superhero.

Additionally, Tulip's nonconformity to common expectations regarding gender and womanhood corresponds with Reynolds' argument that the super-hero, like the hero of the Western, "is marked out from society."[14] As a young girl, Tulip develops a love of pastimes and pop culture more typically associ-ated with male consumer bases, such as baseball, war stories and films, comic books, hunting, fishing, and shooting. Her tastes alienate her from male and female classmates alike; when she attempts to start a conversation with them by asking, "Did you guys see *Kelly's Heroes* on Saturday night? Wasn't it cool?" the girls respond with hostile confusion, saying, "That's a boys' movie, Tulip …"/ "You're weird, Tulip …"/ "We don't want to play with you. …" Just two pan-els later, the boys give a remarkably similar response: "What would you know, O'Hare?"/ "That's a boys' movie, O'Hare!"/ "Go an' play with the other stupid little girls!"[15] These matching panels are nearly identical in layout, with Tulip in profile at the left of each panel, her classmates in a group at the right of each panel, and the child in the middle of each group holding a magazine or comic book (emphasizing the role of her cultural tastes in her isolation). Likewise, the following panels featuring her male and female classmates respectively share an almost identical layout in the way that each group of children is positioned and in the sequences of their dialogue balloons. The correspondences between these sets of panels visually reflect the constructed nature of the separation between masculinity and femininity by depicting the boys and girls in Tulip's life as essentially similar beings.

Tulip's unconventional tastes are due in large part to her home environment, as her father facilitates her engagement in these "weird" activities in a way that aims to discredit perceived gender division. When her teacher suggests that she adopt "more feminine pursuits [. . .] and attitudes," her father repudiates this restrictive gendering: "I always figured it was best to encourage her in what she liked."[16] Likewise, in response to young Tulip's question, "Daddy, can I be in the paratroopers when I grow up?" he says, "When you grow up, you can be whatever the hell you want," rejecting the idea of professions being restricted to a single gender.[17] At the same time, Mr. O'Hare is aware of his daughter's femininity, conferring upon her the affectionate nickname of "Little Petal" and informing her of the social rules that govern interactions between "Us fellas" and "you ladies."[18] In adulthood, she works as a hitwoman for a club owner, who at first mistakenly thinks she is applying for a job as one of his "waitresses and lap dancers."[19] Tulip is therefore "marked out" as an anomaly in the highly gendered world of *Preacher*, a decidedly feminine yet masculine-coded woman.

Paying the Bills: All Work and No Play

Since the refusal to conform to proscribed standards of womanly behavior places Tulip in opposition to *Preacher*'s villains and their insistence on perpetuating traditional gender roles, it is fitting that her socioeconomic background provides a corresponding source of opposition to their affluence. As a child raised in the southern United States who enjoys hunting, fishing, and guns and who attends what appears to be a public grade school, she is coded as working-class. Although she does attend a private boarding school following the death of her father, her status is that of a ward of the state, with no home outside of school besides "this horrible old orphanage."[20] When she enters the workforce, she is more concerned with earning money than with fulfilling any sort of calling; as a young adult, she is employed for one night as a diner waitress and subsequently works a series of "lousy" jobs.[21] Despite developing a hatred of

Tulip tries—and fails—to connect with the boys and girls at her school. *Preacher* #51. Writer: Garth Ennis. Artist: Steve Dillon, 1999.

guns after her father is shot in a hunting accident, she is forced to renounce this stance, first to save another woman from the depredations of men and again to "pay the bills," becoming a hired assassin in order to clear the debt she has incurred by borrowing money for an alcoholism rehabilitation program.[22]

Marie l'Angelle's initial criticism of Tulip—"Too skinny by far. Look at those hips; those aren't breeder's hips ... What kind of children would a woman like that bear you?"—draws together the gender and class aspects of Tulip's characterization.[23] Denigrating her on this specific physical basis points out that her body and agency are, unlike those of the l'Angelles, not dedicated to the single aim of serving as a reproductive receptacle for the products of male sexuality. Describing Tulip's physique as excessively thin, as per a more classical mode of aesthetics that connects fat to wealth and thinness to poverty, implies a perception of her as lacking sufficient socioeconomic privilege.

Tulip's backstory also lends a more literal dimension to her working-class status by revealing that a defining factor in her childhood was the denial of access to traditional arenas of play. Her father's burgeoning awareness of sexism, for instance, is initiated by her exclusion from her school's baseball team: "[The coach] said girls ain't allowed to play baseball an' that's all there is to it."[24] The panels detailing how her pop-culture consumption alienates her from prescribed gender roles at an early age highlight the play-oriented nature of this alienation; the girls inform her, "We don't want to play with you," and the boys echo them with, "Go an' play with the other stupid little girls."[25] In fact, despite the girls' implicit intention to engage in play, femininity in *Preacher* is associated with labor and obligation, as noted in Mr. O'Hare's supposition that male chivalry toward women may be "to make up for ladies generally havin' less fun."[26] For Tulip, this translates into the pursuit of survival-related pastimes such as fishing and deer hunting, which while enjoyable are also concerned with providing sustenance. As an adult, she parlays her facility with firearms into clearing a debt, not to fulfill some abstract code of honor but to avert the threat of physical harm.

In contrast to the lack of play and predominance of work in Tulip's life, labor and vocation are either absent or confines from which to escape for *Preacher*'s male leads. There is scant, if any, attention given to how Cassidy earns enough money to continue residing in his apartment, travel, and buy the numerous alcoholic drinks he consumes over the course of the comic, as well as to procure heroin in his earlier years. (Although he does perform oral sex in exchange for drugs at least once in the 1940s, this is a matter of feeding an addiction rather than the everyday maintenance activities in which most people engage.) Likewise, Jesse's career as a minister represents the multiple oppressive structures that govern much of his early life and pose a threat of monstrous proportions. Thus, in issue #1 we see him instigating a fight with the male members of his congregation when he visits their bar—"you think you can sing a few goddamn hymns an' act like savages the rest of the week?"—while issues #8–10 reveal that his entry into the ministry resulted from years of abuse and manipulation on the part of his grandmother.[27] For him and Cassidy, work is never a financial or otherwise individual obligation.

Jesse's life in particular is governed by play, in the sense that his behavior is largely shaped by the Western films he watched as a child—that is, recreational pursuits. His father employs quotes from cowboy movies to teach him to speak in early childhood: "Say—pilgrim! Say—son of a bitch! Say—Take 'em to Missouri!"[28] The ghostly manifestation of John Wayne's onscreen persona that appears to Jesse throughout his life as a sort of spirit guide offers advice on how to approach hardship based on the behavior of the fictional characters played by Wayne. This is not to discount the influence of media that perpetuates the Western mythos—indeed, a prevailing theme of *Preacher* is the potency of myth—but to emphasize the luxury he enjoys in having continual access to popular culture for recreational purposes. In other words, Jesse is afforded the freedom to relate to popular culture that Tulip is denied.

This discrepancy between the relationships of Tulip and her male counterparts to work and play reflects the concept of women's unpaid emotional labor put forward by Jess Zimmerman, which argues that, in addition to their visible career and domestic duties, women are assigned the duty of engaging in "the constant labor of placating men and navigating patriarchal expectations" without receiving any rewards for this labor.[29] While the focus of Tulip's labor is more economic than emotional, the association between womanhood, the erasure of spaces devoted to leisure, and patriarchy that this concept posits nevertheless applies to her story arc, as well as those of *Preacher*'s female characters in general. Other women enter the story as underappreciated employees of male-owned, male-dominated organizations, such as Featherstone, who works for and is in love with Starr despite the constant barrage of insults he levels against her and her colleagues; and Cindy Daggett, a highly competent, intelligent woman unable to advance beyond the post of deputy sheriff of Salvation due to the fact that she is black in a town controlled by dedicated racist, sexist, and Ku Klux Klan leader Odin Quincannon. Even Marie l'Angelle never has an opportunity to escape the duty of "breedin' the next generation," as she gives birth to Jesse's mother far beyond typical childbearing age, at sixty years old.[30] Regardless of their background, women receive no permanent release from their duty to perform unrewarded labor for men and, without active intervention, are doomed to have "less fun."

It should be underscored that, as exemplified in the cases of Quincannon and Starr, the men controlling these institutions and structures are portrayed as evil individuals devoid of positive human emotion, and that by extension the assignation of unrewarded labor to women within such patriarchal institutions and structures is founded upon similar evils. *Preacher* thus implicitly portrays the marginalizing subjugation of women as an abhorrent, detrimental construct—which provides a distinct contrast to Tulip's individualistic upbringing, which does not insist on compliance with a restrictive gendered code of behavior and instead centers on the media, hobbies, and skills that she as an individual enjoys. Yet even the apparently unbreakable Tulip is subject to socioeconomic domination, since according to the rules of this society, all women are part of a working class whose primary role is to perform labor for the benefit of men. It is this injustice she strives to combat, not only through annihilating the leaders and military powers that perpetuate it or adopting the traditionally male role of the hero, but through her very nature, which has developed in defiance of the harmful male-dominated constructs that aim to maintain women's collective status as an underclass, and upon which she is never afraid to act. As an individual fated to stand apart from society whose labor focuses mainly on survival and, at the same time, who exercises her agency in the heroic defense of others, Tulip serves as an excellent contemporary example of the working-class superhero.

Notes

1. Nicolas Labarre, "Meat Fiction and Burning Western Light," in *Comics and the U. S. South*, ed. Qiana J. Whitted and Brannon Costello (Jackson: University of Mississippi Press, 2012), 242–67; Julia Round, *Gothic in Comics and Graphic Novels: A Critical Approach* (Jefferson, NC: McFarland, 2014).

2. Douglas J. McReynolds, "Alive and Well: Western Myth in Western Movies," *Literature/Film Quarterly* 26, no. 1 (1998): 46–52.

3. Christopher Frayling, *Sergio Leone: Something to Do with Death* (London: Faber and Faber, 2000), 291.

4. Matthew Carter, Myth of the Western: New Perspectives on Hollywood's Frontier Narrative (Edinburgh: Edinburgh University Press, 2014).

5. Will Wright, "The Structure of Myth and the Structure of the Western Film," quoted in John Storey, *Cultural Theory and Popular Culture: A Reader*. Vol. 1 (Upper Saddle River, NJ: Prentice Hall, 2006), 316.

6. Labarre, "Meat Fiction and Burning Western Light"; Garth Ennis and Steve Dillon, *Preacher* #9 (New York: DC Comics 1995).

7. Ibid.

8. Ennis and Dillon, *Preacher* #46 (New York: DC Comics 1999).

9. John Shelton Lawrence and Robert Jewett, *The Myth of the American Superhero* (Grand Rapids, MI: William B. Eerdmans, 2002).

10. Will Wright, *Sixguns and Society: A Structural Study of the Western* (Berkeley: University of California Press, 1975), 41–48.

11. Ennis and Dillon, *Preacher* #11 (New York: DC Comics,1995).

12. Wright, *Sixguns and Society*.

13. Judge Learned Hand, 1952, quoted in Peter Coogan, "The Definition of the Superhero," in *A Comics Studies Reader*, ed. Jeet Heer and Kent Worcester (Jackson: University P of Mississippi, 2009), 77.

14. Richard Reynolds, *Super Heroes: A Modern Mythology* (Jackson: University Press of Mississippi, 1994), 16.

15. Ennis and Dillon, *Preacher* #51 (New York: DC Comics, 1999).

16. Ibid.

17. Ibid.

18. Ibid.

19. Ennis and Dillon, *Preacher* #8 (New York: DC Comics, 1995).

20. Ennis and Dillon, *Preacher* #52 (New York: DC Comics, 1999).

21. Ennis and Dillon, *Preacher* #8.

22. Ennis and Dillon, "introduction," *Preacher: All Hell's A-Comin'* (#51–58), (New York: DC Comics, 2000).

23. Ennis and Dillon, *Preacher* #8.

24. Ennis and Dillon, *Preacher* #51.

25. Ibid.

26. Ibid.

27. Ennis and Dillon, *Preacher* #1 (New York: DC Comics,1995).

28. Ennis and Dillon, *Preacher* #9.

29. Jess Zimmerman, "'Where's My Cut?': On Unpaid Emotional Labor," *The Toast*, http://the-toast.net/2015/07/13/emotional-labor/ (accessed November 9, 2015).

30. Ennis and Dillon, *Preacher* #9.

Bibliography

Primary Sources

Ennis, Garth, and Steve Dillon, *Preacher* #1. New York: DC Comics, 1995.

———. *Preacher* #8. New York: DC Comics, 1995.

———. *Preacher* #9. New York: DC Comics, 1995.

———. *Preacher* #10. New York: DC Comics, 1995.

———. *Preacher* #11. New York: DC Comics, 1995.

———. *Preacher* #46. New York: DC Comics, 1999.

———. *Preacher* #51. New York: DC Comics, 1999.

———. *Preacher* #52. New York: DC Comics, 1999.

———. *Preacher* #64. New York: DC Comics, 2000.

———. *Preacher* #65. New York: DC Comics, 2000.

———. *Preacher: Alamo* (#59–66). New York: DC Comics, 2001.

———. *Preacher: All Hell's A-Comin'* (#51–58, *Preacher Special: Tall in the Saddle*). New York: DC Comics, 2000.

———. *Preacher: Dixie Fried* (#27–33, *Preacher Special: Cassidy—Blood and Whiskey*). New York: DC Comics, 1999.

———. *Preacher: Gone to Texas* (#1–7). New York: DC Comics, 1996.

———. *Preacher: Salvation* (#41–50), introduction. New York: DC Comics, 1999.

———. *Preacher: Until the End of the World* (#8–17). New York: DC Comics, 1997.

Ennis, Garth, Steve Dillon, and Peter Snejberg. *Preacher: War in the Sun* (#34–40, *Preacher Special: One Man's War*). New York: DC Comics, 1999.

Ennis, Garth, Steve Pugh, and Carlos Ezquerra. *Preacher: Ancient History* (*Preacher Special: Saint of Killers* #1–4, *Preacher Special: The Story of You-Know-Who, Preacher Special: The Good Old Boys*). New York: DC Comics, 1998.

Secondary Sources

Carter, Matthew. *Myth of the Western: New Perspectives on Hollywood's Frontier Narrative.* Edinburgh: Edinburgh University Press, 2014.

Coogan, Peter. "The Definition of the Superhero." *A Comics Studies Reader*, edited by Jeet Heer and Kent Worcester, 77–93. Jackson: University Press of Mississippi, 2009.

DiPaolo, Marc. *War, Politics and Superheroes: Ethics and Propaganda in Comics and Film.* Jefferson, NC: McFarland, 2011.

Frayling, Christopher. *Sergio Leone: Something to Do with Death.* London: Faber and Faber, 2000.

Labarre, Nicolas. "Meat Fiction and Burning Western Light." In *Comics and the U. S. South*, edited by Qiana J. Whitted and Brannon Costello, 242–67. Jackson: University of Mississippi Press, 2012.

Lawrence, John Shelton, and Robert Jewett. *The Myth of the American Superhero.* Grand Rapids, MI: William B. Eerdmans, 2002.

McReynolds, Douglas J. "Alive and Well: Western Myth in Western Movies." *Literature/Film Quarterly* 26, no. 1 (1998): 46–52.

Reynolds, Richard. *Super Heroes: A Modern Mythology.* Jackson: University Press of Mississippi, 1994.

Round, Julia. *Gothic in Comics and Graphic Novels: A Critical Approach.* Jefferson: McFarland, 2014.

Wright, Will. *Sixguns and Society: A Structural Study of the Western.* Berkeley: University of California Press, 1975.

———. "The Structure of Myth and the Structure of the Western Film." Quoted in *Cultural Theory and Popular Culture: A Reader.* Vol. 1, by John Storey, 303–317. Upper Saddle River, NJ: Prentice Hall, 2006.

Zimmerman, Jess. "'Where's My Cut?' On Unpaid Emotional Labor." *The Toast*, http://the-toast.net/2015/07/13/emotional-labor/. Accessed November 9, 2015.

ALAN MOORE AND ANARCHIST PRAXIS IN FORM
Bibliography, Remediation, and Aesthetic Form in *V for Vendetta* and *Black Dossier*

James Gifford and Orion Ussner Kidder

The most obvious problem with Alan Moore's works is anarchism. Anarchism provokes his readers, tempts them to buy tie-in Guy Fawkes masks for ever-greater profitability of the publishers, and confuses mainstream and academic readers alike. Anarchism is a problem for which Moore's works are an answer, somehow. Yet anarchism also provides a lucid conceptual method for reading Moore's works—it finds an early and explicit expression in *V for Vendetta* and slowly transforms praxis through an aesthetic enactment in *The Black Dossier*. This movement from content to form reflects both Moore's career and the trajectory of much anarchist art across the twentieth century. Moore's work moves from propaganda to praxis and hence links Moore to a larger context of activist art independent of specific, protean, or explicit calls to action. By privileging anarchism as a movement, a philosophy, and a methodological paradigm, we extend its operation as an organizational concept across Moore's oeuvre, most particularly to his later works that are often without explicit anarchist content or for which critical consensus has been elusive. In essence, we critique the surprise that some readers experience over anarchism in Moore's work, even when he is explicit, and we outline how his career parallels anarchism across the twentieth century by moving from the explicit to the aesthetic while remaining politically active.

In *V for Vendetta*, Moore and David Lloyd give voice to the most frequently cited expression of Moore's anarchism, often misunderstood, and more often provocatively overlooked. Nonetheless, the presence of anarchism and a protracted discussion of modes of anarchist thought are undeniable features of the comic and an obvious challenge to a neoliberal or reactionary readership. The peculiarity, then, is the continuous tidying and recontextualization of anarchist content to more comfortably minimize its expression across each form of the comic, culminating in the film version that famously ignores the political concerns of the comic and elicited Moore's condemnation of the poverty of filmic adaptation of comics generally. Moore's early articulation of anarchism after *Watchmen* was led down a path of commercial remediation that relentlessly minimized its political content while broadening its market share, and following on this experience Moore's anarchist theory turned as praxis to expression through form and aesthetics in *Black Dossier* in parallel to his talismanic enactment of anarchism in magic. Stated directly, the hegemonic operations of the remediating commercial process of republication and adaptation repurposed the anarchist discourses in *V for Vendetta*, which then drove Moore's explicit articulation of anarchism into subversive and productive innovations in *form*. The reader moves from *voicing* anarchism in *V for Vendetta* to a formal aesthetic that *enacts* anarchism as praxis in *Black Dossier* without bringing it to the level of discourse. In a key way, while Moore's works are deeply entangled with proletarian concerns, he sets his revolutions against systems of domination rather than economic exploitation, and hence the move from explicit to aesthetic anarchism is an advance rather than a retreat, as critics like David Weir would see it. Where a Marxist paradigm would find the accumulation of capital and class war, Moore opens his work to proletarian concerns while resisting the accumulation of authority, most obviously state authority but also the work's over the reader.

A Is for Anarchism

In brief, the central problem in anarchism is the tension between authority and autonomy, specifically the former's attempts to eradicate the latter. Robert Paul Wolff's *In Defense of Anarchism* argues that authority is different from power and persuasion. That is, power is the ability to compel someone based on threats, force, or consequences, and persuasion is when someone chooses to agree with a rationally or emotionally presented argument (6), but "to claim authority is to claim the right to be obeyed" (Wolff 6) as if that right were an inherent quality of an individual or, more commonly, the rank or status attached to an individual

(7). That is, "authority" may be given as shorthand for a just expectation of obedience, while "persuasion" and "power" (in its myriad foucauldian forms or as
persuasively enumerated in three forms of three dimensions by Steven Lukes)
are not definitionally reliant on the concept of "justness." Wolff claims that the
most common reason people obey such authority "is simply the prescriptive
force of tradition" (7). He does not go into more detail on this point, but the logi-
cal extension is that figures and institutions naturalize their authority, presenting it as if it were self-evident, thus socializing people into obeying authority as
a matter of habit, and, if necessary, using power—that is, threats—or persuasion
against those who have not been properly socialized. Authority, then, is the mask
that power wears. Anarchism, when understood as the refutation of authority
as such (while still recognizing the reality of power and persuasion), endeavors
to restore the Enlightenment expectations of freedom to agree or disagree with
a rationally presented argument, and then act accordingly through self-determining choice. That is, insofar as one is a rational creature capable of exercising
reason in the pursuit of self-determining choice, and while power and persuasion are inevitabilities, no natural or just expectation of obedience is ethically
viable. This ethical dimension may become complex when a rational individual
is unable to exercise reason or when a person capable of exercising reason is in
a state of irrationality, but neither complexity relies on a return to the justness or
naturalness of an expectation of obedience. While many anarchists may question Wolff's commitment to social action or his misappropriation by American
libertarian movements of the right wing, the great convenience of this argument
is its clarity for asserting that institutions that claim authority over individuals and perpetuate that authority over time are anathema to anarchist thought
and the project of the Enlightenment (without overlooking its own tendency
to dominate the natural world as the object upon which reason acts). Moore
and Lloyd's *V for Vendetta* implicitly claims through Evey's story that we always
did have that freedom; we have just been taught to ignore it. It also presents the
ethical status of V's usurpation of authority and exercises of power, often violent
power, rather than coercive or contextual power (the first rather than the second or third dimensions in Lukes's formulation) as also unethical despite their
necessity. Hence, we see both V and Susan making recourse to the language
of necessity justifying the "justness" of their actions as ethical. It may also be
a matter of convenience to classify this understanding of anarchism as "quiet-
ist" or "pacifist," as a contrast to insurrectionary or revolutionary forms of the
movement, but they all share the underlying refutation of rule predicated on a
just expectation of obedience. This aspect of anarchism is also implicit in *Black
Dossier*'s plot; however, for the reasons elucidated across this essay, the *aesthetics* of the book are more fully anarchistic than the plot or the content of direct
discourse, and that bears some explanation.

Allan Antliff's *Anarchy and Art* examines anarchist art over the course of the twentieth century and concludes that "diversity is inevitable: after all, the artist's creative freedom goes hand in hand with a politics that refuses power over others" (Antliff, *Anarchy* 14). Anarchist art resists generic conventions— for example, narrative closure—because they, too, are kinds of authority. Antliff also observes that anarchist art is often "radically reflexive" (14), which under- mines not only the authority of the artist but the habitual expectations of the audience. *Black Dossier* matches Antliff's analysis: its shifts between modes and voices, the found-document format, and especially the comics within the comic all defy conventional expectations while they reflect upon those expectations. Linda Hutcheon describes metafiction as first establishing and then crossing its own narrative frames (Hutcheon 109). It thus attains one discreet element of what Patricia Waugh calls "radical" metafiction (Waugh 53) in that it "den[ies] the reader access to a centre of orientation such as a narrator or point of view" (136). Without the centering authority of a single narrator, a privileged mode, or one demonstrably real narrative world, the audience of *Black Dossier* is at least ostensibly free to interpret the book any way that it wants to. The form of it thus resists the authority of its own creators. Moore, in this sense, embraces the same strategy as earlier anarchist artists, of whom he is well aware, by shifting between explicit or plot-based representations of anarchism to formal anar- chist experiences within his comics.

Remediation as Communicative Paradigm

We use "remediation" to mean the transformation of one media product into another medium, such as a book into a film. While simple, the concept carries more productive problems than "adaptation." Such a remediation might also be a film in theaters remediated into a DVD or YouTube video, or a vinyl record into an .mp3 file—each of these is a transformation of one media product into another with new conditions, biases, relations to consumers, and capacities for expression and revision. Jay David Bolter and Richard Grusin articulate this "remediation" between the two competing senses of the term: one in Marxist literature and the other in linguistics, as well as other competing ideas in media studies. For them, "the logic of hypermediacy [the blurring together of several different mediums] expresses the tension between regarding a visual space as mediated and regarding it as a 'real' space that lies beyond mediation" (334). This is a complex way of saying "remediation" is a problem that sits somewhere between "reality" and "representations of reality." For one media consumer, a medical documentary's scenes may lack "reality" because it does not use the same sound effects for cutting or intervening on the body or the visual cues we are accustomed to finding in our fictional medical-drama representations of reality. Real surgery will not sound like movie surgery, or real gunshots like filmic gunshots, so reality disappoints us in innumerable ways because it fails to live up to our mediated expectations. Specifically, for Bolter and Grusin, "the representation of one medium in another" defines their use of the term "remediation," and they "argue that remediation is a defining characteristic of the new digital media" (338), although as this essay contends, it extends backward from the digital historical moment.

This remediation could be "passive," such as a DVD of visual artworks that seeks to provide the same viewing experience as a gallery—the digital remediation attempts to be as passive as possible in the viewer's experience, even though the bias in time and space, as well as industrial production of the physical DVD, has significantly changed the social relations of the cultural product to its consumers. The experience of viewing the *Mona Lisa* in the Louvre or on Twitter enacts this problem of remediation, despite the passive nature of the remediation that attempts to render the transfer invisible. It must *surely* be the same smile in both forms, regardless of the glass, crowds, fees, and security in the former and the juxtaposition to other "tweets" on a mobile device typically owned on contract and used while in transit. The social relations I have to a "tweet" or an email are different from the relations I have with a hand-printed book with woodblock engravings for illustrations and a hand-sewn binding, even if the contents are precisely the same, just as a digital comic differs from the "pulp" print product. One may be inclined to duplicate and distribute the "tweet," and less likely to give away a print run of *Warrior* magazine, regardless of the "sameness" of their possible contents. As another example of remediation, I might also say that a postcard of a painting or a film adaptation of a novel changes the contents from one medium to another but profoundly alters its social uses, material context, fetishization as an object, and the intellectual interpretive energy brought to it. Yet Mona Lisa's remediated smile acts much like V's remediations in his smirking mask.

Remediation, however, may also be "aggressive," which happens when the new medium "can try to refashion the older medium or media entirely, while still marking the presence of the older media and therefore maintaining a sense of multiplicity or, as [they] have called it, hypermediacy" (Bolter and Grusin 340). A film adaptation of a Jane Austen novel might, for instance, dispense with chapter headings to break up scenes, even while reminding viewers of the film's origins in a novel by placing a copy of the original book surreptitiously on a desk or bookcase. *V for Vendetta* is a highly remediated work in both passive and aggressive forms, and in addition to its reproduction or "adaptation" to new mediums, it undergoes procedures of revision and repurposing as each remediation brings the work to a new series of economic pressures and cultural expectations—its anarchist contents conflict increasingly with its material instantiation.

C Is for Context

The revisions to *V for Vendetta* begin the process that profoundly challenges Moore's attempt to express if not an anarchist manifesto at least a narrative treatise on anarchism in relation to the rise of neoliberalism during the Thatcher and Reagan years. In its historical context, *V for Vendetta* began as a comic series in the anthology collection *Warrior* magazine in 1982, two years prior, but very much in the lead-up, to the widespread and much anticipated celebrations of George Orwell's novel *1984*. Orwell is a clear influence on the comic, and we might note that Margaret Atwood's *The Handmaid's Tale* was published in 1985 under the sway of Orwell's long influence as well as Terry Gilliam's 1987 film *Brazil*. Orwell's *1984* was still at the height of its Cold War popularity and was the inspiration for the now-famous marketing campaign that launched Apple computer's breakthrough Macintosh line of personal computers in 1984, and across the 1980s this mixture of nuclear and totalitarian fears infiltrated media everywhere. Historically this was also the period of Conservative Britain with the Tories led by Margaret Thatcher (1979–1990). There were still tense relations with Soviet Russia, Reaganomics was growing, and other rises in Conservatism flourished after the New Left of the 1960s. There were also popular nuclear fears that led during *V for Vendetta*'s run to Derek Hines's British television miniseries about nuclear holocaust, *Threads*, in 1984, *The Day After* in America in 1983, and the apocalypse-averted film *WarGames*, also in 1983, that did much to popularize the generic expectations of the 1990s. As Wolk reminds us,

> a handful of stories Moore published in the late '80s ... imagine the end of culture as we know it. ... Shortly thereafter, a lot of mainstream comics began to involve enormous, city-destroying or world-ending calamities, although their creators imagined them as disasters rather than revolutions leading to something glorious. (245)

This was the height of narratives about a nuclear apocalypse, and it is not difficult to guess why without making explicit recourse to material conditions contextualizing cultural expressions of subjectivity—Wolk's contrast of disasters to revolutions is likewise telling, suggesting an allegorization of class struggle, yet in Moore the disaster is a manifestation of rule's corrupting influence rather than the dialectical progress of history. At the same time, there were in Britain ongoing IRA conflicts (1981 was a particularly intense year for public violence), and in 1981 the world witnessed the first public recognition of AIDS as an emerging, feared, and misunderstood global pandemic. Only in 1987 would AZT, the first treatment, become available.

This digression relates to Section 28 of the Local Government Act 1988 in Britain, which amended the United Kingdom's Local Government Act 1986. The amendment stated a local authority "shall not intentionally promote homosexuality or publish material with the intention of promoting homosexuality" or "promote the teaching in any maintained school of the acceptability of homosexuality as a pretended family relationship." This was also a reaction to ongoing popular proposals, based on homophobia, in the United Kingdom and the United States for containment camps for those infected with AIDS. For Moore, who is heterosexual but whose marriage at the time involved a mutual girlfriend with his wife, the struggle against homophobia became a significant part of his work. Moore's work against homophobia and government discrimination is already present in *V for Vendetta*, anticipating his later more explicit work. These historical circumstances also go a long way to understanding the comic's interest in a fascist British government, nuclear holocaust, global pandemic illnesses, concentration camps, and arrests of homosexuals. As Kidder claims, "A culture's bedrock assumptions are thus uniquely visible in its most fanciful stories. As a concrete example, this genre can easily contain a man who can fly, but very rarely can it contain a woman who can have an identity outside of a heteronormative relationship" (249).

The rationale for concern over these issues makes better contextual sense once we place the work coherently in its time period, this period's bedrock assumptions, and the expression of its ideology in actions, not simply words or articles of faith.

B Is for Bibliography

Moore and Lloyd's *V for Vendetta* first appeared in *Warrior* magazine, a British periodical that ran for twenty-six issues between March 1982 and January 1985. It was created by Dez Skinn, who had left Marvel UK and hoped to create an anthology with greater artistic freedom and less reliance on established distribution networks and specialty comic shops. However, this led to irregular publication, an unfounded yet coercive lawsuit from Marvel Comics, and the continual threat of cancellation while writing in a periodical genre. Twenty-six chapters for *V for Vendetta*, twenty-four of which are part of the main narrative, appeared across all but two of the twenty-six issues of *Warrior*, and these were given in the format of two "Books." At this point, with the end of *Warrior*, the narrative had resolution. Its protagonist is a revolutionary man mysteriously named "V," in a dystopic future version of Britain run as a totalitarian state, and he had not yet brought the fictional world to a close. This led to "Book III," published in three issues by DC Comics in America from February to May 1989. This four-year break echoes smaller discontinuities during *Warrior*'s continually interrupted publication schedule. It has been a thoroughly worked, reworked, revised, recreated, and duplicated working-class text aching for the bibliographic attentions more typically lavished on the plural print histories of H. G. Wells's *The Time Machine* or endlessly erroneous variants by editorial rather than authorial hands of Ernest Hemingway's *In Our Time*.

It is important to contextualize this initial set of print witnesses of the text. The first "chapters" of *V for Vendetta* appeared in *Warrior Magazine* with uncertainty for continued publication, its duration, the time frame for subsequent chapters' appearance, and without the kind of formal completeness implicit in its most common form today as a graphic novel. In many respects, this fragmented presentation in serial form was also a safety mechanism to minimize risk if it failed to attract a readership or sufficiently entice the readers who took it up, since an underperforming narrative in an anthology series could simply end without risking the continued sales of the serial as a whole. Hence, Moore and Lloyd could develop higher-risk materials with fewer inherent contextualizing pressures from the material conditions under which it was produced. "The Villain" opens the narrative in March 1982 as a six-page narrative, which of course for a reader in this first moment may or may not continue as a serial. The reader later reaches "Vertigo" in September 1982, which would become a supplement in the graphic novel, removed from its original publication sequence in relation to the other "chapters." Hence, the narrative sequence of the comic is disjunctive from the start and revised in its subsequent editions. In "The Vortex," the first plot line reaches its finale in July 1983, at which point the contemporary reader of the period would be entirely reasonable to anticipate no further development of the narrative—this would be its terminus. Readers today, of course, realize this continued with the brief five-page interlude "Vicious Cabaret" in August, followed by what would then become "Book II" of the graphic novel, beginning with "The Vanishing" in September. After "A Vocational Viewpoint," the strip went on vacation for an issue, which would again disrupt the expectations of a reader in its first form, an experience impossible to replicate for the kind of global reader encountering *V for Vendetta* today in its graphic novel form. The July 1984 chapter "Vincent" would also be later relegated to a supplement status rather than an integral part of

the narrative in its original form, and the original black-and-white series concludes in "The Verdict" in February 1985 with the final issue of *Warrior* itself.
Only four years later would DC Comics in America publish a stand-alone
comic *series* titled *V for Vendetta* that colorizes and resizes the original *Warrior*
publications. This is a far more mainstream publication, meant to reach a large
and profitable audience, and unlike the British tabloid magazine, it is intended
to capitalize on a largely juvenile readership that is more likely to regard V in
the role and generic context of a superhero. While Moore's profitable status
mitigated direct pressure to alter his anarchist vision, bibliographically minded
readers must recognize this new set of witnesses in what is a second edition
and expansion of the work. This began with an extension of Book II through
Moore and Lloyd's "Chapter 13: Values" and "Chapter 14: Vignettes" (15–21), the
second of which in the same issue of the new comic series *V for Vendetta* is
followed by the republication of the excised "Vertigo" (23–28) and "Vincent"
(29–32) chapters from *Warrior*, which leads to "Book 3: The Land of Do As You
Please" (issues 8–10 from February to May 1989). From February to May 1989
across a prologue and eleven chapters, this newly written third book revises
the original depiction of V and anarchism from the *Warrior* witnesses in a new
size and colorized format and with a resulting new sense of authority's operations in anarchist thought, which is then retrospectively curated by the conceptual clarifications afforded by the newly written third book. This DC edition is,
however, more than a new witness and addition to the text—it also comprises
what we will identify below as the first remediation from *Warrior* in the United
Kingdom to *V for Vendetta* as a series by DC in the USA.

The standard edition of *V for Vendetta* is now, after the DC series, a graphic
novel in a single volume, first published by Collected Books in 1990, then
revised for Vertigo in 1995, and revised in minor ways again in 2008 to proudly
proclaim "Now a Major Motion Picture" in order to advertise its remediated
cousin. This 2008 Vertigo edition can now be found in virtually any mainstream
bookstore or comic shop in North America. Each of these forms of the graphic
novel constitutes a unique witness of the text, but for convenience they may be
considered as a whole classified as the third edition of the work. Subsequent
witnesses and editions include the Deluxe Collector's Set and the *Absolute V for
Vendetta*, which restores previously excised contents in a new format.

Anarcho Allusion

The allusive content of *V for Vendetta* should also strike us as fairly obvious,
from Guy Fawkes and the Gunpowder Plot to the importance of Shakespeare.

When V first appears in the comic, he quotes from Shakespeare's *Macbeth* (Moore and Lloyd, *V* 11), and *Macbeth* is the most obvious first allusion because the play encapsulates themes of regicide and power, and also alludes to the Gunpowder Plot itself.[1]

In addition to this "thick" allusion, the reader also encounters other books in the background of various frames (Moore and Lloyd, *V for Vendetta* 9:7, 18:5). We see in these scenes Thomas More's *Utopia* (1516), Karl Marx's *Capital* (1867), Adolf Hitler's *Mein Kampf* (1925–1926), Richard Matheson's *I Am Legend* (1954), and Thomas Pynchon's *V.* (1963). Matheson's novel sets the protagonist as the villain, much as V is presented in *V for Vendetta*. Moreover, when V leaves Madam Justice after his soliloquy, he again quotes Shakespeare's *King Henry VIII* Act I.iv suggestively: "O Beauty, 'til now I never knew thee . . ." (Moore and Lloyd, *V for Vendetta* 41:9). In *King Henry VIII*, Henry says this while taking Anne Boleyn's hand. Anne was his lover and second wife, whom he later had executed; hence, V's romantic attachment to Justice is coded in violence and false rule. We may therefore ask if this allusion compares Anne Boleyn to Anarchy, or if it suggests that V is untrue to both of his "lady loves"—Anarchy as well as Justice.

We also encounter allusions to Enid Blyton's children's novel *Magic Faraway Tree* (1943). In this story she creates the magical "Land of Take-What-You-Want," but the children must recognize that it is a time-limited world that they may visit but must leave before the cloud that supports it floats past their vine that climbs to the sky. If they do not leave, they will become trapped, which alters the "Land-of-Do-As-You-Please" in *V for Vendetta*. It is a fantasy that cannot occur as V sees it. With this in mind, a literary reader attentive to allusion would be unlikely to believe anything from V. It then seems more plausible that Evey offers the "right" revision to his ideas through her pacifism, or, more to the point, if V is tied to so many problems in his allusions, it becomes increasingly difficult to regard him as Moore's spokesman in the graphic novel, a role that Evey fulfills more effectively as the speaker against rule by either violent villain, regardless of the sympathies we may feel.

Remediating *V for Vendetta*

When DC Comics began by publishing the previous materials in seven issues of the self-titled series *V for Vendetta*, as described above, this new series and republication was the first instance of remediation. The British publication was a distinct state of the text in black and white at tabloid size, with each chapter in a unique sequence in different issues, most often without cover art. The

American republication was resized and colorized, which reworked the original visual materials, and a new sequence emerged in the chapters themselves. The self-contained narratives in the chapters "Vertigo" and "Vincent" initially appeared as the sixth and twentieth chapters in *Warrior*. They later became the "Interlude" at the conclusion of the seventh issue in the DC Comics edition, as the twenty-fifth and twenty-sixth chapters respectively. In the later graphic novel, they are removed to an appendix. In this sense, these are not simply different printings or even different states but qualify as distinct editions of a substantively revised text. The medium has undergone remediation from a British black-and-white serial anthology to a resized American colorized series in a limited ten issues suitable for the craze of collectors in the 1980s. This changes the nature of the content in more than one way.

Moreover, the narrative is expanded for a further book made up of eleven chapters and a prologue across three issues, as well as two more chapters that are added to the conclusion of the second book, which did not appear in *Warrior*. These macro-level revisions stand out fairly overtly to even the casual reader—for those familiar with *Warrior*, the serial is suddenly a "book" that has new chapters and a whole new book, as well as a new sequence.

The graphic novel has come of age—comics are no longer the fodder of childhood, and Vertigo specifically publishes material only for adults. Moreover, Indigo, Chapters, Barnes & Noble, Borders, and Amazon all make an excellent margin selling them. The neighborhood comic shop in a low-rent strip mall had faded steadily since the 1980s. These conditions are, of course, contrary to those initially envisioned in *Warrior*, which relied on avoiding mainstream distribution networks, so the fact that a periodical anthology in black and white is now readily available mainly through big-box industrial stores in a colorized, single-volume format is intriguing on its own.

The one-volume graphic novel, which is the most industrially produced and widely distributed edition of *V for Vendetta*, is also the most socially sanctioned and ideologically "cleaned up" version of the text. Where the initial black-and-white, underground production of the first two books in *Warrior* contained a high degree of self-reflexivity with regard to its position within mass media, the graphic novel cuts self-reflexive moments. Where the original is aware of itself within the culture industry and promotes this awareness, the culture industry's graphic-novel edition cuts such reminders. Althusser might argue that "the specific function of the work of art is to make *visible* ... the reality of the existing ideology" (Althusser 1972, 241–242), but as he later concluded, the culture industry and society make this visibility in art increasingly difficult to notice. The reader cannot squint enough to see as it becomes opaque.

This "making visible" and subsequent commercial process via revision and remediation of "making invisible" the ideology of rule becomes clearer as we return to the bibliographical history to compare the different witnesses of the text. They are remediated transformations, each moving to a new production context, the pressures of capital, and a new medium. In the scene in which V watches films in his underground theater, the colorized and resized DC Comics edition establishes the protagonist, the Villain, as our object while we zoom back to a general shot akin to film. We begin with famous faces in film, playing across a screen that is at first only visible in each frame, but zooming back to include V as the audience watching these film images. This is duplicated in our graphic novel (Moore and Lloyd, *V for Vendetta* 85). The next page juxtaposes the leader of the fascist state, Adam Susan, seated in front of his mass observation computer, which is named Fate. He observes the citizens through Fate while the detective Eric Finch tells him about V's activities. This ends the first book, with the words "Happy Christmas," showing only a contemplative Susan dismissing his servant, Finch. This is followed by the game of dominoes that appears between each of the three books. In this instance, we find V watching films while Susan watches people, but this comparison is only implicit. They are, in effect, different parts of a similar problem. In contrast, the DC colorized edition presents an additional sequence of frames that offers a similar zoom-back sequence, nicely rounding out the issue, which begins with a zoom in. The issue opens zooming in on V and closes by zooming out from V watching films and then zooming in on Adam Susan, then finally zooming out again to implicate the reader in the final shift outward from Susan to the reader's frame viewing the comic. This makes the parallel between V, Susan, and the reader as the watching audience explicit. That Moore could make this explicit bridge between V and Susan is a reflection of his profitable status with DC and resulting free hand to mark out his understanding of anarchism without the typical pressures to ameliorate or inoculate the bogeyman of the New Left or neoliberalism, a process the later remediations and the film in particular would experience as a natural market pressure to reach investors and diverse audiences.

This first remediation by DC Comics of the original comic does not delete visual materials, even though it adds color, restructures the chapters, and expands the narrative and credit images that themselves recontextualize and comment on the preceding contents. In this longer version, the zoom-back on V in the theater watching famous film stars is paralleled by a zoom-in on Susan followed by a zoom-out that places the reader in the position of watching V on a television screen. The effect is a self-conscious reminder to the reader that he or she is also a part of this scopophilic game. Susan wishes his servant a happy

In a scene from the original *V for Vendetta* serial, the freedom fighter V, the Fascist leader Adam Susan, and the reader of the comic book are all implicated in voyeuristic practices by a cleverly rendered montage of images about "looking"—especially looking at surveillance footage on screens and at images on comic book panels. Courtesy DC Comics (2005 reprint edition).

Christmas, then turns to his screen to engage in scopophilia by watching the *image* of a happy Christmas without having the reality. As with pornography, his thrill is in the scopophilia of watching rather than participating. We, in turn, *watch him watching* until the spectacle is disturbed by our frame zooming back to include the screen upon which we are, just like him, watching, and then going further to include the "credits" for the comic itself. This provides us with what we might call "conformist deviance"—we can watch what we cannot have. Our looking at the comic is kindred to Susan gazing at his computer that monitors the population, just as it is akin to V consuming his films in the darkened theater—we are disturbed, albeit mildly, from our unselfconscious consumption and are prompted to recognize how the materials in our hands can be employed for the same functions as what we watch others watching: propaganda. In effect, "the specific function of the work of art is to make *visible . . .* the reality of the existing ideology" (Althusser, *Lenin* 241–242). We are also, in this moment, reminded of the ongoing doubling of V and Susan as pairs rather than as opposites. That is, of course, until the product undergoes another iteration through the culture industry, at which point all of these disruptive, liberatory materials are culled when the remediated form of the DC Comics series is itself remediated into the graphic novel. Ideology is again rendered invisible, and the guilty pleasures of pulp become repressive when these images vanish.

The last three remediations are the 2005 film and the 2006 novelization and audio book of the film (which reproduces the film's dialogue almost verbatim), all three of which are designed to be the most profitable and commercially viable products. For films, this is an absolute necessity, since the cost of production is very much greater than the cost of producing a black-and-white comic in an anthology, which is where this work began. A film cannot afford to "flop" in the same way that a comic written by one person and drawn by another (neither of whom is relying on it as their sole income) can afford to have a failure, risk alienating its audience, or fail to satisfy its audience's every desire. Hence, the increasing operations of commercial interests from *Warrior* to DC Comics is increased as further remediations bring the contents to film and to mass market paperback production for sale in bookstores and on drug or grocery store racks. As has already been very widely recognized, a simple comparison of the graphic novel and the film shows the excision of the political contents, a heroic presentation of V, and a profound subversion of the political and conceptual ambitions of the original product.

In the original comic, the anarchist V has a protracted soliloquy with Madam Justice, again in direct contrast to Adam Susan's soliloquy (Moore 2005, 37–41). The titles are set as "First Version" and "Second Version" in the comic so that the comparison is overt. This is the political core of the work's anarchist philosophy,

The poster for the film adaptation of Alan Moore and David Lloyd's comic book miniseries *V for Vendetta* (1988–1989). Directed by James McTeigue and written by the Wachowski Brothers, the film starred Hugo Weaving as the mysterious anarchist known as V, and Natalie Portman as Evey, his working-class protégé. Photo copyright Warner Bros., 2005.

in which Moore articulates the distinctions between Justice, Law, and Freedom. For Moore, anarchism is a political philosophy that privileges pacifism and antiauthoritarian forms of social organization, as well as justice over the rule of law. Moore closes the comic series with his female protagonist, Evey, giving what appears to be the "moral of the story" following V's death and the collapse of the fascist government. At least, this is a moral insofar as an anarchist work *avoids* imposing its morals on others while opening possibilities and frustrating privileged positions or perspectives reliant on authority:

> The people stand within the ruins of society, a jail intended to outlive them all. The door is open. They can leave, or fall instead to squabbling and thence new slaveries. The choice is theirs, as ever it must be. I will not lead them, but I'll help them build, help them create where I'll not help them kill. The age of killers is no more. They have no place within our better world. (Moore and Lloyd, *V for Vendetta* 260:5–6)

The ending that follows remains equally ambiguous. It leaves the reader in a position of choice, much like Evey's notion of "the people" at a door in a moment of decision, which is itself a moment of freedom that she chose during the narrative when she left her own prison. Eric Finch, the detective and representative of Justice in the work, rejects power, a new armed force following on the collapse of the government, and a series of rulers—this scene then closes the comic as a whole.

Moore's V violates the law to revolt against unjust rule, in which the law is complicit. The most striking feature, however, is that V expressly describes his antiauthoritarian political philosophy as anarchism. This description is quite right in a literal sense, but it is contrary to the popular media that portrays anarchism in a very different light. Since the formal repression of antiauthoritarian and syndicalist anarchists by the Communists in the Spanish Civil War and the Russian Revolution, the mainstream media has systematically portrayed anarchism as violent and subversive rather than as pacifist, antiauthoritarian, and intent on both justice and responsibility. As would be expected, this scene and *every* explicit reference to anarchism as well as to fascism is absent from the 2006 film version.

The same omission follows for the novelization of the film and of the audiobook created from that novelization. The deeply political comic becomes apolitical in its film remediation, as has been noted by several critics. Reynolds makes the most striking claim:

> The film suggests terrorism is justifiable—[so long as] it seeks to reinstate the terms of Western hegemony. And so V's terrorism is acceptable; but his anarchist beliefs are

not. Ironically, by erasing the anarchist politics of Moore's work, the film rehearses the kinds of oppression it purports to attack. The erasure … thus has moral overtones, because it banishes a clear political stance in favour of creating a consumer-friendly product that is at best reduced, at worst censored, by adaptation. (Reynolds 132)

In effect, by censoring the work's primary political voice—which privileges freedom of choice, pacifism, and antiauthoritarian views—the film creates an ideologically empty product that practices Herbert Marcuse's notions of "repression tolerance" by reductively celebrating the terrorism and violence perpetrated by the figure whom Moore and Lloyd designate, on the second page of the first chapter, as "The Villain" (Moore and Lloyd, *V for Vendetta* 10). For Wolk, "*V for Vendetta* is set up as a three-act mystery: Who is V? The mystery formula dictates that by the end, he'll be dramatically unmasked. By the end of the actual book, we haven't found out who he is; instead, we've found out why it doesn't matter who he is" (234).

In the comic, we may accept Evey, but V is deeply problematical. In the film, however, he becomes our protagonist hero whose violence is wholly acceptable as a generic necessity, and his death in the film becomes the glorious sacrifice of a martyr to win freedom for all—the subversion of Moore's work here runs deep not only in the heroism and elision of V's villainy but in the act of winning freedom for others rather than their making it for themselves, which had been the crux of Evey's more authentic form of anarchism in the comic.

There is a useful way of considering this reversal from endorsing pacifism to celebrating violence, and from a subversive to a hegemonic cultural product. Gramsci's theory of "cultural hegemony" argues that one group in a society rules over another (or over all others) by presenting its own values (and the perpetuation of the values that keep it in power) as normal and natural social values. This is much akin to the earlier contention, via Althusser, that the industrial production of culture first and foremost entails the "reproduction of the conditions of production"; otherwise, it would immediately lead to its own self-destruction as an industry. In order to be effective, Gramsci's notion of cultural hegemony must be normalized and brought into quotidian, everyday reality—cultural norms must appear to be "natural" or "inevitable," while disagreement or alignment with a different form of social organization is immediately cast as "deviant," which is very much what the original comic book contends. This idea of control tends to conjure up some conspiracy-theory image of backroom dealings between a handful of people ruling the world—nevertheless, the opposite is the intent. Through naturalization of these normative social values, this system of control is just a self-reinforcing social system independent of any natural notion of subjectivity or autonomous subjects. No one needs to direct it, because it manufactures the taste by which it judges itself, as we have already heard. Likewise, no one needs to censor anarchism from *V for Vendetta*; they just need to make a film that sells—and a salable film cannot promote anarchism while courting mainstream funding. The fine distinction is that such overtly anarchist films need not be prevented, since they will simply fail to attract investment because it would fail to draw the mainstream audience upon release.

Transforming Mediated Media

V for Vendetta first appears as an openly anarchist underground comic in an irregularly produced independent anthology magazine. However, it slowly transforms itself across each remediation into a more mass-produced item with progressively less of its "deviant" content and less ability to promote self-reflexivity in the reader. The question for us is whether this was somehow an aim of the artists or an inevitable part of the nature of the culture industry. Alan Moore's response is clear—he demanded a public retraction by the film producers for what he called their "blatant lies" and went on to say *V for Vendetta* is "specifically about things like fascism and anarchy. Those words, 'fascism' and 'anarchy,' occur nowhere in the film. It's been turned into a Bush-era parable by people too timid to set a political satire in their own country" (Moore "Last," n.pag). Moore's position is fairly clear, and we would have great difficulty mistaking his views.

David Lloyd makes the matter easy as well. In his introduction to the first graphic novel edition by Collected Books in 1990, edited by K. C. Carlson, he offers a lengthy commentary on Thatcher-era mass media in the United Kingdom. This leads him to intermingle television soap operas, game shows, newsprint, and their consumers:

> It was Tuesday and I could hear the television in the background still running the latest episode of "Eastenders"—a soap about the day-to-day life of cheeky, cheery working-class people in a decaying, mythical part of London....
>
> After "Eastenders" came "Porridge"—a re-run of a situation comedy about a cheeky, cheery prisoner in a comfortably unoppressive, decaying Victorian prison....
>
> At 8:30, following "Porridge," came "A Question of Sport"—a simple panel quiz show featuring cheeky, cheery sports celebrities answering questions about other sports celebrities, many of whom were as cheeky and cheery as themselves.
>
> Jocularity reigned....

"The Nine o'Clock News" followed "A Question of Sport." Or at least for 30 seconds it did, before the television was switched off and cheeky, cheery pop music took its place. . . .

As [the barman] filled the glass, I solemnly asked him why he'd switched off the News. "Don't ask me—that was the wife," he replied, in a cheeky, cheery manner. . . . (Moore and Lloyd, *V for Vendetta* 5)

The striking content from this short anecdote is not simply the contrast between the popular media and the comic for which this formed part of the introduction, but rather Lloyd's language of "prison," "reign," and "class." This language may lead the reader to ask how familiar Lloyd is with Lukes's discussion of power, the Frankfurt School's concept of coercion, Marcuse's repressive desublimation, or Gramsci's cultural hegemony. A comic may not be a good place for an overt manifesto (a notion certainly open for debate), but Lloyd's terms mark his cheeky, cheery pub patrons as subject to an authoritarian state in which they become the very things performed for them in their mass media: cheeky and cheery in their unoppressive prison, the same prison opened in the closing pages of the novel. Lloyd might just as well have paraphrased Adorno and Horkheimer in *Dialectic of Enlightenment*:

The escape from everyday drudgery which the whole culture industry promises may be compared to the daughter's abduction [by her fiancé] in the cartoon: the father is holding the ladder in the dark. The paradise offered by the culture industry is the same old drudgery. Both escape and elopement are pre-designed to lead back to the starting point. Pleasure promotes the resignation which it ought to help to forget. (142)

As with Lloyd's cheeky, cheery patrons, the culture industry produces the normative behaviors in its consumers that are most conducive to their consumption. *Eastenders* teaches the London pub patrons how to be themselves by constructing everyday life as itself a consumable product, and in doing so we enter Lukes's third dimension of power, which, unlike direct force or coercion, operates contextually by seeming natural to all involved, often over significant gaps of time and distance while remaining largely unrecognized by those involved, very much akin to Gramsci's theory of cultural hegemony.

V for Vendetta appears to be a work built from a conscious understanding of this process, yet as it was processed through the culture industry, each new witness of the work in each remediation increasingly promoted the "eternal consumer" of Adorno and Horkheimer. This is why it is of particular value as an example—not only soap operas and romance novels, but even an anarchist underground comic book, can be successfully processed by the culture industry as a tool for cultural hegemony and repressive tolerance.

Black Flag, Black Dossier

Moore and O'Neil's much later work, *The League of Extraordinary Gentlemen: Black Dossier*, in contrast, reverses the process that *V for Vendetta* underwent. Its creators learned the lessons of dealing with the culture industry in general and DC Comics in particular. *Black Dossier* reacts to editorial interference by remediating the previous volumes of *League*, as well as yet another Hollywood adaptation. The result is that the larger text of *League* has even stronger anarchist implications at the levels of both plot and form. The plot is anti-imperialist and antifascist, which *could* be anarchist but could also be comfortably acceptable within neoliberal hegemonies that claim to be democratic (i.e., America, Britain, etc.). The form, however, enacts an anarchist praxis by rejecting authority entirely and, instead, inviting readers to make their own determinations, in essence, to *think like anarchists* in the act of reading. This move is similar to *V for Vendetta* but without using the word *anarchism*, which is easily censored and also tends to distract the audience with clichéd nineteenth-century images of bomb-throwing terrorists. This move also parallels twentieth-century anarchist art's move from explicit to implicit, from content to form, which is less a depoliticization than it is an effective tactic.

This movement to form reflects a praxis developed from the more overt statement of anarchist theory. In effect, the explicit discussion of anarchism and the thinking through of anarchist approaches to rebellion and authority becomes praxis in aesthetic form. The most overt broaching of this concept appears in David Weir's *Anarchy & Culture*, where he contends, "Anarchism was, quite simply, an outmoded ideology in the period between the world wars, too antiquated to be of use to anyone . . . [but] anarchism succeeded culturally where it failed politically" (4–5). By this, Weir means that anarchism failed as a political movement in Spain while going on to success as a mode of artistic and aesthetic practice. Weir's over-polite rebuke reflects his Marxist position very much in alignment with Fredric Jameson, the critical touchstone of his project, but the notion that anarchist theories of activism could redeploy themselves as praxis through artistic form is well established. Antliff has presented this in direct terms through the British poet and art critic Herbert Read: "Read searched for art that prefigured anarchism's open structures on a metaphorical level, as form, [while] contemporary anarchists are developing art that fosters anarchist politics in practice, by transforming art-making into an egalitarian process that is itself unbounded" (Antliff, "Open" 6). In Antliff's analysis, the contrast to Weir becomes pointed as they approach the complexities of form. Antliff presents Read's understanding of anarchist form by writing "its revolutionary import lay elsewhere, in its potential to infuse the man-made environment with universal aesthetic qualities that mirrored the organicism of the natural world" (11), or in another sense, the open form of abstract art could model the absence of rule in organic environments. The contrast, however, lies in the language, for with Antliff, "not only did these artists refuse the didactic programmes of communism and fascism; they created art that, like anarchism, mirrored the open structure of nature itself" (11). In contrast, for Weir, this sense of organicism reflects Raymond Williams' contention, understood in Weir via Jameson, that "organic" is a Marxist term "and that in both the Marxist and the conservative traditions, the organic is opposed to and threatened by the atomistic" (223), which is to say the organic indicates the communal or collective as well as the material. For Antliff, the organic relates to form as a reflection of anarchist social organization, while for Weir the matter remains one between the atomistic and the communal. As we turn to Moore's *Black Dossier*, the anarchist contents of *V for Vendetta* that has been overtly expressed as a refutation of rule and authority are transformed from a stated theory and call to activism into a praxis that expresses itself through form. That is, *V for Vendetta* seeks to express anarchism, as an idea, whereas *Black Dossier* seeks to enact anarchism within its readers as praxis.

Theory, Praxis, Contextualizing Power

Black Dossier itself falls between the second and third volumes of *The League of Extraordinary Gentlemen*, and it deviates significantly from the established form of the series in order to enact its anarchist praxis. Published under some duress and not exactly a story, it literally does not look like the previous two volumes, and it is often remarkably hard to read on a practical level. The only consistent element is the antiauthoritarian thread that we have just described. *Black Dossier* depicts a continuity of illegitimate authority, first in imperialist and then fascist Britain, and it rapidly switches between modes—both in pictures and prose—thus defying linear storytelling. As a result, it rejects authoritative systems, both aesthetic and political, and the roots of that rejection lie in the context of how the book was published.

Black Dossier constitutes a distinct break from the way that previous parts of *League* reached their audience. The first twelve issues were published by Wildstorm Comics between 1999 to 2003, in two six-issue story arcs that came out serially. They were then collected into what can now be purchased in two more-or-less standalone volumes, much like *V for Vendetta* was collected into a single book. This was and remains common practice in mainstream American comics. It allows publishers to sell the same material twice with minimal revisions, and it also allows them to minimize risk, because they can publish a series one issue at a time, gaining profits continuously, rather than commissioning a whole book, as is the model for novels. However, Wildstorm had been purchased by DC Comics in 1998, a year before *League* first appeared, and Moore had by then decided to never work for DC again because of a dispute that went back to *Watchmen* in 1986.[2] Moore was "perfectly happy to allow [Wildstorm] to continue publishing *The League of Extraordinary Gentlemen*" (Moore, "Opening"), which he did for the first two volumes, but not without complications. All parties were aware of the previous friction, including Moore's audience, but DC stayed out of the editorial process, and that was good enough for both Moore and O'Neill.

Black Dossier itself had started in Moore's mind as a sourcebook that would provide non-narrative information about the "universe" of *League*. It would consist mostly of text with only minimal artwork, just enough to get Kevin O'Neill a paycheck. It was not meant to be, and truly is not, a third volume of *League* stories. It quickly evolved, however, into something much more complex. Instead of just a sourcebook, it would contain a frame narrative that would depict the heroes reading what came to be called "the Black Dossier" (hence the title of the book), which itself would be a collection of intelligence documents about the League's activities. Thus, the framing device occasionally interrupts the dossier and depicts the heroes, Allan Quartermain and Mina Murray, escaping across Britain from agents of the British government, agents who are working for the people who compiled the dossier to begin with and who very much want it back. *Black Dossier* thus marries the content of a simple sourcebook to something akin to a MacGuffin plot, but the MacGuffin is, itself, another layer of story.

The "Black Dossier" *in* the book is a collection of documents spanning four centuries, and thus they are visually designed to reflect different time periods and printing techniques as well as styles of art and writing. Thus, *Black Dossier* was originally going to include a Tijuana bible insert, a 3-D section, and a playable vinyl record, two out of three of which did make it into the final book. For the majority of the production, Moore says that he and O'Neill had no problems with DC. Their editors agreed to publish *Black Dossier* the way the creators had planned it, without interference, and they agreed not to bother O'Neill with deadlines, as was their standing arrangement with Wildstorm (Moore, "Opening). However, when Moore and O'Neill announced that they were going to move *League* to Top Shelf Comics after finishing *Black Dossier*, Moore claims that DC began meddling with the process: pulling the vinyl record, pestering O'Neill to finish the art in time for Christmas, and then not publishing it until after Christmas anyway (Moore, "Opening). At that time, Warner Bros. was also touting its *V for Vendetta* film, and promotional materials spuriously claimed that Moore was in support of the project (Johnston, "Lying"), which, as we have already established, he was most emphatically not.

It is worth noting that none of DC's expectations were particularly unusual in comic book publishing; working to deadlines and cooperating with marketers and their schedules is a given, but Moore considers it to have been a violation of his and O'Neill's agreement with Wildstorm as well as an insult to their artistic integrity. It is also worth noting that DC eventually decided that it could not publish *Black Dossier* in the United Kingdom at all, because of copyright laws surrounding the contemporary characters it depicts. The Victorian characters in the first two volumes had long since passed into the public domain, so Moore and O'Neill were free to turn Allan Quartermain into an opium addict, and Captain Nemo into a psychopath, for example, but modern characters presented too much legal risk. Moore specifically cites an image of the Lone Ranger they were required to change (Moore, "Opening" par. 8), and the character "Jimmy," a James Bond analogue, who is depicted in Black Dossier as a sexual predator and a sadist, so there may have been misgivings there, as well. As a result, one could order the book online in the United Kingdom, but it was not available in comic shops and other bookstores. The upshot, then, is that Moore and O'Neil ultimately gave DC an odd beast of a book: not quite a comic book not quite a story, with very unusual physical elements *and* cut off from a major English-speaking market, *and* ultimately late to that market.

Now, to be clear, Moore and O'Neill have never said that *Black Dossier* was any kind of protest or attempt to harm DC's profits. Indeed, its format and content had been settled long before the trouble started, and Moore is quite clear that he and O'Neill very much believed in the project. There is but one gentle reference in the book to the whole kerfuffle. On the credits page, which is fashioned to resemble a map of the London Underground, a box off to one side says: "ABC: Closed for the Duration" (*Dossier* xi), which references the fact that America's Best Comics would come to an end after *Black Dossier*. However, all of these delays in publication and troubles with the publisher were reported at the time, and readers in the United Kingdom found out that the book would not be as easily available to them. To fans and consumers, then, it looked a lot like either yet another instance of DC meddling in Moore and his collaborators' creative process, or Moore throwing another temper tantrum,[3] or perhaps a bit of both.

This, then, is the context in which much of his audience read *Black Dossier*: as a thumb in the eye of DC, a corporate entity that had a reputation—rightly or wrongly—for exploiting its creatives and aggressively acquiring its competitors' intellectual properties (e.g., Wildstorm Comics itself), sometimes allegedly after having driven them out of business. From this point of view, if the book *is* a critique of DC's corporate-capitalist practices, then it is an accidental one born simply of Moore and O'Neill wanting to do something different from a standard sourcebook. However, that explanation does stretch the meaning of the word "accidental," and it does not account for the anarchist aesthetics and ethics behind Moore and O'Neil's decisions. That is to say, the same force that drove them to transform *Black Dossier* from a simple sourcebook into a multimodal collage of writing and visual styles drove them to insist on *total* artistic freedom and, once they realized they did not have it, to simply reject the authority of their publisher by leaving. The point, then, is that the anarchist politics behind how *Black Dossier* was published is not separable from the anarchist politics behind how it was created, which is why that sense of anarchism is implicit in both the plot and the form of the book. To understand the anarchism of the plot, we have to juxtapose the first two volumes with *Black Dossier* and, a little, to the subsequent volumes.

The first two volumes of *League* are essentially the adventures of a Victorian superhero team that fights monsters and super-criminals, and while there is an underlying anti-imperialist critique, it is somewhat muted. *League* depicts the sexism, racism, and brutality of the British Empire, and the protagonists are not heroes but rather monsters and outcasts who happen to have been recruited into the spy service. Wilhelmina Murray is an outcast by contemporary standards because she is, in effect, a rape survivor. She wears a red scarf around her neck that covers the massive scar from Dracula having attacked her in Bram Stoker's novel. Likewise, Allan Quartermain is an aging opium addict rather than a dashing colonial adventurer. Captain Nemo, H. G. Wells's Invisible Man, and Mr. Hyde are all psychopaths whom Murray is tasked with commanding. She consistently acts as a capable leader, even managing to tame Mr. Hyde, while Quartermain is mostly an unreliable junkie with a gun. His addiction and Captain Nemo's deep hatred of the British Empire, along with the general brutality of the team's experience, do constitute a critique of imperialism itself, but the majority of the team is still some combination of white, male, English, or upperclass, and they still defend the Empire from foreign threats: the Chinese in the first volume (although led by Professor Moriarty, who is working for Britain at the time), and Martians in the second volume. The series thus inevitably takes the perspective of the empire, rendering everything outside of itself as alien (sometimes literally) and/or villainous. A more explicit critique of empire does not appear until the end of Volume II, when the British government destroys half of South London in order to repel the Martian invasion (26.5), at which point two members of the group are dead (Hyde and the Invisible Man), and the other three (Murray, Quartermain, and Nemo) quit in protest.

League had, by this point, already suffered from some of the very same forces of remediation as *V for Vendetta*: specifically, the film by 20th Century

Fox (2003), which was produced without any input from Moore and O'Neill and was often promoted as "*LXG*," thus ruining its deliberately wordy, antiquated title. The adaptation of its characters and plot also invert two key elements from the book: gender and imperialism. Mina Murray is no longer a rape survivor and capable leader, but rather a sexy vampiress as depicted both in the film and in promotional materials, and with all the abilities of cinematic vampires: strength, flight, transformation, fangs, blood drinking, etc. Thus, it is no longer her culture that spuriously defines her as a monster. Rather, she is an actual monster, and so the film turns a deconstruction of victim blaming into actual victim blaming. This shift also relegates her to an all too common trope in superhero comics in which a woman's strength, literal or otherwise, is ultimately attributed to a sexual assault in her history. Likewise, Quartermain is restored to his colonial adventurer roots—an expert with a gun and a highly capable fighter—as well as being played by Sean Connery, who despite his age, is still overwhelmingly associated with perhaps the ultimate figure of modern British imperialism and sexism: James Bond. Just as the Wachowskis excise precisely those elements of *V for Vendetta* that constitute an anarchist argument, *LXG* inverts precisely those elements of *League* that critique rape culture and imperialism.

The film further rejects any critique of empire by including Tom Sawyer, depicted as a secret service agent and yet another expert with firearms, and it symbolically passes the imperial torch to him at the end of the film. During Quartermain's death scene, he explicitly states that the twentieth century belongs to America, whereas the nineteenth century belonged to Britain (*LXG*). While this assertion is entirely contrary to anything a loyal British imperialist would have believed at the time, it does articulate a form of American *manifest destiny* in which the United States simply inherits the right to rule the world from its colonial parent. There is also a final scene in which Quartermain is buried in Africa, and an African mystic proclaims that Africa itself will literally not let him die. A lightning bolt strikes the grave, setting the stage for a sequel that was, mercifully, never produced. The scene displays no self-awareness of its colonialist implications: primitive magic attributed to Africans, the assumptions that Africans are supernaturally linked to the soil, the assertion that a colonial invader is a true African, and the continent itself exerting supernatural energy to restore the life of that colonizer. Taken together, the two scenes legitimize imperialism, whether by the British or the Americans, but of course, privilege America, although there is the slight implication of shifting from a class system represented by Quartermain to an American-style "common man": Sawyer. Nevertheless, these changes to the comic book are recreations of exactly the kinds of colonialist narratives that Moore and O'Neill's comics are critiquing, and anathema to their own anarchist narrative in which the *continuity of authority* is the ultimate enemy of freedom, whether that authority comes in the form of a queen, a dictator, or a democratic hegemony. Unlike this cinematic remediation, however, *Black Dossier* retroactively recontextualizes the whole *League* "text" such that its anarchist ideology is both more powerful and more covert.

Black Dossier's frame narrative opens sixty years after the end of Volume II and just after the fall of "Ingsoc": English Socialism as depicted in George Orwell's *Nineteen-Eighty Four*. Thus, the previous book closes with a pointed critique of the British Empire, and *Black Dossier* opens with the aftermath of fascism, which implicitly equates the two, as if Britain had merely traded the queen for Big Brother. This plot element is also the first clue in the text that the diegesis does not just include a handful of Victorian pulp and horror novels, as Volumes I and II do, but rather as many works of myth, fantasy, science fiction, and so-called genre fiction as can be stuffed in. Murray and Quartermain return to Britain only to retrieve the "Black Dossier," which means that they spend the entirety of the frame narrative fleeing from analogues of Emma Peel of *The Avengers* and James Bond. The whole moral axis of the narrative flips, then, as the British government has now been thoroughly associated with fascism and violence, which makes them straightforwardly the villains, while the protagonists represent sexuality and freedom, having acquired eternally young bodies that they use to have rather a lot of sex with each other, and anyone else who is game, throughout this book and the next two volumes. This element of the book links Moore's anarchism with his theory of "magic" as articulated in *Promethea*, which is consistently depicted as both sexual and linguistic.[4] Briefly put, magic, language, sex, and anarchism are all intimately linked for Moore, if not quite equated with each other, and, as noted earlier, this same concept is prefigured in the American poet Robert Duncan, who offers a similar model, so its idiosyncrasy is not without a critically recognized tradition.

Black Dossier's specifically anarchist critique of empire, however, emerges from the mystery that drives the frame narrative, which is the search for the true identity of Big Brother, a mystery that is implied but never fully explored in Orwell's original text. This mystery includes the identities of Big Brother's colleagues, the other men behind Ingsoc, the ones who are in command of Bond and Peel. Through a series of deductions and revelations, Murray discovers that Big Brother was General Sir Harold Wharton, otherwise known as Harry Wharton, who, in Moore's words, was "the leader of the gang at Greyfriars" (Moore, "Alan Moore"). "Greyfriars" refers to Greyfriars School (not the London neighborhood), which is the setting for a series of boys' adventure stories published from 1908 to 1961 in a weekly boys' story paper called *The Magnet*. The

Greyfriars stories mostly involve school-boy shenanigans, football matches, and a bit of defending the Empire against foreign spies during wartime. In *Black Dossier*, Moore and O'Neill transform Greyfriars into a recruiting house for British intelligence, one that was established all the way back in the Renaissance; in effect, it is a Hogwarts for spies.[5] According to Moore (Moore, "Alan Moore" par. 25), he and O'Neill struck on this idea partly based on Orwell's own critique of the Greyfriars adventures in an article called "Boys' Stories," published in *Horizon* in 1940. Orwell argues these stories are merely propaganda for Edwardian imperialism, racism, and classism—the idea that boys educated in the traditional upper-class atmosphere were the norm of all behavior and the protectors of the values of the British Empire—and that they long outlasted the Edwardians, thus implicitly perpetuating the period's values. He also laments the lack of left-wing entertainment for British boys to balance off things like Greyfriars; i.e., "why is there no such thing as a left-wing boys' paper?" (Orwell par. 34). *Black Dossier*, ABC, and most of Moore's output in the nineties constitute a response to that lament; they are left-wing entertainment that is, ostensibly, for younger readers and, unlike the Greyfriars stories, largely told from a lower- or working-class point of view or containing an anticlassist message.[6] It is only consistent, then, that *Black Dossier* should also extend Orwell's thought and depict Greyfriars itself as the womb from which emerges Big Brother and English fascism. Moore and O'Neill neatly synthesize Orwell's text (*Nineteen Eight-Four*) with Orwell's critique of Greyfriars, thus producing an anarchist and anticlassist critique of the Greyfriars stories and of authority in general.

Which is to say, Greyfriars represents the continuity of upper-class authority that is the ultimate moral outrage to anarchism: not just authority concentrated in one person but aristocratic authority perpetuated over time and without the consent of the population at large, literally the *archons* of an-archy. In *Black Dossier*, Greyfriars' position at the center of British power lasts for centuries, through the fall of the British Crown, the dominance of Big Brother, and his replacement by O'Brien (as implied in *Nineteen Eighty-Four*), and even after the ultimate fall of IngSoc (as depicted in *Black Dossier*). Those forces are part of a legacy of class rule that simply puts on a new hat when it needs to create the illusion of consent to the will of the people. This is Moore and O'Neill's most direct attack on the Empire: revealing the horror that basically the same people have been exploiting Britain, and by extension the world, for hundreds of years, and with no legitimate justification. Thus, the "game of allusion-hunting" (Jones 101) that makes up most of the book produces a distinctly anticlassist, anti-imperial, and antifascist argument. However, the audience must recognize those allusions for the critique to function. At the very least, they would need to know both *Nineteen Eighty-Four* and the Greyfriars stories, and it would help to know Orwell's "Boys' Stories," so this element of the book is easy to miss. Unlike this complex critique, though, the book's aesthetics conspire to create an anarchist experience that is far less reliant on audience knowledge and also far more difficult to censor or excise, as in the remediations of *V for Vendetta*.

You Not Do This! Form Unbound

Black Dossier is formally anarchistic while the previous two volumes are not. Volumes I and II are traditional American comics: saddle-stapled pamphlets that consist of left-to-right panels, in color, and with dialogue in word balloons and narration in narrator boxes. Kevin O'Neill's drawing style has its own special flair—a geometrical quality to his faces and heavy use of inked lines as shading rather than coloring effects—but it is stylistic rather than radical. The narratives are consistently linear and, while the first twelve issues do contain illustrated prose pieces, such as "Allan and the Sundered Veil" in Volume I, and the credits pages are drawn to resemble period newspapers in the collected editions, the majority of the story occurs at the level of the panels, not distanced from the audience by a framing device, as in *Black Dossier*. O'Neill's art *just is* the real world of these stories, despite their sometimes cheeky self-referential packaging.

Black Dossier does away with all of these formal conventions as a result of the evolution of the project. The "Black Dossier" rapidly switches between modes as it emulates individual styles and historical periods. For example, "Faerie's Fortunes Founded" is ostensibly a lost Shakespeare play. The title is a play on *Love's Labour's Lost,* of course, and the typeset looks Elizabethan. Its illustrations diminish the effect, but they effectively synthesize a quarto and a comic book. There are similar stylistic touches in "What Ho, Gods of the Abyss," which combines Lovecraftian drawings and descriptions of elder gods with the comedy of P. D. Wodehouse's *Jeeves and Wooster* stories. Likewise, the "The Crazy Wide Forever" is a rambling short story that resembles Jack Kerouac's stream-of-consciousness prose from *On the Road* and uses what looks like a typewriter printed on yellowed pulp paper. Again, it is not quite realistic, but it does combine visually recognizable signifiers of the referent. Aside from the frame narrative, there are two other comic book sequences, and they both emulate specific visual styles: British humor comics of the fifties in "Trump Traveller's Club" and Tijuana bibles in "Sex Jane." The audience has to rapidly shift, then, not only between modes (prose and comics) but between narrative voices, typefaces, page formats, and the like.

As a result, a specific relationship develops between the sourcebook content and the frame narrative. The sourcebook material needs the frame to create a clear sense of story, but it could stand on its own as pure information. However, the frame's mystery has no resolution without the sourcebook content, in which Wharton's identity is revealed in a handwritten note on an IngSoc report. Without the content in the sourcebook, Murray uncovering Big Brother's identity has no significance. Those documents are also out of chronological order, so the audience has to piece together the causality of sixty years' worth of diegetic history along with everything else.[7] Finally, while the frame story is in O'Neill's *League* drawing style, which indicates something like unmediated reality, the majority of the plot points are revealed in the sourcebook pages, which are in the dizzying variety of styles that we have already discussed. In effect, this arrangement dislocates "the real" in two ways. First, it is no longer reliably located in the comics sections, and second, while the prose does contain the necessary information to understand the mystery (that Big Brother is Wharton), it is not in any one reliable form or format.

The book is also just plain difficult to read, with prose spanning the width of a standard comic book page and fonts that are simply hard on the eyes, and by virtue of sheer density. That difficulty is potentially productive, though, in that it can produce an anarchist reading subject. Thus, we argue that *Black Dossier* remediates *League*, a comic book and later a film, through form, and in so doing it effectively breaks history itself into something not built from a consistent visual aesthetic, normative gaze, or political theory. History, in *Black Dossier*, is built of perspectives as embodied by documents that are, themselves, subjective. They do not function as direct observations of *League*'s diegesis. They are not unmediated reality, unlike the comic book format of the first two volumes, and once *League* comics make that transition, they are never the same again. While the subsequent volumes of the series, *Century* and *Heart of Ice*, return to O'Neil's direct depiction of the narrative, they are no longer published as single issues, and they take great leaps in time between volumes: decades, in both cases. This transition is, no doubt, a product of moving to a new publisher with more lenient format restrictions, but again, that itself is part and parcel of Moore and O'Neill's artistic sensibilities, which are anarchistic. Thus, ultimately, *Black Dossier's* format makes the audience work to understand it and, in the process, gives them the option of not just *an anarchist reading* but *reading it like an anarchist*. The large-scale rejection of *Black Dossier* by many of Moore's fans signifies, in part, that they declined that option. Ironically, that is consistent with an anarchist text in which coercing the audience would constitute a form of power, as defined by Antliff.

V for Vendetta and *Black Dossier* perform inversely parallel remediations. The first is remediated in such a way as to excise the anarchist content, which is particularly easy to do when that content is explicit. It starts by removing pages that foreground the viewer's own complicity with authority, and it ends with the Wachowskis writing a script that does not even contain the word *anarchism*. *League* receives the same treatment in its film adaptation, and *Black Dossier* at first receives the same treatment from its editors. By virtue of Moore's massively bankable name, however, he and O'Neill managed to construct a book that does not need to use the word *anarchism* to create an anarchic experience for its audience. This shift in sensibility, from explicit anarchist philosophy to implicit anarchist formalism, mirrors the shift in anarchist art in the twentieth century. Explicit anarchist art has, at times, resulted in swift censorship, and the word itself has been evacuated of meaning for most people, either signifying a bomb-throwing madman (e.g., V himself) or meaning nothing at all, hence the seeming inability to fathom what *V for Vendetta* was even about on the part of its remediators. Moore, therefore, learns the lesson of twentieth-century anarchist art and constructs something that invites the audience to think like anarchists rather than reading about anarchism as a named philosophy.

Notes

1. When V appears, he is quoting the sergeant retelling the victories of Macbeth and Banquo, which establishes V's identity as an antihero and leads us to expect a tragedy caught up in a national upheaval and overturning of rulers. *Macbeth* is taken as itself alluding to the Gunpowder Plot, because Catholic conspirators were popularly equated with Jesuits. Henry Garnet's *A Treatise on Equivocation* was found in the possession of one of the Gunpowder Plot conspirators. This treatise addresses how Catholics should answer authority if questioned about religion. Hence, popular belief was that the Jesuits were trying "to lie like truth" (in Shakespeare's terms). The equivalence of opposites ("fair is foul and foul is fair"), double-dealing, deception, and of course "equivocation" are major themes in *Macbeth* and the many other "Gunpowder Plays" of the time. In *Witches and Jesuits*, Wills argues Shakespeare's audience would have seen Henry Garnet (the Jesuit) as addressing the Porter in this famous scene (greeting him three times, as the witches hailed Macbeth under three titles). Part of Garnet's defense was famously "equivocation." Because of this, several Shakespeare editors suggest *Macbeth* was written in 1605 to 1606, mainly because of these allusions to the Gunpowder Plot and its trials.

2. In brief, the contract stated that the rights to the story would revert to Moore and David Gibbons after a certain amount of time if the book was out of print, but DC has kept it in print ever since, which was unheard of in American comics at the time, thus retaining the rights.

3. This is the phrase that Moore occasionally, cordially, uses to describe his own actions (e.g., Dunn par. 9).

4. Kidder has material on this subject. See "Self-Conscious Sexuality in *Promethea*," *Sexual Ideology in the Works of Alan Moore* (McFarland, 2012) as well as "Telling Stories about

Storytelling" (diss., University of Alberta, 2009). The most obvious point of comparison in anarchist practice is the major American poet, anarchist, and pre-Stonewall gay rights writer Robert Duncan, who regarded his poetry as the enactment of a magical praxis that would enact anarchism.

5. Moore also pillories the Harry Potter books in *League of Extraordinary Gentlemen: Century*, so they are not off the hook.

6. What Moore thinks is appropriate for younger readers is not necessarily the norm, but then, that is part of his anarchist approach to art.

7. The dossier documents four hundred years of history, but the mystery spans only about half a century.

Works Cited

Althusser, Louis. *Lenin and Philosophy, and Other Essays*. New York: Monthly Review Press, 1972. Print.

Antliff, Allan. *Anarchy and Art: From the Paris Commune to the Fall of the Berlin Wall*. Arsenal Pulp Press: Vancouver, BC, Canada. 2007. Print.

———. "Open Form and the Abstract Imperative: Herbert Read and Contemporary Anarchist Art." *Anarchist Studies* 16.1 (2008): 6–19. Print.

Bolter, Jay David, and Richard Grusin. "Remediation." *Configurations* 4.3 (1996): 311–358. Print.

Horkheimer, Max, and Theodor Adorno. *Dialectic of Enlightenment*. 1979. Trans. John Cumming. New York: Continuum, 1989. Print.

Hutcheon, Linda. *A Poetics of Postmodernism: History, Theory, Fiction*. Routledge: New York. 1988. Print.

Jones, Jason B. "Betrayed by Time: Steampunk & the Neo-Victorian in Alan Moore's *Lost Girls* and *The League of Extraordinary Gentlemen* 3.1 (2010): 99–126. Print.

Kidder, Orion Ussner. "Show and Tell: Notes towards a Theory of Metacomics." *International Journal of Comic Arts* 10.1 (Spring 2008): 248–267. Print.

Moore, Alan. "Alan Moore." Interview with James Knight, Jonathan Worth, Jose Villarrubia. "Alan Moore." *Vice.com*. 1 Dec. 2009. Web. 3 Feb. 2015.

———. "Alan Moore: The Last Angry Man." Interview with, Jennifer Vineyard.. MTV Networks. Mar. 2006. Web.

———. "Opening the *Black Dossier*: The Alan Moore Interview." Interview with Kurt Amacker. *Mania: Beyond Entertainment*. 7 November 2007. Web. 3 Feb. 2015.

Moore, Alan, and David Lloyd. *V for Vendetta*. New York: Vertigo, 2005. Print.

———. "Chapter 13: Values." *V for Vendetta* 7 (Jan. 1989): 8–14. Print.

———. "Chapter 14: Vignettes." *V for Vendetta* 7 (Jan. 1989): 15–21. Print.

———. "Vertigo." *V for Vendetta* 7 (Jan. 1989): 23–28. Print.

———. "Vincent." *V for Vendetta* 7 (Jan. 1989): 29–32. Print.

Moore, Alan. and Kevin O'Neil. *The League of Extraordinary Gentlemen: Volume I*. America's Best Comics (Wildstorm Comics, DC Comics). 2002. Print.

———. *The League of Extraordinary Gentlemen: Volume II*. America's Best Comics (Wildstorm Comics, DC Comics). 2004. Print.

———. *The League of Extraordinary Gentlemen: Black Dossier*. America's Best Comics (Wildstorm Comics, DC Comics). 2008. Print.

Moore, Stephen. "Boys' Weeklies." www.orwell.ru. 30 August 2013. Web. 1 May 2014.

———. *V for Vendetta*. New York: Pocket Star, 2006. Print.

Orwell, George. *Nineteen Eighty-Four*. Penguin Books: London, UK. 1989. Print.

Reynolds, James. "'KILL ME SENTIMENT': *V for Vendetta* and Comic-to-Film Adaptation." *Journal of Adaptation in Film & Performance* 2.2 (2009): 121–136. Print.

Waugh, Patricia. *Metafiction: The Theory and Practise of Self-Conscious Fiction*. Methuen: New York. 1984. Print.

Weir, David. *Anarchy & Culture: The Aesthetic Politics of Modernism*. Amherst: U of Massachusetts P, 1997. Print.

Wills, Garry. *Witches and Jesuits: Shakespeare's MacBeth*. Oxford: Oxford UP, 1996. Print.

Wolff, Robert Paul. *In Defense of Anarchism*. The Anarchist Library. 16 Aug. 2010. Web. 1 May 2014.

Wolk, Douglas. *Reading Comics: How Graphic Novels Work and What They Mean*. New York: Da Capo Press, 2007.

TRUTH, JUSTICE, AND THE SOCIALIST WAY?
The Politics of Grant Morrison's Superman

Phil Bevin

I won't choose between any one life and another! All of these people are under my protection, you got that? Every living thing!
—Superman to Brainiac, *Superman and the Men of Steel*[1]

Superman has been in existence and continuous publication for more than seventy-five years, and while it is true that many people may have a favorite incarnation—one they deem the "true" interpretation of the character—his longevity is a result of his adaptability to new circumstances and the ability of successive writers to reinvent him.[2]

In 2011 Superman was beginning to look tired. He had not been the star of a number of his own comic books, leaving the impression that writers did not know what to do with him.[3] The malaise was even dramatized in *Superman: Grounded*, a storyline that saw Superman travel America seeking his lost sense of purpose, the direction of which also became muddled when the original writer, J. Michael Straczynski, left the book halfway through, confusing its message and intent.[4]

Shortly after the conclusion of *Superman: Grounded*, DC Comics brought in Grant Morrison, a writer with a reputation for reinventing superheroes, to re-envision Superman in *Action Comics* for DC's New 52 continuity reboot.[5] He gave the character a new sense of direction and purpose by seemingly infusing him with what many surprised commentators have interpreted as a "socialist" political stance. This essay analyzes Morrison's *Action Comics* in order to understand his socialist Superman and discover the truth behind the apparently radical, left-leaning politics of the New 52 Man of Steel.

Morrison has prior experience writing stories featuring Superman, most notably the critically acclaimed *All-Star Superman*, a "stirringly mythic, emotionally resonant" out-of-continuity account of the lead-up to Superman's death from a radiation overdose precipitated by Lex Luthor.[6] In *All-Star Superman*, Morrison and penciller Frank Quitely paint a portrait of a majestic, pacifist Superman, who avoids conflict on principle and who looks beyond binary divisions to the unified field of the imagination, seeing the underlying connections and interdependences between individuals.[7]

The idealistic nature of this Superman is expressed perfectly in Morrison's autobiographical history of superheroes, *Supergods*:

> A Vitruvian Man in a cape, our restorative Superman would attempt to distill the pure essence of pop culture's finest creation: baring the soul of an indestructible hero, so noble, so clever and resourceful, he had no need to kill to make his point. There was no problem Superman could not overcome. He could not lose. He would never let us down because we made him that way.[8]

This Superman can see the potential good in everyone and frequently guides those he meets—even people who are initially antagonistic toward both the Man of Steel and the humanity he protects—into making positive contributions to broader society by finding them roles that allow them to express their unique personalities and beliefs in ways that benefit rather than conflict with others. *All-Star Superman* received high praise from critics, and it is likely a consequence of the success of this limited series that DC commissioned Morrison to reboot Superman's continuity, perhaps hoping that a similar approach would be as successful in the character's ongoing monthly adventures.[9]

Surprisingly, however, at first glance, Morrison's run on *Action Comics* seemingly departs from a number of the earlier series' principles. The Superman of his tenure on the title is certainly no pacifist; the first page of *Action Comics* #1 opens with him violently threatening media and property magnate Glen Glenmorgan—the initial villain of Morrison's story who is responsible for poor-quality construction in Metropolis and biased reporting—by holding him above the edge of the balcony of his penthouse apartment.

As we can see, Rags Morales, the series' main penciller, has rendered the Man of Steel as an inscrutable and threatening force: a clear sign that the Superman of the rebooted *Action Comics* continuity is a new, confrontational character. In the above panel, the reader's first encounter with Superman, the top half of

A new Superman: this Man of Steel is not the same benign, reassuring presence as his predecessor. He is unpredictable, dangerous, exciting, and intriguing. Grant Morrison and Rags Morales, *Superman and the Men of Steel* (New York: DC Comics, 2012), 5.

the hero's face is draped in shadow, penetrated only by his glowing red eyes, an image that recalls Batman's intimidating cowl-like mask.

An explanation for Superman's newfound aggression and the seemingly stark shift in tone from *All-Star Superman*'s representation of the Man of Steel is hinted at by Morrison's description, in *Supergods*, of Siegel and Shuster's original character as a "socialist," as well as by the status of the New 52 as a reboot that reset the superhero's continuity to its beginning, taking him back to his roots.[10] It seems appropriate to note here that Morrison's conception of "socialism" is akin to the popular, journalistic use of the term—a loosely defined synonym for "progressive" or "liberal" or "FDR Democrat" or "believer in Keynesian economics"—which obviously differs from the formal uses of the term found in economics and political science scholarship. That having been said, in this context, the acceptance of the binary division between rich and poor, powerful and marginalized by Morrison's New 52 Superman can be seen as an embrace of the 1938 character's politics, at least as Morrison sees them.[11] This reading is supported by a number of incidences in Morrison's *Action Comics*. In this series, Clark Kent investigates Mr. Tide, an unscrupulous subway car manufacturer, who has laid off the entirety of his workforce in the pursuit of increased mechanization and higher profits, and the Man of Steel tackles the corrupt media and construction magnate Glen Glenmorgan, who "used illegal cheap labor" and "no safety standards" in his building projects.[12] Glenmorgan's crimes in particular seem designed to link the New 52 Superman's politics to those of Siegel and Shuster's original protagonist, who frequently challenged businessmen over "bad safety conditions" and "inferior metals and parts" used in manufacturing processes.[13]

These early stages of Morrison's *Action Comics* run even seem to reproduce the underlying binary division between the exploitative capitalist bourgeoisie and the oppressed proletarian underclass that features prominently in orthodox Marxist analysis. Marx argues that in the development of modern capitalism "self-earned private property"—the means through which individuals previously sustained their personal livelihoods as an outcome of their own efforts and labor—was "supplanted by capitalistic private property, which rests on exploitation of the nominally free labour of others, i.e., on wage labour."[14] Resulting from this "process of transformation," "labourers are turned into proletarians, their means of labour into capital."[15] For Marx, "that which is now to be expropriated is no longer the labourer working for himself, but the capitalist exploiting many Labourers."[16] In essence, modern capitalist society, as well as the generation of wealth within it, is fundamentally dependent upon the exploitation of the poorer classes.

This world of exploitative capitalists leeching off the downtrodden proletarian masses is the setting for the first three issues of Morrison's *Action Comics*. In issue #1, Glen Glenmorgan endangers the lives of destitute squatters living in his poorly constructed "Moravian Quarter" by letting Luthor use them as bait in his plan to trap and kill the socialist Superman, who is threatening to ruin his reputation and his business prospects. The demolition caused by Luthor's plan even stands to benefit Glenmorgan financially, because he has already "earmarked it for development."[17]

In modern America, as it appears in Morrison's *Action Comics*, people are used and discarded according to the interests and whims of their corporate masters. Morrison's new Superman's intention to shift the balance of power is clear in his own words as he apprehends Glenmorgan. Responding to the police's instruction to "put that man down" Superman quips, "Just as soon as he makes a *full* confession to someone who still believes the law works the *same* for rich and poor alike."[18]

Here, Superman is drawing a division between rich and poor, and he is separating himself from the police—the representatives of conventional law and order—who, apparently naively, still believe in the efficacy and fairness of the traditional justice system. Essentially, Superman is drawing an opposition between himself as a crusader for the poor, who are underserved by the existing legal and social frameworks, and the police, who, in their pursuit of the flawed practices of traditional law enforcement, effectively serve the wealthiest and most powerful individuals, who are able to play the system. He is, of course, also creating a binary division between himself, a social reformer who serves the interests of the downtrodden, and wealthy, corrupt types like Glenmorgan. This incarnation of Superman is therefore, at least initially, a challenge and perhaps a threat to the social order and very different from previous portrayals, including the relaxed, assured, and reassuring hero of *All-Star Superman*. Whereas *All-Star Superman*'s hero sought to look beyond ideological divisions and antagonisms between individuals, *Action Comics*' Man of Steel positively embraces them in his fight to represent the less fortunate and to bring down the wealthy and corrupt.

Whilst Morrison seems keen to link his new Superman to the political project that he ascribes to Siegel and Shuster's original, in some respects he amplifies the character's social activism. Whereas Siegel and Shuster's Clark Kent veered between a crusading reporter and a spineless coward, Morrison consistently presents his Kent as a crusader for justice who fights the same cause as Superman but with his pen rather than his fists, and who is willing to stand up to representatives of law enforcement when they side with the "wrong" people.[19] Moreover, although Morrison's Kent is still working in the middle-class profession of journalism, he works for the struggling *Daily Star*, lives in a small, dingy apartment, has difficulty paying his rent and is harassed by the authorities. Even though he is offered a job at the more prestigious and profitable *Daily Planet*, he chooses not to accept it, describing the offer as an attempt by Glenmorgan, who owns the paper, to "*co-opt* me, shut me down."[20]

Such integrity emphasizes Clark's commitment to the cause he fights as both Kent and Superman; he lives what he preaches, and his poverty underscores his class consciousness. Kent could climb the social ladder but actively chooses not to, presumably to stay close to the experiences of those he defends, so that he will never forget how it feels to be vulnerable or the necessity of protecting the poor from powerful and malign forces. Therefore, while Kent may not be working class in the traditional sense, he holds to a class consciousness that affects his day-to-day life and how he relates to Metropolis's other inhabitants.[21]

Given the existing evidence that supports reading Morrison's *Action Comics* as a narrative about a socialist Superman, it is not surprising that that this interpretation has gained prominence, or that several critics—including journalist Laura Sneddon, who describes Morrison as "the father of the new socialist Superman," and comics analyst Cody Walker, who dubs Morrison's Man of Steel "the ultimate socialist hero"—have emphasized it.[22]

The reading is even supported by Morrison himself in an interview with Brian Hiatt for *Rolling Stone*, where the author explicitly states, "[T]he original champion of the repressed Superman, the socialism and stuff, I wanted a bit of that [in *Action Comics*]."[23]

However, while the socialist interpretation of Morrison's New 52 Superman is a legitimate reading of the character, it is only a partial one that does not account for the full significance of Morrison's story.[24] Notably, while Superman's socialism and class awareness are initially strongly represented in the storyline, as early as issue #4, when Brainiac invades Earth, they apparently begin to be overlooked in favor of more fantastical narrative concerns, a trend that continues as the series becomes increasingly experimental in its handling of abstract concepts and reveals its true villain, the fifth-dimensional imp Vyndktvx. Indeed, during his battle with Brainiac in issue #7, Superman appears to have renounced his specific working-class consciousness, declaring to Brainiac: "*I won't choose between any one life and another, all of these people are under my protection, you got that? Every living thing!*"[25] This statement indicates that Superman has stopped making judgments based on assumptions grounded in class and that he will not even make distinctions between the different peoples and cultures from diverse worlds found within the Collector's spaceship: he will fight to protect everyone and everything.

These developments might indicate that Morrison lost interest in telling a politically charged, socialist story in favor of writing a more traditionally outlandish superhero tale.[26] In fact, the idea that Morrison's approach to his material changed over the course of his run is supported by his comments in an interview with *Newsarama*'s Vaneta Rogers:

Initially the idea was to do a six-issue story, which was all that I'd come in to do back then. When Dan came to me and said I'd be relaunching Superman, or restarting Superman, I had some ideas left over from *All-Star*, where I'd do a young Superman story. I really wanted to do a T-shirt and jeans and a different idea.

So then that didn't quite fit in with the fact that Jim Lee had designed a new Superman suit, and that was going to be the official look. So the idea then became to have a modern Superman within the world of modern politics, and to show how he might transform into the new modern DC Superman.

So initially, that's all it was, and that was going to be the Brainiac story, and this superhuman character suddenly brought about a whole culture of superheroes, all wearing costumes. And that was it.

But then we had the Legion story, and suddenly it evolved these time travel complications. And in that way, I thought, well, I haven't done a big Mr. Mxyzptlk story or a Fifth Dimension story.[27]

However, a closer examination of the narrative indicates that the development of Morrison's *Action Comics* run is far less accidental than his comments imply. The early issues feature a number of signposts to the future development of the storyline. Although he is not named or identified, Vyndktvx appears in issue #1 and is marked as a significant and even powerful figure by a panel composition that depicts him as if he were being viewed from a low-angle camera shot.[28]

As we can see here, the appearance of the "little man" in *Action Comics* #1 is not just an afterthought.[29] He is signposted as an important figure, even holding the tie that he uses to initiate Glenmorgan's undoing later in Morrison's first story arc.[30] Also in the inaugural issue of Morrison's run, Mrs. Nxly, Clark Kent's landlady, makes reference to his friends "*two* men and a *woman*—a blonde, *very* nice, very good-looking."[31] She is referring to the Legion of Superheroes members Saturn Woman, Lightning Man, and Cosmic Man, whom we do not see her meet until issue #17.[32]

It is therefore clear that, whether or not Morrison initially intended his run on *Action Comics* to extend to eighteen issues, the final storyline—as it appears in print—is meticulously planned and plotted, and it seems as if Morrison knew how it would eventually develop from the first issue. This cautions against the assumption that Morrison's decision to sideline Superman's socialism and class consciousness is a result of the author's loss of interest or change of mind. Rather, it implies that the shift in focus is intended as an integral part of the story's progression and that Morrison had a purpose in transferring the focus of his narrative away from Superman's social activism to the character's battles against Brainiac and an evil imp from the fifth dimension.

Small but mighty: beneath Vyndktvx's puny appearance lurks a cruel mind and vicious, powerful magic. Grant Morrison and Rags Morales, *Superman and the Men of Steel* (New York: DC Comics, 2012), 5.

A clue to why the narrative transition takes place can also be found in the early stages of Morrison's run, specifically in issue #3. In this issue, Glenmorgan uses his media influence to rally public support against Superman; he claims, about Superman's forcing him to confess to his crimes, "I was *threatened*, tortured to a point where I would have confessed to pretty much *anything*."[33] After retracting his confession and accusing Superman of using excessive force in extracting it, Glenmorgan moves to raise doubts about the superhero's humanity, claiming, "I have expert evidence that this monster is an *alien creature* from *another world*."[34] Glenmorgan's bias is predictably supported by his own news channel, GBS, which describes the media boss as "the most recent victim of an increasingly violent and unpredictable individual."[35]

Glenmorgan's rhetoric is surprisingly effective in persuading people Superman previously helped to turn against him. A number of squatters saved by Superman from the derelict tenement that was nearly destroyed by the military in their attack on the Man of Steel in issue #1 now condemn him, blaming him for the damage to their homes, overlooking the role played by the authorities in their haste to criticize an unknown other, "whatever he is."[36] It transpires that Glenmorgan bought their favorable opinions by providing "*real* hope for the *future*" through "*fresh* accommodations."[37] Later, when Superman rescues a small girl from an oncoming truck, he is chased away by a mob holding placards that scream "ALIEN GO HOME" and "UNWANTED FLYING OBJECT," suggesting that the crowd has been won over by the same "us-versus-them" perspective that prompts Luthor to refer to Superman as "it," not "he."[38] Crestfallen, Superman retreats to his apartment in an apparent admission of defeat: "Ma. Pa. I'm so sorry. I tried."[39]

Here, the limitations of a philosophy like Marxism—which encourages division by privileging the interest of one group of people above another—as a vehicle for progressive change is revealed. Superman, who fights for the benefit of the poor against the rich, unintentionally helps to foster a blame culture that encourages people to hold those different to themselves responsible for social ills. This backfires on him spectacularly, because, as a powerful alien from a foreign galaxy, he is more of an outsider than most and a very easy target for those looking for a scapegoat. It is not surprising that those targeted by Luthor and Glenmorgan in their attack on Superman side with the corporate villains against the superhero, because, as humans in common, they are a class apart from the imposing illegal alien immigrant. Certainly, it is much easier for Glenmorgan and Luthor, who trade in cynicism and vindictiveness, to exploit social divisions than the outsider Superman.

It is clear from *Action Comics* #3 that Superman's methods are not working, and he has failed to transform society through his class-focused social

Working-class protestors depicted taking a strong stand against the "wrong" person, supporting the wealthy robber baron over the populist alien who has fought for their rights. Grant Morrison and Rags Morales, *Superman and the Men of Steel* (New York: DC Comics, 2012).

activism. Rather, despite his heroic intentions, he has helped to foster a divisive, sectarian culture of which he is now a victim.

We can better understand why Superman's social activism fails if we now move beyond Marxism to consider Morrison's admission—cited earlier—that, despite their apparent incongruity, aspects of his run on *Action Comics* have been developed out of unused concepts from *All-Star Superman*.[40] This implies that *Action Comics* does not represent as clean a break from the themes *of All-Star Superman* as first appears, and the connections between the two series, as well as the reasons for the apparent failure of the New 52 Superman's socialism, can be explored if we return to Morrison's understanding that individuals are inextricably linked through the unified field of the imagination.[41] Although it is articulated in *All-Star Superman*, this concept is unpacked more explicitly in *Supergods*.[42] Reminiscing about a life-changing, perception-altering hallucinatory experience or alien abduction in Kathmandu, Morrison recalls his vision of the connectedness of all life: "[T]ime was a kind of incubator, and all life on Earth was one thing, a single weird anemone-like mega-Hydra with its single-celled immortal root in the Precambrian tides and its billions of sensory branches, from ferns to people, with every single detail having its own part to play in the life cycle of a slowly complexifying, increasingly self-aware super-organism."[43]

Morrison terms his new ability to see beyond the conventional sensory limits and temporal linearity that characterize everyday experience in ordinary three-dimensional space, as well as his capacity to see the connections between all living things, "fifth-dimensional," or "5-D," perspective, which is a kind of super-power in itself.[44] In fact, the concept of 5-D perspective encapsulates the way that Superman perceives the world in *All-Star Superman* or, as Lex Luthor recognizes after having stolen the superhero's powers, "I can actually *see* the machinery and wire connecting and separating everything since it all began. . . . This is how he sees all the time, every day. Like it's all just us, in here, together. And we're all we've got."[45] Here, Luthor sees that, as a single "organism," all life ultimately shares the same consciousness, which, as Morrison believes, forms Einstein's "long sought unified field," which connects everyone and everything.[46]

In *All-Star Superman*, it is Superman's ability to view the world from a 5-D perspective, more than his physical powers, that makes him special, as he recognizes the intricate connectedness of all forms of life. In *All-Star Superman*'s interlinked world, negative actions that hurt others and selfish feelings are damaging not just to individuals but to society, the world, and even the universe as a whole. Here, Superman is an idealistic figure who exists as a manifestation of positive consciousness, created to reconcile differences and defuse negative emotions for the betterment of the universe. To this end, he is able to recognize and understand the unique traits of everyone in society, even his would-be enemies, and to find ways of accommodating their personal aims and values into the common good that do not infringe upon their individuality and right to self-determination. This Superman does not force people to change but encourages them to positively rethink and reconceptualize their place in society. For instance, Kryptonian supremacists Bar-El and Lilo initially appear as authoritarian antagonists, seeking to force the people of Earth to abide by Kryptonian culture, whether they like it or not. Superman remonstrates with them, arguing that he—and by implication the other Kryptonians—has no "right to impose [his] values on anyone."[47] Eventually, Superman even finds a constructive role for Bar-El and Lilo to play in a universe without Krypton, although it is made possible only when the two authoritarians realize that they are suffering from a terminal overdose of Kryptonite poisoning and require his help.[48] They realize the validity of Superman's role on Earth, and he saves their lives by placing them in the Phantom Zone, giving them the freedom to exercise their authoritarian instincts without harming humanity by policing the dangerous, disembodied Kryptonian convicts who reside there.[49]

If Bar-El and Lilo's attempts to build a "*new* Krypton" in the "squalor" of Earth speak of a dictatorial approach to interspecies relations, Superman's restraint and quiet persuasiveness are more akin to the anthropological methods characterizing Morrison's own attempts to intervene as a writer in the cultures of superhero universes.[50] For Morrison, the DC Universe is a real, concrete place that physically exists in comic book form and which functions according to its own rules and parameters. Given that a universe that has enabled the growth of superheroes is inevitably distinct from our own reality, Morrison believes that those writers who, like Alan Moore, enforce upon their characters "the same familiar human doubts and failings we all shared"—traits common in everyday "reality"—are engaging in a form of cultural imperialism.[51] They are imposing our understanding of the world onto a fictional population who would behave quite differently if it were not for the malign influence of comic book creators seeking to reshape a universe in their own alien image. Morrison's anthropological approach is quite different:

> I chose to see some writers as missionaries who attempted to impose their own values and preconceptions on cultures they considered inferior—in this case that of superheroes. Missionaries liked to humiliate the natives by pointing out their gauche customs and colourfully frank traditional dress. They bullied defenseless fantasy characters into leather trench coats and nervous breakdowns and left formerly carefree fictional communities in a state of crushing self-doubt and dereliction.
>
> Anthropologists, on the other hand, surrendered themselves to foreign cultures. They weren't afraid to go native or look foolish. They came and they departed with respect and in the interests of mutual understanding. Naturally, I wanted to be an anthropologist.[52]

Morrison has applied this logic to relations between different cultures within his invented fictional universe of *All-Star Superman*, and in this world it is Superman who is the anthropologist. He understands distinct cultures and tries to facilitate cooperation between them, an approach that requires giving primacy to the ties and connections that bind them together rather than to the differences that some would use to construct barriers. In *All-Star Superman*, Superman is the perfect hero who can solve any problem, which heavily indicates that his anthropological approach is the "correct" one.

As I mentioned earlier, this approach is quite different from the New 52 Superman's initial embrace of binary divisions in *Action Comics*. However, the differences between Morrison's two versions of Superman increasingly blur following the New 52 superhero's failure in issue #3 to change society through his socialist politics. In fact, in the following issue, the plot shifts focus and centers upon Brainiac's invasion of Metropolis, which in turn appears to prompt a change in Superman's methods. When Brainiac attacks Metropolis and the military is unable to stop him, Superman is the only person capable of rescuing the city's inhabitants, and, if he is going to save them, he must challenge his own physical and perceptual limitations. In order to enter the invader's spaceship, Superman must run far faster than his previously recorded best of "*600 M.P.H*" to a massive "*25,000 miles per hour*," which he accomplishes with a burst of "extra-effort."[53]

Superman continues to push past his limits as he enters Brainiac's ship. In a panel that recalls the imagery of Morrison's fifth-dimensional hallucinatory experience in Kathmandu, Superman encounters Brainiac's collection of bottled cities, thinly separated from one another by walls of glass but in fact existing side-by-side in a single location.[54] Just as Morrison felt himself hovering outside of the third dimension following his abduction by alien "silver blobs," able to see the connections between different peoples and time periods and to perceive all life on Earth as a single organism, Superman experiences something akin to a revelatory 5-D experience, viewing a number of different cultures with their own distinct customs and history all at once, and he can see that they are connected by the same peril.[55] If the ordinary people of Metropolis are insects to the wealthy elites like Luthor and Glenmorgan, even these high-powered individuals are minnows in comparison to a colossal threat like Brainiac. Everybody, however big or small their social stature, is vulnerable to something and in need of protection from the forces that threaten them.

So, when Brainiac tries to force Superman to make a choice between rescuing Kandor, the capital city of his home-world, and Metropolis, the Man of Steel—seeing the interconnected fate of all the captured societies—refuses the premise of the question "*are* you loyal to *Krypton* or *Earth*?" and instead declares that all life—including the societies with which he has no previous association—is under his protection.[56]

This decision represents a significant shift in allegiance on Superman's part. Whereas he had once tried—and failed—to win the support of one section of Metropolis society by defending it against another, he now fights for the common interests of all the inhabitants of his adopted city and those of other civilizations, in a move that sees the hero transcend his previous class consciousness. He dons chameleonic Kryptonian battle armor, which—in a symbolic nod to Superman's new multiple allegiances—is capable of responding to the traits of its environment, changing color according to the dress and customs of the society to which he is physically closest. His new costume therefore allows him to become a visual embodiment of the multiple cultures he seeks to protect and their will to resist oppressive forces.

Here, the story hints that, though all people have the potential to cause great harm to themselves and others by focusing on differences and divisions, when they unite and pool their strength, passion and compassion, to common ends, collectively, the human race becomes a much stronger, more powerful entity. If it is Brainiac who collects, categorizes and compartmentalizes different cultures in confining glass bottles, it is Superman who smashes these barriers and unites the people as the singular manifestation of their collective positive will

From the outside looking in: this new perspective for Superman allows him to see that all creatures are small, vulnerable, and in need of protection. Grant Morrison and Rags Morales, *Superman and the Men of Steel* (New York: DC Comics, 2012), 109.

to resist tyranny and willingness to transcend the artificial limitations of the confined existences that Brainiac has imposed upon them.

As we can see, Superman's battle with Brainiac instigates a significant change in the nature of his heroism. He realizes that he cannot protect humanity by siding with one faction against another. Indeed, following his former approach, he has helped to sow division and incur the enmity of some of those he wishes to protect. Even if that were not the outcome, Morrison suggests that rivalries between binary oppositions lead to stagnation and repetition as two opposing forces continuously fight it out, resulting in the same conclusion time and time again. This is confirmed when Vyndktvx, a manifestation of the negative potential of the collective imagination when it is turned towards bitterness and vengeance, and the ultimate villain of Morrison's story, reveals that Superman's fight against Glenmorgan only "cleared the way for the rise and rise of *Lex Luthor*," another corporate villain and "a new monster, far worse than the old one."[57]

Furthermore, it was while "Superman was preoccupied in a cat and mouse game" with his multimillionaire opponent that Vyndktvx crept into the Man of Steel's universe and, like a malign editor, revised it into a darker place, where his earthly parents Jonathan and Martha Kent are no longer alive to give him comfort and moral guidance.[58] In this respect, Superman's preoccupation with binary divisions is both a dead end and a distraction, and, in response to Brainiac's attack, he decides instead to encourage humanity by example, discarding his prejudices in order to represent everyone, rich and poor, good and bad.

In being able to see beyond divisions and differences, Superman is able to become a manifestation of positive, progressive consciousness who demonstrates the heroic aspects of humanity, in particular our ability to constantly expand our understanding of the world and capacity to empathize with different peoples and cultures, whilst challenging the prejudices that hold us back. In embracing this role he is better able to wage a symbolic battle against the negative forces of materialist cynicism and reductive, obsessive tyranny. Specifically, these forces manifest in Luthor, who justifies his jealousy and resentment toward Superman in the language of scientific empiricism, Brainiac, whose single-minded obsession with collecting societies in glass containers forces them into an unnatural stasis and curtails their potential to develop, and finally Vyndktvx, a hypostasis of humanity's collective potential for bitterness and hatred.[59]

Superman's decision to protect the whole of society rather than a particular class allows him to be more successful, as people from all walks of life may now be inclined to see him as heroic. Following his defeat of Brainiac, Superman has a broader reach and may be hindered by fewer enemies. Even General Lane, who, alongside Lex Luthor, facilitates attacks on Superman in *Action Comics* issues #1 and 2, is forced by necessity to accept the Man of Steel's assistance during Brainiac's invasion. Superman's new status as an unproblematically heroic figure who stands up for society as a whole is cemented at the end of issue #8, when the mayor of Metropolis hands him the key to the city, a symbol of official recognition and an indication that he is no longer feared by large sections of the populace.

It is now possible to understand why Morrison seemingly intentionally discards his early focus on Superman's class-conscious crusade for social justice. It is, in fact, likely that he never intended his work for *Action Comics* to be a traditionally left-wing fable about a socialist Superman fighting corrupt capitalist media magnates and industrial bosses. Rather, he is using Superman's early socialism and its limitations to prove a point about the need for mutual understanding and empathy between different cultures and perspectives, while suggesting that aggressive partisan divisions do little to make the world a better place.[60]

By the end of Superman's battle with Brainiac and Morrison's first *Action Comics* story arc, Superman has developed into a symbol of idealist positivity and collective consciousness, a role akin to that of *All-Star Superman*'s idealistic protagonist. In this sense, despite initial appearances, *All-Star Superman* and *Action Comics* represent something of a coherent statement. If *All-Star Superman* is a depiction of Superman at the height of his power and symbolic resonance, *Action Comics* illustrates how the Man of Steel managed to rise to this status by seeing beyond and outgrowing his own initial prejudices and preconceptions, while dramatizing the shift in perspective that was required to transform him into a universal hero who has the willingness and the power to protect all life, even if that means defending humanity from its own negative, self-limiting and self-destructive impulses.

This does not mean that Morrison dislikes socialism or that his *Action Comics* storyline is antisocialist. Indeed, his comments in an interview with the left-leaning *New Statesman* magazine affirm that his modern conception of Superman is an attempt "to go back to first principles and ask: how would a champion of the oppressed act today?"[61] The answer, he suggests, is that "the Superman I would write would be a much more international figure" and thus, it seems, a representative of numerous different peoples, cultures and perspectives.[62] For Morrison, a modern socialism would be a more embracing concept than its class-centered Marxist progenitor. Therefore, the Superman of *Action Comics* does not, as far as Morrison is concerned, abandon his socialism along with his class-focused attitude. Rather, he transforms himself and his socialism, reconfiguring his ideals into a universal moral framework that applies the values of solidarity and collectivism more broadly than ever and is not limited to serving the interests of a particular class culture, national interest, or even a single dimension.

Morrison's vision of a perfect hero capable of bringing into being a perfect society is not itself flawless, and as a left-wing political narrative, it is even disappointing. In shifting his storyline's focus from an emphasis on social problems to grand, symbolic existential superhero conflicts, Morrison appears to be glossing over the difficult solutions, contingencies, and compromises that would be required to solve such issues as the protection of workers' rights in the face of advancing technology and the difficulties faced by those taking on overbearing media monopolies, which have the power, the influence, and the platform to frame the popular narrative. Morrison does not provide detailed analyses of or solutions to the problems posed during the early issues of *Action Comics*, and his storyline seems to insinuate that Superman's embrace of his role as multiuniversal savior—something like his equivalent in *All-Star Superman*—who can "overcome" any "problem" is enough of a solution in itself, which can feel like an evasion.[63] Indeed, it is possible that Morrison's reformed "socialism" actually bears a greater resemblance to modern social liberalism than the working-class focused approach of conventional Marxist socialist theory and politics.[64]

However, it is important to note that Morrison is probably not seeking to use Superman to provide a detailed roadmap for a better society in the "real world." As we have seen, while Morrison is keen to emphasize the reality of comic book universes, he insists that they are real only on paper, and their reality is therefore defined by the established, expected conventions of comic book superhero fictions, which are quite different from the rules that presently govern our own world.[65] As we have seen, he believes that there is something distasteful, even disrespectful, in trying to force superheroes into behaving like real people. Rather, Morrison's Superman is an ideal: inherently unrealistic in the sense that he does not reflect human beings as we currently are. He is able to be better than we are because the conventions of his fictional world can facilitate the existence of a character who is inherently good and who displays an unlimited capacity for empathy.

In this respect, while the Superman of *Action Comics* may not provide detailed, pragmatic, and well-thought-out solutions to specific, complex social problems as they currently exist for nonfictional people, his development does show us how we might help to create the conditions for a better world by simply imagining one through broadening our perceptions and our capacity for empathy, while recognizing our inherent connectedness to others. If we could establish a world in which we were profoundly aware of and sensitive to the impact of our thoughts and actions upon those different to us, detailed solutions might follow. Morrison's Superman therefore retains aspects of the collectivist ethos of socialism as he develops it into something more, to show us the vision of an imaginary better world, even if he is not, in the end, a traditional socialist. In this, he represents a profound reaffirmation of the values of mutual respect and common decency.

Morrison's Superman is an impossible fictional ideal from a fantasy comic book universe. Still, when viewing him from the confines of our own presently bitterly divided world that is often characterized by aggressively intolerant politics, we can be forgiven for suspending our disbelief in the hope that we, who inhabit real life, will one day all come to share and embody his positive, progressive values.

Notes

1. Grant Morrison and Rags Morales, *Superman and the Men of Steel* (New York: DC Comics, 2012), 117.

2. Phillip Bevin, The United States of Superman: An Analysis of Superman and Relevance (unpublished thesis, Kingston University, 2015).

3. For instance, the 2010–2011 storyline *Superman: Black Ring* features Lex Luthor and focuses on his personal philosophy and his endeavor to gain enough power to defeat the Man of Steel. Paul Cornell and Pete Woods, *Superman: Black Ring* (New York: DC Comics, 2011).

4. Michael J. Straczynski and Eddy Barrows, *Superman: Grounded*, vol. 1 (New York: DC Comics, 2011); Michael J. Straczynski, Chris Robertson, and Eddy Barrows, *Superman: Grounded*, vol. 2 (New York: DC Comics, 2011); Cody Walker, "Humanity, Heroism, and Action: Grant Morrison's *Action Comics* #12," *Sequart*, September 6, 2013, http://sequart.org/magazine/23862 /humanity-heroism-and-action-grant-morrison-action-comics-12/.

5. Marc Singer, *Grant Morrison: Combining the Worlds of Contemporary Comics* (Jackson: University Press of Mississippi, 2012), 251.

6. Grant Morrison and Frank Quitely, *All-Star Superman* (New York: DC Comics, 2011 [2006–2008]); "The Must List: March 3, 2006," *Entertainment Weekly*, February 24, 2006, http: //www.ew.com/article/2006/02/24/must-list-march-3-2006.

7. Singer, *Grant Morrison*, 266.

8. Grant Morrison, *Supergods: Our World in the Age of the Superhero* (London: Jonathan Cape, 2011), 410.

9. The series received glowing reviews from a number of journalistic publications, including *IGN*, *Comic Book Resources*, and *Entertainment Weekly*. Dan Phillips, "Morrison and Quitely's Wonderful Story Comes to an End," review of *All-Star Superman* #12, DC Comics, *IGN*, September 17, 2008, http://uk.ign.com/articles/2008/09/18/all-star-superman-12-review; review of *All-Star Superman*, DC Comics, *Comic Book Resources*, September 17, 2008, http: //www.comicbookresources.com/?page=user_review&id=365; "The Must List: March 3, 2006," *Entertainment Weekly*.

10. Morrison, *Supergods*, 6–7.

11. I argue in my thesis that there is little explicit textual evidence to support the idea that Superman was a politically left-wing advocate of the New Deal in his early comic book appearances. In fact, if the character can be deemed a working-class hero, it is less a result of his explicit politics than of the fact that the content and tone of his early stories were influenced by pulp narratives typically targeted at a working-class audience and published in a medium that was read by a similar demographic. Nevertheless, the understanding that Superman was originally a left-wing socialist is widely held, and it is a view that Morrison clearly accepts. Bevin, *United States of Superman*, 57–105.

12. Morrison and Morales, *Superman and the Men of Steel*, 10, 72, 65–67.

13. Jerry Siegel and Joe Shuster, "The Blakely Mine Disaster," in *The Superman Chronicles*, ed. Anton Kawasaki, vol. 1 (New York: DC Comics, 2006 [1938]), 31–44: 36; Jerry Siegel and Joe Shuster, "Superman Declares War on Reckless Drivers," in *The Superman Chronicles*, ed. Anton Kawasaki, vol. 1 (New York: DC Comics, 2006 [1939]), 153–66: 161. Interestingly, Glenmorgan's Scottish-sounding name and his status as an owner of a powerful media organization render him loosely analogous to real-life right-wing news magnate Rupert Murdoch, adding further left-wing political connotations to Morrison's story.

14. Karl Marx, "The Historical Tendency of Capitalist Accumulation," in *The Portable Karl Marx*, ed. and trans. Eugene Kamenka (New York: Penguin Books, 1983 [1845]), 490–93: 492.

15. Ibid.

16. Ibid.

17. Morrison and Morales, *Superman and the Men of Steel*, 70.

18. Ibid., 5.

19. As Gerard Jones has noted, in *Action Comics* #3's "The Blakely Mine Disaster," it is not Superman but brave "crusading newspaper reporter" Clark Kent who forces a corrupt mine owner to change his ways. By contrast, *Action Comics* #9 features Superman playing Clark as a "contemptible weakling" who cannot stand up for himself. Gerard Jones, *Men of Tomorrow: The True Story of the Birth of the Superheroes* (London: Arrow Books, 2004), 142; Siegel and Shuster, "The Blakely Mine Disaster"; Jerry Siegel and Joe Shuster, "Wanted: Superman," *The Superman Chronicles*, ed. Anton Kawasaki, vol. 1 (New York: DC Comics, 2006 [1939]), 111–24: 113.

20. Morrison and Morales, *Superman and the Men of Steel*, 66, 68.

21. Karl Marx emphasizes the centrality of the working class in changing society. For him, because of their total lack of "control" over their essential socioeconomic role, which is defined by their wholesale exploitation at the hands of the bourgeoisie and their lack of access to "the conditions which would place" them "in the other class," it is the working classes who are particularly placed to wholly reform society: "if they [the proletariat] are to assert themselves as individuals, [they] will have to abolish the very condition of their existence hitherto." As we have seen already, Superman's endeavors to reform society in the early issues of *Action Comics* lend themselves quite readily to a Marxist interpretation, because his efforts are — in the case of Mr. Tide's former employees — centered upon aiding the working poor and — in the case of the tenement squatters — the socially excluded, all of whom are isolated from the benefits of the existing social structure, which serves individuals like Glenmorgan. Karl Marx, "Communism as the End of History," in *The Portable Karl Marx*, ed. and trans. Eugene Kamenka (New York: Penguin Books, 1983 [1845]), 189–95: 194–95.

22. Laura Sneddon, "Grant Morrison: Why I'm Stepping Away from Superheroes," *New Statesman*, September 15, 2012, http://www.newstatesman.com/blogs/voices/2012/09/grant-morrison-gay-batman-superheroes-wonder-woman; Cody Walker, "Humanity, Heroism, and Action: Grant Morrison's *Action Comics* #9," *Sequart*, July 26, 2013, http://sequart.org/magazine/19651/humanity-heroism-and-action-grant-morrison-action-comics-9/.

23. Brian Hyatt, "Grant Morrison on the Death of Comics," *Rolling Stone*, August 22, 2011, http://www.rollingstone.com/music/news/grant-morrison-on-the-death-of-comics-20110822.

24. Cody Walker's analysis is nuanced and touches upon a number of other themes addressed by Morrison's *Action Comics*, but his series of articles currently remains unfinished, and it is therefore unclear whether he continues to see socialism as such a prominent aspect of Morrison's New 52 Superman.

25. Morrison and Morales, *Superman and the Men of Steel*, 117.

26. Morrison is well known for changing his mind, particularly in relation to his creator-owned series *The Invisibles*, which altered its stylistic direction a number of times. Singer, *Grant Morrison*, 98.

27. Vaneta Rogers, "Morrison Closes Out *Action Comics* Run, Teases *Multiversity*," *Newsarama*, February 6, 2013, http://www.newsarama.com/10882-morrison-closes-out-action-comics-run-teases-multiversity.html.

28. Morrison and Morales, *Superman and the Men of Steel*, 5.

29. Ibid., 5, 127.

30. Ibid.

31. Ibid., 21; Grant Morrison and Rags Morales, *Superman: At the End of Days* (New York, NY: DC Comics, 2013), 106.

32. Morrison and Morales, *Superman: At the End of Days*, 106.

33. Morrison and Morales, *Superman and the Men of Steel*, 69.

34. Ibid.

35. Ibid.

36. Ibid., 70.

37. Ibid.

38. Ibid., 70, 13.

39. Ibid., 71.

40. What Morrison is doing is criticizing what he sees as the limitations of class-based politics in favor of his own more "liberal" "socialism"; whether or not this is an original, theoretically valid, or particularly unique strand of thought is beside the point. The attribution of socialism to Morrison's Superman is by Morrison himself, and his is a popular understanding of socialism, not a systematic academic one. I think this point is fairly self-evident (Morrison is a writer of comic books, after all). Marxism and socialism are not synonymous, and one can be a class-based activist without being a socialist, but Marxian forms of socialism do tend to put an emphasis on class politics.

41. Morrison, *Supergods*, 275; Singer, *Grant Morrison*, 266.

42. Morrison, *Supergods*, 409.

43. Ibid., 273.

44. Ibid., 274.

45. Morrison and Quitely, *All-Star Superman*, 287.

46. Morrison, *Supergods*, 275.

47. Morrison and Quitely, *All-Star Superman*, 207.

48. Ibid., 219.

49. Ibid.

50. Ibid., 207.

51. Morrison, *Supergods*, 217.

52. Ibid., 218.

53. Morrison and Morales, *Superman and the Men of Steel*, 101; Richard Reynolds, *Superheroes: A Modern Mythology* (Jackson: University Press of Mississippi, 1992), 41.

54. Morrison and Morales, *Superman and the Men of Steel*, 109.

55. Morrison, *Supergods*, 272.

56. Morrison and Morales, *Superman and the Men of Steel*, 116.

57. Morrison and Morales, *Superman: At the End of Days*, 108.

58. Ibid., 106.

59. Morrison and Morales, *Superman and the Men of Steel*, 30.

60. Somewhat surprisingly for a writer from a working-class background, Morrison is ambivalent about traditional left-wing politics, criticizing in *Supergods* "eighties [British] leftist politics, with its regular recourse to incoherent angry victimhood." Interestingly, Superman's initial anger toward wealthy individuals can be read as an embrace of "angry victimhood." Morrison, *Supergods*, 217–18.

61. Helen Lewis, "Superman Is a Socialist," *New Statesman*, July 7, 2011, http://www .newstatesman.com/blogs/helen-lewis-hasteley/2011/07/superheroes-superman-graphic.

62. Ibid.

63. Morrison, *Supergods*, 410.

64. It is worth remembering that, while Karl Marx "refined and systematized the socialist way of thought," Marxism is not the be-all and end-all of socialism. For instance, in British left-wing politics there have been many attempts to find a "third way" between Marxist orthodoxy and market capitalism, a compromise still described as "socialism" by many who advocated it. Introduction to *The Portable Karl Marx*, ed. and trans. Eugene Kamenka (New York: Penguin Books, 1983 [1845]), xi.

65. Lewis, "Superman Is a Socialist."

PART II

MARVEL COMICS, NETFLIX, AND THE WORKING-CLASS SUPERHERO

FROM THE STREETS TO THE SWAMP

Luke Cage, Man-Thing, and the 1970s Class Issues of Marvel Comics

Blair Davis

Class issues are frequently visible in Marvel comic books. Peter Parker struggles to pay his bills and support his ailing Aunt May in *Amazing Spider-Man*. Ben Grimm's upbringing in the Lower East Side of New York is regularly referenced in the pages of *Fantastic Four*. Tony Stark is a wealthy industrialist whose business ventures funded the technology behind his heroic alter ego in *Iron Man*. Matt Murdock transcended his lower-class upbringing in Hell's Kitchen, New York, to become a lawyer in *Daredevil*. In the early 1970s, Marvel Comics introduced several new characters that expanded the scope of the publisher's representations of social class. Two of these new characters are seemingly antithetical on the surface—Luke Cage and Man-Thing. One is a former gang member and prisoner who acquired super-strength and an impenetrable body, while the other was once a promising scientist transformed into a distorted swamp creature; one patrols the urban streets of New York City, while the other haunts the Florida Everglades. Yet a comparison of the two characters reveals a similar commitment to exploring issues of class conflict—even while the discourses surrounding how class is represented in their books' narratives are often radically different.

Luke Cage positions himself as a "Hero for Hire," often helping working-class citizens of New York City from his squalid Times Square office. Unlike other superheroes, however, Cage charges for his services in order to support himself financially (which often proves difficult). Man-Thing also emerges as a defender of some of society's more vulnerable members, albeit as a largely inadvertent hero. The character is an empath who can sense the emotions of others but possesses no rational consciousness himself. He has no need for nourishment or material goods and hence is altogether a classless being. Luke Cage's and Man-Thing's comic books demonstrate varying degrees of subtle and overt commentary on class issues in 1970s America, albeit using a narrative split between urban and rural settings. Issues of class, power and socioeconomic status connect across their disparate adventures, yet these two less-well-known books from this period take strikingly different positions about the role of the working class within American society.

Luke Cage, Hero for Hire

Working-class politics were prominent in the 1970s. Kieran Walsh Taylor notes how the rise in unemployment, inflation, and wage stagnation led "nearly 2.5 million workers [to go] on strike in 1970," with "unauthorized wildcat strikes in the early 1970s surg[ing] to levels unseen since the 1930s."[1] Comic book publishers sought to make their titles more socially relevant overall as the 1970s began, with their heroes battling real-world problems to do with race, class, gender, and youth in addition to the usual array of rampaging monsters, cosmic threats, and escaped supervillains. In 1971, for instance, drug abuse was confronted in the pages of both Marvel's *Amazing Spider-Man* and DC's *Green Lantern/Green Arrow*, as Peter Parker's friend Harry Osborn overdoses on pills, and Green Arrow's sidekick Speedy is revealed to be a heroin addict. Publishers were increasingly concerned with offering their readers social relevance along with escapist fantasy. DC writer Mike Friedrich describes being "very concerned about social issues and want[ing] to bring them into the stories [he] wrote. It was a culturally and politically turbulent time"; he notes how *Superman* editor Julius Schwartz "actually seemed to encourage the social commentary" so long as stories still had plenty of action.[2]

In 1970 DC offered a survey within the pages of its monthly titles, soliciting feedback on who was reading its comics, overall patterns of media consumption, and the types of storylines respondents might be interested in reading about. The survey wasn't subtle, however, in how it asked readers about questions of race and ethnicity: "How interested are you in reading about: a) pollution, b) black people, c) space flights, d) National Problems, e) City Problems, f) sports, g) hobbies, h) romance, i) astrology."[3]

Marvel was similarly interested in exploring new storylines about national and city problems, and while ultimately being less interested in astrology and romance, they devoted a new series to "black people" in *Luke Cage, Power Man* starting in 1972. In his critical study *Super Black: American Pop Culture and Black Superheroes*, Adilfu Nama notes that because the series debuted "during the increasing popularity of the Blaxploitation film craze of the 1970s, convention dictates that Cage is primarily understood as the comic book analogue to the over-the-top black masculinity paraded across the big screen in nearly any assortment of black films that came out from 1971–1976."[4] Despite the character's many detractors, Nama sees Cage as "in many ways the most inherently political and socially profound black superhero to emerge, regardless of his connection to the Blaxploitation film fad," with the character used to explore "issues of unjust black incarceration, black political disenfranchisement, and institutional racism in America."[5]

Additionally, Cage's working-class politics are at the forefront of his series. Historian Jefferson Cowie describes how 1970s American culture reflected a larger ideal of "a conscious, diverse and unified working class acting as a powerful agent in political social and economic life,"[6] and reading *Luke Cage, Hero for Hire* through this lens allows us to see how working-class politics are reflected throughout the series. After being given a reward for stopping a man from robbing a diner in the first issue of *Luke Cage, Hero for Hire*, Cage declares that he has "an idea how to turn what I got goin' for me into a livin'!" in reference to his newfound super-powers.[7] After distributing business cards around town for his "Hero for Hire" services, he struggles with the practicalities of starting up a new enterprise. We find him calling his answering service in a Times Square phone booth at the start of the second issue, where he learns that a potential client has cancelled on him. "Crud! Answerin' service alone ain't makin' it. Gotta get me an office," he says.[8] His steady financial struggles and the emphasis on the process behind starting a new business quickly set *Luke Cage, Hero for Hire* apart from most other titles of this era. If superhero comics offer readers the potential for vicariously triumphing over life's challenges, *Luke Cage* depicts a protagonist who toils in desperation. While Marvel was known for having their characters face real-world problems in the 1960s, a character like Luke Cage takes this notion to a new level, given his socioeconomic background as an African American male and a former gang member/ex-convict from Harlem.

Cage is decidedly a working-class hero, and given that he is "for hire," his work as a superhero therefore constitutes paid labor. The fact that he earns his living by charging a fee for his services (even if, for altruistic reasons, he doesn't always collect) sets him apart from nearly every other superhero. "The super-hero fella. I've heard about how you've helped neighborhood merchants against syndicate protection men . . . for a *fee*. Bit disillusioning from a so-called

Luke Cage makes a cup of coffee on the stove of the office (where he also lives, out of economic necessity). *Luke Cage, Power Man*, no. 34, August 1976. Written by Don McGregor, Art by Frank Robbins.

hero, isn't it?" someone asks Cage. "Folks hire security guards, doc . . . private detectives . . . why *not* someone like me?" he replies.[9]

If the idea of being a superhero who charges for his efforts seems irregular, this is due to the long-standing convention of superhero narratives that being a hero is meant to be an act of altruism rather than financially motivated—echoed in Peter Parker's belief that there is a great deal of responsibility that comes with having super-powers. Supervillains use their powers to acquire wealth illegally, while superheroes use their powers for the public good whether it results in financial reward or not. Most heroes work independently rather than for the government or another institution that would provide a salary. While some are provided room and board on larger teams like the Fantastic Four or the Avengers (the latter putting up its members in a mansion and offering them the services of a butler named Jarvis), the majority of heroes must pay their own way through their day jobs.

Unlike most other superheroes, however, Cage doesn't have a secret identity (although as an escaped convict he changed his name from Carl Lucas to Luke Cage to avoid detection). Instead, he adopts a public persona in which his role as a hero for hire serves as his sole source of income. Whereas others keep their professions separate from their heroic deeds as a way of preserving an alter ego, Cage specifically ties his labor potential to his super-powers. Tony Stark uses the profits from his company, Stark Enterprises, to fund the suits of armor that secretly let him be Iron Man, while Cage does not divide such roles. While Peter Parker must hide the fact that his wall-crawling ability allows him to take salable photos of his efforts as Spider-Man, Cage has the potential to increase his customer base the more he displays his powers.

The series uses inner-city New York as its primary setting, a creative choice allowing for very different class dynamics to be explored in its stories than those taking place near the Fantastic Four's Manhattan headquarters, Peter Parker's suburban home or the X-Men's upstate campus. Cage rents a run-down office above a grindhouse movie theater on West Forty-Second Street between Broadway and 8th Ave., an area the book's narration describes as possessing "a perpetual aura of gaudy filth and danger." He explains how it is the only space he can afford—"'Least I'll know any client who comes this far must want me bad," he rationalizes.[10]

While he earns a meager living as a hired hero, he still struggles to afford anything approaching luxury. Of his humble living quarters, Cage says, "I've got to go next door to turn over in my sleep!"[11] When he needs to travel from New York to Los Angeles, he takes the bus rather than a plane, because it's all he can afford. We see him regularly riding the subway, given that he doesn't own a vehicle. The series also shows the practical expenses of being a superhero, with

Luke Cage returns home to a pile of unpaid bills. *Luke Cage, Power Man*, no. 27, October 1975. Written by Bill Mantlo. Art by George Perez.

Cage pointing out that while his skin may be impenetrable, his clothing is not: "Yeah, superhero gig surely is rough on shirts. Only dude makin' coin on it are the garment workers ..."[12]

When a group of criminals ambush Cage in his office, he is more concerned about the fact that they broke his phone than the attempt on his life: "Crud! An' double crud! Those creeps ripped my phone out! That costs me money! Deposit on a phone's so steep in Manhattan. I hadda settle for a pay box to begin with. Now I'll really have I.T.T. on my back!"[13] The same is true when a different villain throws Cage through his own office door: "Why you—! It cost me fifteen bucks to get my name painted on that door! Fifteen bucks! An' you went and ruined it in fifteen seconds!"[14]

While Cage usually struggles to pay his bills, he also demonstrates a clear responsibility for supporting himself financially. When the infamous supervillain Dr. Doom hires Cage and then refuses to pay him, he borrows a jet from the Fantastic Four and tracks down Doom in the (fictional) European country of Latveria. "You came all the way here for that? A paltry $200!!! . . . this is all for some stupid debt?" bellows the villain. "Not stupid to me, Doom. Put in an honest day's work—expect my bread for it!" replies Cage, who takes moral offense to not getting paid for doing a job. This ethos is further reflected in the working-class rhetoric used in the book: "'Nother day, 'nother dollar!" says Cage after trouncing a group of villains.[15] "No one said being a paid hero was easy work. If it were there would be a helluva lot more people pounding the pavement alongside Luke," the book's narration surmises.[16]

The narration also links masculinity with employment: "But once he turned his prison-walled world topsy-turvy, and he found a new life—- a new chance to be a man—in so doing. . . . Yet he is a man for hire—and he does his job!"[17] In *Working-Class New York: Life and Labor since World War II*, Joshua Benjamin Freeman describes how there is also a "widely held view that the problem of poverty [lies] in the morality and habits of the poor, rather in a lack of appropriate jobs."[18] Luke Cage regularly ties his own morality to his ability to remain steadily employed, particularly as he attempts to distance himself from his former criminal persona.

The series often defends working-class values, while at the same time offering a critique of upper-class life. When Cage is captured by a well-off villain named Piranha Jones and taken to an East Side penthouse apartment, the story's narration tells of how the "East Side is quieter than its uptown neighbor, Harlem. The 2 A.M. sounds are more muted. The desperation is more subtle. The laughter is more artificial. The rent is phenomenally higher—though residents can claim that they live in the same area Paul Simon once did, if that's the kind of thing that turns them on." Later, the narrator describes a woman and her dog as "definitely East Side inhabitants—they both have that sleek, well-bred look."[19]

This mockery of one of New York's upper-class districts is paralleled by the comments of Jones's henchman, Roach, as he beats Cage with the handle of a sawed-off shotgun. When Cage keeps fighting back after receiving two powerful blows from the gun's handle, Roach exclaims "How about that? Street-tough black's still game. Now, I calls that class. Real class."[20] Here, Roach uses Cage's connection with the lower-class streets of Harlem (and its "desperation") to

Luke Cage confronts Doctor Doom over an unpaid $200. *Luke Cage, Hero for Hire*, no. 9, May 1973. Written by Steve Englehart. Art by George Tuska.

mock his efforts to resist his attacker, reminding Cage of the class distinctions between where he is from and where Jones lives.

While this contrast between the "real" quality of inner-city life and the "artificial" nature of New York's East Side shows a recurring discourse in favor of working-class values, this dynamic was challenged later on in the series. With its fiftieth issue, the title's name was changed to *Power Man and Iron Fist*, as Cage teamed up with martial artist Danny Rand, a.k.a Iron Fist. The cover proclaims the duo as "The Most Unlikely Team Of All," while the book's opening credits describe them as "Two men from different worlds . . ." Whereas Cage was "a child of the streets, and Iron Fist was raised in "the mystic city of K'un L'un,"[21] this difference also stems from how Rand inherited his industrialist father's fortune and now serves as the CEO of a large corporation.

With the help of a lawyer, Cage expands his business and opens up a new office in a Park Avenue tower. The narration tells us that Cage "begins to feel an inner satisfaction as his natural shrewdness is augmented by the beginnings of business acumen. Somewhere between the pressing of the flesh and the plethora of paperwork, he is mildly astonished to realize that it is not, as he might have once supposed, the least bit beyond him."[22] As the series progresses, Cage undergoes a change in his class status, moving from his inner-city origins to his lavish new accommodations. At the same time, however, he keeps his old Times Square office open for his "old clients" who might be intimidated by the new location (and unable to afford his new fees).[23] Through becoming a small business owner, Cage eventually transcends his initial working-class status to attain a higher socioeconomic position in society; he still maintains an active connection with his old neighborhood and customer base, perhaps as a reminder to never lose sight of his roots and the ways in which his working-class background formed his personal identity, morals, and values.

"Whatever Knows Fear Burns at the Touch of the Man-Thing!"

On the surface, Luke Cage and Man-Thing seem to be antithetical characters. One is a former prisoner, the other a former scientist. Cage patrols inner-city New York, Man-Thing haunts the swamplands of rural Florida. Cage has exceptional street smarts, while Man-Thing has no rational mind (existing as an empath who can sense emotions but does not possess actual consciousness). While Cage actively helps those in need, Man-Thing is largely an inadvertent hero who offers (sometimes accidental) aid to the victimized in the process of responding to that which directly threatens his existence. The types of stories told in *Luke Cage, Hero for Hire/Luke Cage, Power Man*, and *Man-Thing* (with the character first appearing in the titles *Savage Tales* and *Adventure into Fear*) are naturally very different, given that their premises are so dissimilar, yet the two characters are regularly used to explore issues of class conflict and the abuses that various institutions inflict upon the lower class.

Man-Thing was once a biochemist named Dr. Ted Sallis, whose work (on a project to recreate the Super-Solider serum that gave Captain America his powers) led him to the Florida Everglades. When he learns that his wife has betrayed him to a terrorist organization that turns up to steal the serum, Sallis flees and injects the serum into his arm rather than allow it to fall into the wrongs hands. When his car crashes into a nearby swamp, the "highly unstable" serum interacts with the water, "twisting" his body and mind and changing Sallis "into a grotesque Man-Thing!"[24] Unable to remember his former life, Sallis instinctually roams the Everglades while occasionally intervening in various disputes he encounters.

The rural Florida setting does not offer the same sorts of conflicts and characters as *Luke Cage, Hero for Hire*, and in turn we would expect working-class concerns to function differently as well. Freeman describes working-class life in New York City as being defined by "large rental apartment buildings" as opposed to property ownership. "Dense population, small stuffy apartments and shared hallways and stoops meant that life was exposed and often communal," he says.[25] The stories told in *Man-Thing*, on the other hand, often take place in and around small Florida towns without high-rises. Many live in small shacks on the edge of the swamp, and privacy is easy to find for those seeking to escape.

While Man-Thing sometimes comes to the aid of lower-class residents (such as a young woman in an abusive relationship), the biggest moments of class conflict center around the efforts of a land developer named F. A. Schist to build a new airport on swampland (which is home to an indigenous tribe as well as to the Man-Thing). Schist's name (a play on the word "fascist") obviously signals series writer Steve Gerber's feelings toward big business and unchecked industrial development. A group of local townspeople hold a rally to protest the development, only to be interrupted by a group of Schist's construction workers. "You folks've been soundin' off about the birds n' snakes n' their ecology. What about *my* ecology? I don't work . . . my kids don't eat . . . ! That's the simplest ecology there is, right? Heck, we ain't villains—just hard workin' guys tryin' to earn a dollar!" says one of the workers. The confrontation soon turns violent, when one protestor questions the workers' innocence in the role they are playing in turning the town into "a noisy, smog-infested hell-hole."

Man-Thing approaches the site of a new airport set to be built on swampland by the F. A. Schist Construction Company. *Man-Thing*, vol. 1, no. 3, March 1974. Written by Steve Gerber. Art by Val Mayerik.

The worker throws a punch—"I'm sick of you longhairs tellin' me I ain't moral!" he shouts, again invoking the notion that paid labor is inherently honorable.[26]

The book's narration contextualizes the divide between the protestors and construction workers: "A town, angry because its serene existence is about to fall victim to jetliners and endless horizons of parking lots—a work crew, its members angry because they cannot survive without betraying this town: put them together and one blow is all it takes!" The rhetoric here emphasizes victimization and betrayal in how it represents the crew's employment. Character dialogue during the brawl further emphasizes the immorality of their labor: "You'd sell your own mother—to earn a dollar!'" shouts one protestor. The dialogue even becomes overtly hostile toward the crew's very profession: "You crummy hard-hat! I'll bet your brain is hard too!" yells another protestor.[27]

While *Luke Cage* regularly espouses the value of gainful employment, the discourses surrounding the working class are more complicated in *Adventure into Fear/Man-Thing*. When Cage is hired by Dr. Doom, the hero rationalizes the job by telling the supervillain, "Well, I don't dig it . . . but you got a right to hire me like anybody else."[28] In assisting Doom, Cage is committing a morally questionable act (given that he was hired to eliminate the enemies of a man who is himself a villain), yet the work is deemed righteous because it is paid labor. This same dynamic becomes criticized when applied to the men who work for F. A. Schist, with the construction workers positioned as immoral because they choose to remain employed when given a job with ethically debatable consequences.

When Schist is rebuked by scientists whom he attempts to hire to destroy Man-Thing, he declares, "Don't be fools! You saw the thing! It's deadly! It's hurting people—eating up my profits!" His apparent concern for public safety soon gives way to the economic reality of Schist's hatred for Man-Thing. He then expresses bewilderment for the scientists' disinterest in his offer: "Why—why did they leave? Why did they act insulted? I offered to make them rich!"[29]

While the series shows a blatant disdain for aggressive capitalist ventures, there is also recurrent support for counter-culture figures as a way give a voice to those whose politics are not working class but entirely anti-establishment. Man-Thing is a classless entity, described in the series' narration as "a *thing* that has lost its very humanity."[30] Given that he has no need for food, shelter, clothing, or other basic human necessities, Man-Thing has no need for money. Nor does he have any understanding of the economy, politics, or social order, given his limited consciousness as a purely empathic being. As such, he isn't lower-, middle-, or upper-class, existing outside of such definitions entirely. In turn, the series often explores the counter-cultural values of younger characters (often college students) who, inspired by recent social and political

Protestors clash with F. A. Schist's construction workers. *Adventure into Fear*, no. 16, September 1973. No. 16, Written by Steve Gerber, art by Val Mayerik.

movements, seek to challenge traditional beliefs about employment, gender, and patriotism, as well as the military.

When a bus crashes in the Everglades, a group of survivors with disparate backgrounds must find their way to safety. The group includes a student, a nurse, a salesman, and a former soldier who has returned from Vietnam. The student surmises that their group constitutes "the whole establishment in microcosm" and proceeds to criticize the others while stating that he refuses to help them "on philosophical grounds!"[31] Calling the nurse "cold," he tells her "Life is a commodity to you. You're so busy saving it, you never really experience it!"[32] In reference to the solder, the student surmises "he just came home from a war of attrition. That's where the whole fight is to see which side can kill more people! It's sick! And here at home we dump chemicals in our waters—poison the fish—then we eat 'em and poison ourselves! That's suicide—but it's also our way of life!"[33]

When the salesman (whose car slammed into the bus) complains of having lost his vehicle in the accident, the student accuses him of being more worried about money than the lives that were lost. This prompts the salesman to shoot the student while screaming, "Shut up! Don't you point the finger at me—you filthy commie scum! You deserve to die—for runnin' down this country!" Here, the working-class salesman equates the student's critiques of the country's socioeconomic patterns with communism, calling it his "patriotic duty" to kill him for his perceived contribution to the degradation of the moral fabric of American society. Indeed, working-class politics were often seen by many as being rooted in Communist and/or socialist politics, given the ways in which socialist groups in the United States sought "to build a base in the working class" since the end of World War I. Taylor describes how numerous "young labor radicals of the 1970s" were "mentored by older Communists, Trotskyists, socialists and liberals who had engaged in working-class organizing."[34]

Man-Thing ultimately rescues the nurse while killing the gun-toting salesman, who had wanted to kill anyone who could prove he caused the accident: "I worked too hard to get where I am—to get a piece of the good life!"[35] With his death, the salesman's dream of a better life comes to an end. As it turns out, he is one of many working-class men positioned as villains in the series, willing to kill to maintain his identity as a provider while simultaneously denigrating those who do not share his values.

Man-Thing also comes to the rescue of a young man named Richard Rory, who we are told has recently lost his job. Camped out in his van by the swamp, Richard is saved from an attacking alligator by Man-Thing.[36] When Richard later stops at a motel for the night, the owner mocks him with the nickname "Joe College." Richard grumbles afterward, "I hate people who make 'education' sound like a dirty word. I'll bet he's a reform school reject."[37] The owner's disdain for students is meant to make him seem ignorant, further emphasized by Richard's dig about his personal background.

The series' critique of working-class characters continues when Richard encounters a group of townspeople in Citrusville, Florida, who join a grassroots campaign called the "Mothers' March For Decency." Described as "a crusade against subversion, godlessness and permissiveness," they make their way to the local high school, where they plan to hold a book burning. "We've been reading our children's textbooks . . . and we know what you're really teaching here: communism . . . atheism . . . sex! . . . We don't want our children's minds filled with filth!" The book burning is rationalized as the prerogative of every taxpayer: "Our taxes bought them—we have the right to destroy them!" shouts the group's leader.[38] "Do you see . . . what people can do if they care enough? We don't need judges and courts to make our decisions for us! We can run our own lives!" she cries. Yet while these sentiments may seem to approach an anti-establishment tone, the leader goes on to ground her logic in traditionally working-class principles: "Don't be afraid. You believe in God, don't you? You believe in America—in morality. You believe exactly as I do."[39] The affirmation of God and country and their associated morality connects the campaign to the masses, rather than to the elites or the nonconformists.

The campaign was actually spurred on by the efforts of a longshoreman named Josefsen, who refuses to accept his mandatory retirement. When he shows up for work the day after his sixty-fifth birthday, his boss tells him that union rules prevent him from remaining employed. "Hang the union!" says Josefsen, as he grabs his boss and hoists him in the air. "I'm a man—an' a man's gotta work, or he dries up an' dies! You tryin' to murder me, little boss? You afraid of a man who can lift more'n paper?" he says, referencing the blue-collar/white-collar divide between labor and management.[40] Josefsen snaps when the police arrive to remove him for trespassing, leading to a mental breakdown that sees him adopt the persona of a Viking warrior set upon restoring the town's moral order. What might have started out as a critique of a union's mandatory retirement policies quickly turns into a parody of the societal relationship between employment and masculinity. Josefsen no longer has a job that defines his identity as a man, in turn becoming a mad Viking warrior who declares that he will "show men how to be *men* again!" His first act is to attack a long-haired guitar player: "Filth-monger! Weakling! Your kind wrecked my world! Your kind must die! Sissy dies! Man lives! And this axe here will carve a world for *real men* to live in again!"[41] While the ways in which employment can fulfil a man's need for self-identity are explored with relative earnestness in *Luke Cage, Hero for Hire*, in *Man-Thing* this dynamic seems subject to ridicule through the extremes to which Josefsen goes to prove that retirement has not dampened his masculine vigor.

The crusade to preserve the morals of the country's youth is eventually criticized by a young student who speaks out against her Viking-grandfather: "You raised me to be like you . . . you brought me up to think for myself—to be independent and strong-willed, isn't that so? The world is changing, Grandpa—but kids still can't grow up unless they have their own minds. And now you want to take that away from them!" she urges. "I—don't care!" shouts Josefsen as he strikes his granddaughter. "The world changes—makes room for hippies—sissies—cowards—but not for me! I let you think for yourself and you turn against me—you love the weaklings and the pantywaists! So what if it's wrong? I don't like it!!" he rages. His blow knocks the granddaughter to the pavement, killing her as her head hits the concrete.[42]

The Mad Viking leads a group towards a book burning in small-town Florida. *Man-Thing*, vol. 1, no. 18, June 1975. Written by Steve Gerber. Art by Jim Mooney.

The sheer irrationality of the retired-longshoreman-turned-Viking-warrior and his intolerance toward a younger generation of men whom he blames for "wrecking his world" (and presumably for fostering a culture that supports unions and mandatory retirement policies) casts the character as a tyrannical caricature of a disgruntled ex-employee who seeks revenge upon society. Much like in naming a land developer F. A. Schist, there is little subtlety in the message here; just as capitalism is portrayed in a negative way, so too are traditional working-class values regarding gender, patriotism, and religion set in opposition to societal change and freedom of thought.

When he first arrived in Citrusville, Richard Rory found work at the local radio station. "Congratulate me, ladies. I am employed," he says with a smile. He tells of how he "decided to stay in Citrusville because it's so small-townsy . . . everybody knows everybody . . . and all that." After the book burning, the narration tells of how Rory "will leave behind him the city he chose to make his home because it once seemed 'so small townsy, everybody knows everybody, and all that.'"[43] Ultimately, the series rejects the working-class values of small-town America, casting life in such a setting as too narrow-minded for those interested in challenging social norms. While the overall message of tolerance is admirable, it comes at the expense of negative portrayals of small-town working-class identity. This position is somewhat ironic, given the ways in which the big-city setting of *Luke Cage* is used to affirm the working-class values that *Man-Thing* is ultimately critical of.

Conclusion

As Marvel entered its second decade of superhero comics, the publisher began to offer more nontraditional approaches to the genre as the 1970s began. A black inner-city crime-fighter who charged for his services and a swamp-monster that patrolled the Everglades were each attempts to challenge existing representations of comic book heroism. In turn, the politics represented in each of these characters' books with regard to class issues were often more overtly critical than most other superhero titles of the previous decade. Both *Luke Cage, Hero for Hire* and *Man-Thing* offered readers social commentary alongside displays of exciting action and heroism, even though the positions taken in each book were largely opposite ones.

The 1970s saw a shift in public consciousness concerning class politics. Cowie tells of how "a broad blue-collar revival" could be seen in the United States in this decade, "as working-class America returned to national consciousness through strikes, popular culture, voting booths and corporate strategy." He cites

Newsweek's description of a "far-ranging, fast-spreading revolt of the little man against the Establishment," *Fortune*'s portrayal of "the workers of the early seventies as 'restless, changeable, mobile, demanding,' and headed for a time of epic battle between management and labor given the angry, aggressive and acquisitive mood in the shops," and *Time*'s summation that "blue-collar workers are gaining a renewed sense of identity, of collective power and class that used to be called solidarity."[44] Such concerns became reflected in the narratives of many Marvel comic books. Writer Steve Gerber worked through such "anger" by exploring current social tensions through their titles, using characters like F. A. Schist to provide a thinly veiled attack on the dangers of allowing capitalism to go unchecked. Similarly, writers like Archie Goodwin, Steve Englehart, and Don McGregor explored the economic struggles of an African American ex-con who attempts to find redemption in a new career path.

While *Man-Thing* clearly identifies with society's countercultural forces, the struggles depicted in *Luke Cage* are ultimately grounded in concerns for working-class identity. Cage likens his job to that of a private investigator and is paid to fight crime at a local level, but he encounters the same growing pains that any small business owner faces while starting out. He shows an ongoing concern for affording the basic necessities of life, dodging bill collectors, and taking offense to a proposed rent increase. He also does regular battle with a temperamental soda machine that keeps taking his coins without dispensing his drink properly, prompting Cage's outrage as he wastes the last few cents he has in his pocket. Cage clearly struggles financially, but he has a strong work ethic and is grateful for the opportunity to earn a living from his newfound superpowers. He often appears uncomfortable when he finds himself in upper-class surroundings, skeptical of the "well-bred" nature of their inhabitants.

At the same time, Cage is unwilling to accept being looked down upon because of his lower-class roots, never more so than when he confronts Dr. Doom: "Ever since I started messin' with you, Doom, you been brushin' me off—bein' lord o' the manor—Well—maybe I talk like Harlem, 'cause that's where I was raised, but that don't make me stupid! Hero for hire's a tough gig, baby—and it'd get much tougher if I'd let anybody walk on me! *Anybody!*"[45] The series displays an ongoing discourse that upholds the values of working-class life, the importance of hard work as well as the need to never let an employer walk all over you.

While Cage advocates against discrimination based on socioeconomic background, Man-Thing himself exists as a classless member of society, given that he has no need for the economic basis by which class distinctions emerge. The idea of eliminating class distinctions may even be construed as communist by some, much as the salesman who killed the student for challenging capitalist ideals he believed. In *Man-Thing*, writer Gerber offered an ongoing critique of American society, using the backdrop of rural Florida to explore political issues and class concerns. While he was often less than subtle in how he constructed his criticisms, the series stands as a valuable addition to Marvel's roster of superhero titles in the 1970s, given how it regularly embedded social and political issues within its tales of a tragic swamp monster. *Man-Thing*, like *Luke Cage*, was a forum for its creators to tell genre-based stories with larger cultural significances. Together the two series stand as a vital part of the way in which Marvel Comics sought to make comic books a platform in the 1970s for encouraging social change through the combination of escapist adventure and real-world issues.

Notes

1. Kieran Walsh Taylor, "Turn to the Working-Class: The New Left, Black Liberation, and the U.S. Labor Movement (1967–1981)," unpublished dissertation, Chapel Hill, 2007, p. 8.

2. Jim Kingmen, "Men of Steel: Superman and Julius Schwartz in World's Finest Comics and DC Comics Presents," *Back Issue*, no. 66, August 2013, p. 52.

3. Conor Kilpatrick, "Great Moments in Comics History: 1970 DC Comics Reader Survey, *iFanboy*, February 10, 2011, http://ifanboy.com/articles/great-moments-in-comics-history -1970-dc-comics-reader-survey /.

4. Adilfu Nama, *Super Black: American Pop Culture and Black Superheroes* (Austin: University of Texas Press, 2012), 53.

5. Ibid., 53–55.

6. Jefferson Cowie, *Stayin' Alive: The 1970s and the Last Days of the Working-Class* (New York: New Press, 2013), n.p.

7. *Luke Cage, Hero for Hire*, no. 1, June 1972, 21.

8. *Luke Cage, Hero for Hire*, no. 2, August 1972, 1.

9. Ibid., 4.

10. *Luke Cage, Hero for Hire*, no. 6, February 1973, 1; *Luke Cage*, no. 2, 12.

11. *Luke Cage, Hero for Hire*, no. 23, February 1975, 8.

12. *Luke Cage, Hero for Hire*, no. 5, January 1973, 19.

13. *Luke Cage, Hero for Hire*, no. 10, June 1973, 18–19.

14. *Luke Cage, Hero for Hire*, no. 27, October 1975, 10.

15. *Luke Cage, Hero for Hire*, no. 10, 18; *Luke Cage*, no. 9, May 1973, 11.

16. *Luke Cage, Power Man*, no. 37, November 1976, 5.

17. *Luke Cage, Hero for Hire*, no. 3, October 1972, 9.

18. Joshua Benjamin Freeman, *Working-Class New York: Life and Labor since World War II* (New York: New Press, 2000), 333.

19. *Luke Cage, Power Man*, no. 31, May 1976, 9, 20.

20. Ibid., 6.

21. *Power Man and Iron Fist*, no. 50, March 1978, 1.

22. *Power Man and Iron Fist*, no. 54, July 1978, 6.

23. *Power Man and Iron Fist*, no. 56, September 1978, 6.

24. *Savage Tales*, no. 1, May 1971, 7.

25. Freeman, *Working-Class New York*, 30.

26. *Adventure into Fear*, no. 16, September 1973, 9–10.

27. Ibid., 10.

28. *Luke Cage, Hero for Hire*, no. 8, April 1973, 14.

29. *Man-Thing*, vol. 1, no. 2, February 1974, 7.

30. *Man-Thing*, vol. 1, no. 7, July 1974, 4.

31. *Adventure into Fear*, no. 18, November 1973, 7–9.

32. Ibid., 11.

33. Ibid., 15.

34. Taylor, pp. 9–10.

35. *Adventure into Fear*, no. 18, p. 17.

36. *Man-Thing*, vol. 1, no. 2, February 1974, 14.

37. *Man-Thing*, vol. 1, no. 5, May 1974, 7.

38. *Man-Thing*, vol. 1, no. 18, June 1975, 3.

39. Ibid., 12.

40. *Man-Thing*, vol. 1, no. 16, April 1975, 10–11.

41. Ibid., 13.

42. *Man-Thing*, vol. 1, no. 18, June 1975, 13–14.

43. *Man-Thing*, vol. 1, no. 7, July 1974, 9–10; *Man-Thing*, vol. 1, no. 18, 18.

44. Cowie, n.p.

45. *Luke Cage, Hero for Hire*, no. 9, May 1973, 12.

"IT'S JUST US HERE"
Daredevil and the Trauma of Big Power

Kevin Michael Scott

The caption of the first narrative image in *Daredevil* #1 tells the reader, "You are looking at the entrance to Fogwell's gym in New York's Lower West Side! It is here that our story begins. . . ."[1] The scene described by the caption and the title character's reason for being there create an objective correlative for the fifty years of Daredevil stories that would follow.[2] Fogwell's is no longer a successful gym (if it ever was). Despite depicting architecture, the image is drawn without clean, straight lines (typical in other scenes), giving the street a ramshackle feel. The entrance is sandwiched between two other storefronts, and its sign includes the directions "ONE FLIGHT UP." Old boxing promotional posters surround the door, torn and weather-beaten and drooping. Trash is strewn across the sidewalk, apparently having fallen out of the overturned trashcans that would greet any visitor. A scrawny black cat carefully picks its way through the refuse. Under the next-door window, a political poster provides the simple instruction "Vote *NO*."

When Daredevil first appeared in 1964, there was no other comic that placed its hero so squarely in the realm of the poor and working classes. The Avengers were in their mansion. The X-Men studied in their tony school in Westchester County, New York. The Fantastic Four operated out of their own high-rise, the Baxter Building. Even Peter Parker (Spider-Man), the other working-class superhero, whose success made Daredevil possible, was the product of a clean and comfortable home in Queens, New York. Over at DC Comics, all the heroes had long been ensconced in the jokey, classless, borderline-camp fictional universe that characterized its defensive approach to superheroes.

Matt Murdock assumes the powers that make him Daredevil when, as a boy, he saves an old man from being run down by a truck, only to have some of its radioactive cargo splash him in the face. It is an act of local heroism and

The decrepit storefront of Fogwell's Gym provided a rare image of the environment of poor New Yorkers. Stan Lee (writer) and Bill Everett (illustrator), "The Origin of Daredevil," *Daredevil* vol. 1, no. 1 (1964), page 2.

initiates the theme of intense sacrifice at the community level. The accident blinds him but also heightens his other senses to superhuman levels. (Based on his enhanced senses, Murdock is able to "see" the world around him in 360 degrees, giving him a kind of radar sense.) Murdock grew up in and around Fogwell's, where his father trained as a boxer until, refusing to throw a fight, he was murdered by "The Fixer."[3] The nonlinear origin narrative of *Daredevil* #1 begins in the middle, with an adult Murdock, as Daredevil, revisiting Fogwell's to investigate the very cold case of his father's murder.

This first appearance of Daredevil establishes the strange and often painful binaries that Daredevil/Murdock will face over the next fifty years. Head of a single-parent, working-class home, Matt's father struggles to ensure that young Matt will not "grow up to be an uneducated pug" like himself but instead "amount to something." He studies hard to fulfill his father's dream that he become a professional (eventually a lawyer), but he aches to join his peers as they play amidst the trash in the alleys and streets. After his accident and his father's death, he finds that his powers separate him from the common man, both professionally and as a (super)human. Indeed, he believes that his enhanced senses have a large impact on his academic success.[4] Matt Murdock the lawyer purposes to stay in "Hell's Kitchen" in New York City, specifically to fight for innocents, usually men and women of the working class, but as Daredevil he swings through the city above their heads. He is simultaneously of them and above them. The fact that this condition regularly imperils both of his selves throughout the character's fifty-year span foreshadows the difficulties the character will face when he attempts to maintain his working-class identity while moving his efforts to a macro level in the twenty-first century.

Scholars and fans generally identify three eras of "Daredeviltry": the Stan Lee era, the Frank Miller era, and the modern era (with Brian Michael Bendis as the writer most often associated with it).[5] These three periods are characterized by quite different approaches to storytelling, but, throughout the series' entire run, issues of working-class identity are regular interests of both the narrative and the characters. What begins in the Stan Lee era, however, as overt attacks on the habit of (what I will call) BIG POWER to exploit the common man become, especially in recent years, more like meditations on the nature of power and oppression and the difficulty in finding a pathway to combat Big Power without becoming it. (Here I define Big Power as the corrupting bargain made between government, crime, and wealth to collude in order to maintain their authority and profit from the working classes.) The struggle to find an effective mode of opposition to Big Power in the storytelling mirrors the debates within the academic discourse on class of the last fifty years, between a Marxist, oppositional model and a Weberian, individualistic, and differentiated model.[6]

At the heart of *Daredevil* (and of rhetoric about the working class) is inequality, and the systems that tend to reinforce such class stratification. Such systems regularly bedevil the citizens of Hell's Kitchen, as does the absence of effective countervailing systems of justice. Daredevil, from the beginning, works to correct these flaws. The introduction of such stories to a newly reestablished fictional universe was no small development. Previous to the rising popularity of Marvel in the 1960s, DC Comics had largely reigned supreme and did so by promoting the American "myth of classlessness."[7] The heroes were *essentially* good, and the villains were generally large and garish and uncomplicated in their evil. Little attention was paid, beyond simplistic origin stories, to how social forces can bend individuals toward particular—and sometimes antisocial—behaviors. The elision of these narratives denies the legitimacy of experiences outside the assumed middle-class status of the vast majority of Americans.[8] The writers of Daredevil have contended against this self-aggrandizing impulse often by demonstrating that its impact is the criminalization of anyone operating outside the "classless" middle class.

Hell's Kitchen: A "Good Place to Be Killed"

In New York folklore, the actual origin of the infamous name Hell's Kitchen is not known. A variety of narratives have competed for the honor: a notorious tenement, a local eatery, a gang, a similarly named, and similarly dangerous, London neighborhood. The most common nominee likely achieves its status based more on drama than on any historical validity. It is a story that appeals to the working-class, tough-guy, life-on-the-streets portion of New York's personality, and the narrative was used by Brian Michael Bendis to situate the character of Murdock/Daredevil squarely in the neighborhood's perceived history and socioeconomic condition. The story takes place in the late 1800s during an era of riots (with which Hell's Kitchen has a long history), many arising out of a Catholic/Irish/immigrant ethnic identity and working-class anger. According to the story, Dutch Fred the Cop was breaking in a new rookie partner who was overwhelmed by the carnage and who complained, "This place is hell." Dutch Fred responds, "Hell's a mild climate. This is Hell's Kitchen."[9]

Whether or not the story is true in its details, it effectively represents the experience of history in Hell's Kitchen. The neighborhood attracted Irish immigrants throughout the 1800s, and this influx defined its character until new waves of immigrants complicated its ethnicity but confirmed its working-class personality. During the nineteenth century, the area was known for its class-based riots, most notably the 1863 draft riots, spurred by laws that allowed wealthy men to pay their way out of serving in the Union Army, and the Orange Riots (1870–1871), which began as a fight between middle-class Irish Protestants and working-class Irish Catholics and escalated into antigovernment protest and violence.[10] American workers, primarily white men in these cases, were experiencing and reacting against a transition described by Eric Hobsbawm, a Marxist historian of class and capitalism. In *The Age of Capitalism: 1848–1875*, he argued that mid-century forces—in the United States, like Europe, these would be immigration, industrialization, urbanization, and the end of slavery—changed the status of labor in dehumanizing ways.[11] Instead of the buyers and sellers of labor sharing some relationship (moral or social obligation, proximity, shared cultural experience, and so forth), workers grew more separated from employers and related to them only through contract and paid wages.

In Hell's Kitchen, employers enjoyed not only this power but developed alliances with governmental and criminal forces in order to further separate themselves from interaction with or responsibility to the working classes. Yet Hell's Kitchen provided for its working-class denizens a contradictory environment, one in which they were often abandoned by civil society and thus made vulnerable to predators, and simultaneously one in which this same abandonment was a kind of freedom to build a rich if dangerous subculture and express their political views as flamboyantly as they wished, as the riots demonstrated. According to political scientist Anthony Petros Spanakos, when Daredevil decides to make Hell's Kitchen his home, he enters what "often looks like a Hobbesian state of nature. The characters are rational, make calculations based on fear, threat, opportunity, and, for some, the pursuit of glory."[12] Even today, though the neighborhood has gentrified, much of its "charm" is understood to come from its wild, riotous, working-class roots.

Matt Murdock's origin is embedded in Hell's Kitchen's larger narrative. His father made his living fighting (and dying) under the thumb of others. Murdock is consistently depicted as a "citizen" of gritty streets. In Frank Miller's retelling of Stan Lee's origin story, the grime and struggle of life is emphasized, and alcoholism and child abuse are added to his biography.[13] The character of Matt Murdock could almost be seen as the embodiment of the neighborhood's history and character. He is a red-haired Irish Catholic (Murdock is a Gaelic name), raised in poverty and taught to fight by his circumstances. He struggles against all forms of Big Power: organized crime, government indifference (or worse), and the exploitations of capitalism. After success in college and an immediate hiring to a corporate law firm in a shining high-rise, he returns to Hell's Kitchen to work with his old friend, Foggy Nelson, and to join his class-action lawsuit against a slumlord. A caption informs us that "Matt remembers why he wanted to become an attorney. To fight for justice. To fight the bullies."[14]

The Stan Lee Era

Marvel's approach to comics in the 1960s immediately set it apart from the other giant in the field, DC. At the time, the narratives DC superheroes were known for tended to be what comics fans call "villain of the month" stories that focused on garish supervillains attempting either to rob banks or "take over the world." According to Stan Lee, Marvel's rise depended on a very different approach:

I would guess it's because we tried to make our characters as human and empathetic as possible. Instead of merely emphasizing their super feats, we attempted to make their personal life and personal problems as realistic and as interesting as possible. We wanted to make them seem like real people whom the reader would like to spend time with and want to know better.[15]

Even within the Marvel Universe, Daredevil's powers would be considered "small." He can taste, touch, smell, and hear incredibly well.[16] Compared to the immense strength of the Hulk or the ability to burst into flame like Johnny Storm, Daredevil's powers are more fitted to street-level conflict than to the often cosmic excursions of the Fantastic Four or the Avengers.

For the first several issues of the comic series, while the villains may be costumed or have names like "The Ox," the crimes committed are all street level, such as the auto theft ring he breaks up in issue #2. (It should also be noted that an auto theft ring, in Hell's Kitchen in the 1960s, would have been seen by many as the tool of organized crime and existing only because the government and the police ignored or, worse, profited from its existence.) Such stories, however, are fairly common for Marvel heroes and do not clearly identify Daredevil as specifically fighting for the "working class." Soon this would change. *Daredevil* #9 begins a series of stories that position the hero as specifically oriented against those who operate within Big Power to exploit various forms of proletariat citizenry (even as the stories take Daredevil a bit further away from the streets of Hell's Kitchen). In *Daredevil* #9, Matt Murdock is kidnapped by the dictator of an Eastern European nation, Lichtenbad, who lords his overtly aristocratic power over his country's working class people (knights in armor are his henchmen) and jails their greatest scientists to increase his wealth and authority. Daredevil leads an impromptu coup, telling the other prisoners, "You get started breaking the lease on this place while I try to find us all a new apartment!" Daredevil here uses the kind of language that might make little sense to the citizens of Lichtenbad, but to the readers of Marvel comics, it marks him as sharing the kinds of experiences many of them have endured (and the use of "us *all*" emphasizes the collective nature of his efforts—a theme that never completely leaves his comic). He goes on to make fun of the stilted, "cornball dialogue" used by the villains and describes the dictator's fetishistic reliance of aristocratic trappings as creating a "comic opera kingdom."[17] It is a brilliant moment of social(-ist?) wit and critique, identifying the holders of Big Power as performers of their station—*simulacra*—and not providing actual leadership or service to the people. The tension between the Marxist underpinnings of the story and the fact that it required the American fantasy of the "one good man" to begin the revolution does not negate the clear message here: the goal of power is to increase itself, and heroism is about fighting that, not alone, but alongside the oppressed.

The most important idea introduced during the Stan Lee era is that Big Power regularly deploys all of its various forces against the working class. Sometimes this collusion among crime, government, and wealth is purposeful and planned, and other times it simply emanates from the aligned values of the three powerful forces and the social conditions of the working class. The first clear example is also the character's first two-issue story arc. A candidate for mayor on the Reform Party ticket, Abner Jonas recruits Foggy Nelson to run for district attorney while Daredevil battles an animal-themed crime wave that is embarrassing the incumbent politicians. Jonas is an ascot-wearing stereotype of wealth, an American incarnation of the dictator of Lichtenbad, and Murdock distrusts him immediately when they meet at a fund-raising event on a yacht. As Daredevil discovers that the animal-costumed criminals are led by "The Organizer," Murdock and Nelson begin to suspect that the Reform ticket may also be a ruse designed to seize power. At the climax, of course, Daredevil publicly reveals that Jonas *is* The Organizer.[18] Here, the wealthy Jonas levers his wealth to use crime, and the public reaction it creates, to harness the power of government. To Daredevil and to the working class, each of these forces, individually, can be threatening. When the three combine, however, they grow harder to detect rather than easier. The true threat of Big Power is how easily it can become the status quo. The title of the story arc, "The Organization," implies both the method and the culmination of Big Power.

As Stan Lee grew busier with editing duties and Marvel grew more successful, other writers took on the difficult task of writing a working-class hero who is also a lawyer with super-powers. In general, these writers continued the traditions created by Lee (whose own work had grown increasingly more political),[19] but when Roy Thomas began writing duties with issue #51, the problems in combating Big Power grew ever more difficult and complex. For Thomas, Big Power is so ubiquitous and embeds itself so completely into society that it no longer needs active participation from individual members of wealth, crime, and government to maintain it. In three stories, Daredevil finds himself working to extricate working-class individuals from situations grown beyond their control. In #64, "Suddenly . . . the Stunt-Master!" a Hollywood stuntman who had a brief and failed career as a costumed villain attempts to live the straight life, only to be forced by poverty and criminals into assuming his criminal role again. Daredevil helps him escape their control and to lead the honest, working-class life he desires.[20] In #68, "Phoenix and the Fighter!" Daredevil revisits his own origin story and helps a young fighter, again compelled by his own poverty and organized crime, live up to his decision to live honestly.[21]

By 1965, the ascot worn by Abner Jonas—contemporaneously appearing on the television show *Gilligan's Island*, worn by Thurston Howell III—sends the clearest of signals to readers that the character is an enemy to the working class. *Daredevil*, no. 10. Wally Wood (writer and artist) and Bob Powell (artist).

In such stories, Daredevil extricates the victims of Big Power from the social traps into which they have fallen, but he does not attempt to change to system that placed them there. Indeed, resistance on a systemic level seems impossible to effect without adopting the strategies of Big Power itself. In #69, "A Life on the Line," Daredevil teams up with Black Panther to save a young black man who is depressed by his environment and the impact he believes it is having on his brother (a veteran who is actually undercover for the district attorney). The young man, Lonnie, responds by falling into a life of crime with a gang called the Thunderbolts. Here the implications of the other two stories are made explicit. Black Panther, in his secret identity, is a high school teacher who watches Lonnie lose his faith in social systems and what they consider knowledge. Lonnie fails to see the system as offering any hope and describes all of it as not "relevant" to improving his life; he tells his teacher, "Wake me up when we start learnin' about makin' bombs, baby!"[22] Daredevil and Black Panther are able to save Lonnie and his big brother and end the tyranny of the Thunderbolts, but not only do they not impact the social inequality that disenfranchised Lonnie, they act as de facto agents of Big Power itself—reestablishing a status quo that has already revealed itself to be ineffectual.

As Daredevil faces the 1970s, the idea that Big Power can be combatted by punching someone in the face is growing increasingly less realistic, even in a comic book. Corrupt politicians can be exposed, but the corruption that politicians allow to embed itself into the social order is more difficult to eradicate.

The Frank Miller Era

Writers struggled to write compelling stories that also addressed social issues of power and class during the 1970s, with the result that the series, with some exceptions, backtracked, transforming into a more traditional "villain-of-the-month" structure for most of the decade. Daredevil became more involved in the science-fiction-inspired stories that felt much more appropriate for titles like *The Fantastic Four* and *The Avengers*. As a result, circulation steadily declined, and the title was demoted to bimonthly.

"A Grave Mistake," *Daredevil* #158, opens with an uncommon narrative caption: "From time to time a truly great new artist will explode upon the Marvel scene like a bombshell!" The caption then lists all of the creative team and ends by saying that all of its members "confidently predict newcomer lanky Frank Miller will be such an artist!"[23] Miller's visual approach immediately changed the tone of the book with his explicit referencing of film noir style. Comics nearly always have, as default background, the color white or some other bright hue. In Miller's vision of Hell's Kitchen, the default background colors are often rich, dark hues or even black. The change allows his characters to emerge into the light or be half hidden in shadow in much the same way filmic characters could in film noir. One of Miller's favorite techniques, for instance, involves the use of multiple, narrow, vertical panels, each focusing on the same character and nearly the same pose and lighting. Issue #164 retells Daredevil's neighborhood origins, and after reporter Ben Urich reveals to Daredevil that he knows the hero's secret identity, Miller uses the technique to allow the reader to watch Urich, in four panels, silently light a cigarette, followed by a similar vertical panel of Daredevil's reaction, and then by another vertical panel of Urich using a lighter to set aflame his notes for the story he will never write.[24] It is a moment of immense visual power that visually links the men to each other and to the neighborhood they share. Urich protects Murdock/Daredevil because of what he means to the neighborhood and the people who have no other protector. The scene removes the distance between the two versions of the man.

The effect of Miller's style mimics the lingering close-up common in film noir. There are few explicit connections between a film noir style and working-class themes, though (how does one read a shadow?), and the category of "film noir" has itself been contested. Yet one common trope of the film noir story is that of individuals caught up in forces much larger than themselves. The more intimate camera work and lighting effects highlight the individual struggles, and since so many film noirs end poorly—or, at least, indeterminately—for the protagonist, the result is usually some variation of nihilism. In recent years, scholars have resisted the traditional approach to representing the working class or reading its representations as "powerless."[25] However, in film noir and in much of Miller's work, once he adds to his duties the role of writer, successfully making an impact on one's surroundings is rare, for either superhero or civilian. That said, the vertical panel sequence is also a tacit joining of forces between the hero and the reporter, the creation, possibly, of a Small Power that might hope to stand against its larger enemy.

Miller begins writing *Daredevil* with issue #168, in which he introduces Elektra, Matt Murdock's college girlfriend who disappeared, only to reenter his life a decade later as an assassin for hire.[26] Miller approaches class more obliquely than the earlier writers. He writes fewer parables of class, but the evidence of class difference—the signs of poverty, of working-class struggle—are, if anything, *more* present in his writing and art. There is more street-level action here, like the earliest *Daredevil* comics, except grimier and with more and more realistic violence. Daredevil strong-arms criminals for information. The onetime girlfriend who left Murdock to be a movie star returns as a junkie, a porn star, and a prostitute.[27] In "Daredevil . . . Goes Berserk—" (#173), Matt and Daredevil struggle to understand why rape victims often do not report the crime. While the victim, in the last panel, does finally make a report, the story largely acknowledges the film noir suggestion of powerlessness. The implication in the story is clear—without extrajudicial help from a superhero, the victim would not have found justice.[28]

Miller is also credited with making the aptly named character Kingpin important. Wilson Fisk had been a second-tier Spider-Man villain, but in Miller's hands the character becomes a brilliant, Machiavellian figure of corruption. Kingpin and the foregrounding of corruption, not merely of authority but of identity, are likely Miller's most influential creations. Widely regarded as one of Miller's greatest stories, the "Born Again" story arc (*Daredevil* #226–233) expands this theme in extreme ways. Kingpin represents Big Power in a way that is much more frightening than previous stories or characters had been able to achieve. Although the character is couched in film noir tropes that actually bend away from realism, Miller is able to construct him as so cunning and so corrupt that he perfectly counterbalances Daredevil. Kingpin, offended by the existence of both Murdock and Daredevil (he knows Daredevil's secret identity), wants not merely to kill him, but to ruin him, to corrupt his mind and re-form his identity into something that would no longer serve as a living critique of the Kingpin's own choices. Rather than wishing to merely defeat Daredevil in some individual conflict, he wants to tear the hero down *systemically*.

The plan nearly works (*nearly*, of course), and, frustrated, Kingpin seeks out an assassin to accomplish more bloodily what his schemes could not. Aside from his desire to ruin Murdock, he has spent the story arc consolidating his power in business, in crime, and in government. Given that he is visually represented as a massive man, of both muscle and fat, he becomes for Miller the perfect symbol of Big Power. Kingpin bribes a general to send to Hell's Kitchen—from Nicaragua—a psychotic, amphetamine-popping soldier named Nuke, who has an American flag tattooed on his face.[29] Dozens die. After Daredevil subdues Nuke, Captain America and the Avengers show up to collect him.[30] After Miller's success with Daredevil and, later, Batman, his work took an iconoclastically libertarian turn (evident in works like *Sin City* and *300*), and the roots of that are evident in "Born Again." Built into the story is the *assumption* of the corruption of power—its inevitability, the impossibility of anything else. When Kingpin manipulates Nuke into attacking Americans (specifically, the working-class citizens of Hell's Kitchen), he convinces the soldier that the act will be patriotic. "We who . . . *decide* such things have formed a proud trinity—of state—and military—and business. We must have unity—against the madness that surrounds us—against the infection of the American spirit." It is a harrowing scene made more frightening by its brazen admission

Miller and Mazzucchelli's composition of this scene obscures the identities of the characters pictured and visually suggests the mechanisms of control used by Big Power. *Daredevil*, no. 232. Frank Miller and David Mazzucchelli (creators).

of Big Power values. The Kingpin continues, "I am NOT a villain, my son. I am a CORPORATION—in the conglomerate that is AMERICA."[31] In Miller's version of the world, this is bitter truth.

Near the end of the story, Captain America breaks into a government research lab to investigate Nuke's origins, only to find that *he* is Nuke's origin, that the US government corrupted the program that created Captain America—who is the embodiment of pure and selfless service in the Marvel Universe—in order to create more like him.[32] Nuke was the result. It is as near to sacrilege as is possible in a fictional universe.

After Miller's run, several writers contributed individual stories until Ann Nocenti took over for the longest run of any writer. Nocenti adopted some of Miller's style and kept the urban realism that he had foregrounded, as did nearly all Daredevil writers for the following twenty years. Nocenti, however, became the most overtly political writer to pen the title, addressing issues like feminism, drug and gambling addictions, homeless shelters, environmentalism, and class. Her first Daredevil story is about the US government stealing the American Dream from its own soldiers (#236). Murdock, for the first time, became a working-class man. As Kingpin's assault on his identity had successfully led to his disbarment, Murdock becomes a cook in a diner, and this change in perspective impacts his interpretation of events that occur in Hell's Kitchen (notably, the title of the issue is "Context!"). When Black Widow critiques his new job, he explains, "It's honest work—and satisfying to a man with my sense of smell!" He then accuses her of being a "born again Yuppie."[33] Daredevil's superhero work is similarly local, and he increasingly identifies against the superhero community, and its tendency to exist above the masses.

Nocenti's stories about class are largely like Thomas's—parables of Big Power crushing the little guy, largely in the form of a social order that disempowers the individual. Nocenti's representation of Big Power, though, is more like that of Lee: simple and evil. She presents a union representative who accidentally kills a stereotypical "fat cat" businessman and builds on the event to become an anti–Big Power serial killer/Robin Hood. Daredevil, accused of being in "cahoots" with the media to increase his own social authority, again is forced to act on behalf on Big Power, stopping the "Caviar Killer" without replacing his revolutionary efforts with any legal and effective resistance.[34] The America that Nocenti describes has accepted the kind of corruption that exploits the working class and no longer even recognizes it as corruption.

In "The American Nightmare" (#283), Captain America picks up a magazine and complains, "Not again! We broke international law invading Panama! Now we're breaking the law again with this fabricated 'drug' war [in Latin America]!"[35] Cap then joins Daredevil to try to protect a neighborhood man who has invented a car made from recycled garbage and which runs on "harmonics." The villain: the "auto—oil—military—industrial complex."[36] He goes on to cite Thomas Paine's call to "get rid of the elite ruling class" and argues that America has replaced the British aristocracy with "the royal aristocracy of the corporate elite," painful words to hear coming from the superheroic ideal of patriotism (and words that continue a *Daredevil* theme going all the way back to the dictator of Lichtenbad and Abner Jonas, "The Organizer").[37] After Big Power successfully sabotages the inventor's car, it seems as if he is going to jump off of a building, but he instead *flies away* using another invention, dropping an American flag into Cap's arms.[38] The parable here could not be more broad. The imagery is both heroic and sad. The creativity and work ethic of the working man lives on, but it has to go into hiding to survive. Big Power is not merely systemic in Nocenti's world; it is pointed and purposeful in its oppression of the working class. While Miller's politics are sometimes difficult to pin down, Nocenti's are firmly planted in populist liberalism.

The Modern Daredevil Era

By the late 1990s *Daredevil* was again struggling, largely due to editorial decisions (such as having Daredevil adopt a more technological costume and approach). To resuscitate the title, the editors brought in Kevin Smith, the film director, to write a story arc that seemed to follow the well-worn "attack-Matt-Murdock's-mind" storyline but allowed Daredevil a more clear victory, signaling a new approach to storytelling. This more positive approach does not last, but the occasional explicit focus on issues of class is submerged into stories based on character and place. In the two major storylines of this era, each of which takes at least two *years* to develop, Daredevil adopts the mechanisms of Big Power in an effort to undercut it and serve the people of Hell's Kitchen more effectively.[39]

In the first storyline, Daredevil tires of the constant battle with Kingpin and the mobster's trampling of the people of Hell's Kitchen using the combined authority of crime, government, and wealth. After badly beating him, Daredevil delivers the villain to a group of thugs and publicly declares himself the new Kingpin of Hell's Kitchen. "I am not protecting this city anymore. I am *running* it! And I say, the people of Hell's Kitchen are *my* people. This is *my* territory now—And I say, GET OUT OR CHANGE! Tonight!"[40] Daredevil's plan to make Hell's Kitchen safe works, at least for a while. Because the public believes that Murdock is Daredevil, his "secret" identity becomes immensely popular, and the Democratic Party considers asking him to run for mayor. It is a moment of grace, the moment that occurs in many stories when the reader believes that "things may just turn out okay." The concept of a beneficent Big Power, though troubling to Foggy Nelson (and to Spider-Man, Luke Cage, Reed Richards, and Doctor Strange, who stage an intervention with Murdock to question his thinking in declaring himself Kingpin), seems to be improving the lives of the residents of Hell's Kitchen.[41] Luke Cage argues that Daredevil has simply moved the crime one borough over, but Murdock is so traumatized by the damage he has seen on "his" streets that he accepts that outcome as not his responsibility. By declaring himself a new, peace-minded Kingpin serving his citizens, he is attempting to impact Hell's Kitchen on a macro level and break what he sees as the cycle of acting as a de facto arm of Big Power. The result of Daredevil's actions, though, is the creation of a vacuum in Hell's Kitchen, and Japanese organized crime—the Yakuza, a new Big Power that values individual lives even less than Kingpin does—steps in to fill that gap, resulting in firefights on the streets. Beneficent Big Power has failed.

Scholars have long identified in superhero comics a tendency to bend toward the status quo.[42] Crime must be solved and, often, avenged. Evildoers must be expunged from society. Equilibrium restored. (Doctor Strange even lectures Murdock on "the balance we bring to people."[43]) Narratives in which a hero seeks out and vanquishes a villain are straightforward, are easy to write and comprehend, and satisfy most readers. In fits and starts since the 1970s (the

Dennis O'Neil and Neal Adams series *Green Lantern/Green Arrow* comes to mind), comics have attempted to respond to systemic social issues, to disrupt the equilibrium, but seldom very successfully. In Bendis's *Daredevil*, however, the prognosis is not just difficult, but possibly fatal. In Daredevil's Hell's Kitchen, the removal of crime operates, contradictorily, to create "a big, untapped oasis in the middle of the biggest city in the world."[44] Crime, in this conception of the social order, is so built into the system that removing it leaves a sustained hole, as if human endeavor can influence only the scope of Big Power, not its existence or functions.

Clearly, Daredevil feels burned by his failure, and he recognizes that stopping muggers has real but limited benefit. When he, as Matt Murdock, stumbles upon a support group of people who have been affected by Daredevil-related incidents, he explains his goals:

> I'm trying hard to keep these kinds of things away from you . . . and they just keep coming in every direction. . . . Something needs to be built—I need to do more than fight people. I need to build something so strong they can't attack it. . . . We need to rebuild our lives. And no one is going to help us. Not the cops. Or the feds. Or the heroes. It's just *us* here.[45]

This is a painful moment, but also one of clarity (and one that, again, echoes all the way back to his rallying the prisoners of Lichtenbad—"us all"—to overthrow their own Big Power tyrant). It is also a moment of Weberian hope, of a collective response, with Murdock/Daredevil as one participant in the social action. He proposes new social behavior here, writ large. Big Power has proven itself corrupt, but it does have the advantage of being systemic, and Murdock recognizes that only a systemic approach—not the installation of himself as a kind of Western sheriff—has a chance of effecting real change. It is this realization that renders him vulnerable in what is easily his most epic story arc.

The *Shadowland* comic event—one of the few Marvel Universe–spanning events centered on a single character—begins near the end of Marvel's two-year-long story arc *Dark Reign*. In that storyline Norman Osborn has risen to the unlikely position of the nation's "top cop," the leader of H.A.M.M.E.R., and the supervisor of an Avengers team reconstituted with one-time villains.[46] Osborn takes the example of Wilson Fisk, the Kingpin, considerably further. Once the supervillain Green Goblin, Osborn resuscitated his public reputation through deployment of his wealth (he ran Oscorp Industries) and government service. He is the apotheosis of Big Power, and the fact that, unlike Kingpin, he operates from a position atop the American government makes him one of the most powerful men in the world. Indeed, he adds to the Big Power triumvirate of crime, government, and wealth the authority of corrupted superheroes. As the exemplar of Big Power, Osborn's only goal is to increase his own authority. He swears to deal harshly with anyone who defies the rule of law, because, he says, "I am the rule of law."[47] He is the system become man.

As part of the *Dark Reign* storyline, Osborn creates "The List," which includes Daredevil, and he sends the assassin Bullseye to kill him. Bullseye lures Daredevil to a tenement in Hell's Kitchen that has been condemned so that Oscorp can turn it into condominiums. The "1 percent vs. the 99 percent" storyline here is made even more dramatic by the citizens of Hell's Kitchen who have protested by refusing to leave the building. One resident holds a sign out of a window: "PEOPLE OVER PROFIT."[48] Facing police in riot gear (who are clearly serving the needs of Big Power here), the protesters attempt to accomplish what Daredevil has accomplished on so many occasions: setting right one specific wrong. Unfortunately, Bullseye has lured Daredevil there specifically so that the hero can watch him blow up the building with more than a hundred residents inside. "Just think of all the innocent lives you could have saved if you'd killed me when you had the chance," Bullseye taunts him.[49]

Before this event Daredevil had already been engaged in a plan to take control of a Japanese clan of assassins called the Hand in order to keep the leaderless group from being commanded by a supervillain such as Kingpin. After the tragedy, however, Daredevil begins to use the Hand more aggressively to protect Hell's Kitchen. Once in control, he immediately orders the assassins to use only nonlethal means to police his neighborhood. Peace reigns, and it seems as if Hell's Kitchen could again be an oasis of calm in a nation edging toward totalitarianism. The spiritual compromises Daredevil makes to command the Hand and protect his city, however, make him open to demon possession by the Beast, the primordial spirit that imbues the Hand with its supernatural power. As Daredevil grows more powerful, his leadership shifts toward the very style he rebelled against, and he rules Hell's Kitchen as a tyrant, turning against his friends and changing his attitude about killing.[50]

Again, the allegory of class and power is broad. Big Power is literally demonic, literally corrupting. The demon-empowered Daredevil does bring peace, but at the cost of free will—including his own. The climactic battle takes place in Daredevil's psyche, where he realizes that he has disconnected from the "It's-just-us-here" approach and is now blind "to every point of view but [his] own."[51] In that most common of comic book clichés, he becomes the thing he hates (a fascist, Big Power bully), and he symbolically kills himself, in his own mind, to stop the cycle.

Conclusion

In the evolution of the representation of the working class and of Big Power in *Daredevil*, as the narratives address the issues of class less directly, they actually promote a solution that is likely the only one with a chance at success. In the early stories, when class is addressed, the relationships between the upper and lower classes generally are oppositional and fit fairly neatly into a Marxist model: the rich and powerful hold sway over a pure but powerless working class. The only hope for relief comes from the deus ex machina of the superhero. I have often found the debate about the fascism of the superhero a bit amusing—since when has Superman sought to assume power? But Daredevil in these early stories is more clearly a Marxist *hero*, despite Marx's disdain for extrahuman agency. Daredevil serves not the status quo, but rather, he serves as a member and representative of the proletariat to equalize authority between the working classes and Big Power. He is the walking, talking reification of class struggle—in all of its complexity, and in red spandex.

In the subsequent Daredevil eras, however, the stories are more commonly meditations upon Big Power than successful subversions of it, and it is found to be flawed, incapable to sustain success, for good or ill. The only kind of power that has a chance to offer free agency, the *Daredevil* comics seem to suggest, is actually Small Power, or power that rises from the ground up rather than from the top down and simply wants to increase the free agency of the poor and working classes: The unspoken agreement assumed by Ben Urich, as a member of the press, when he decides not to reveal Murdock's identity. The protection of the inventor of the garbage-powered car. The support group that could become the basis of social action. The moments of power that individuals at street level can enjoy and employ fairly consistently derive from such negotiations between individual and group actions. Such possibilities mimic—with a less violent approach—the freedom that early denizens of Hell's Kitchen found to work around the reach of Big Power.

A final thought: comic fans and scholars for whom Daredevil is a favorite character used to be a fairly small—or, at least, *quiet*—group. The release of the Netflix series *Daredevil* changed that, however. In two seasons, as I write this essay, the series has, if anything, heightened and foregrounded the working-class imagery and themes of the comic series. Setting aside the gentrification of the actual twenty-first-century Hell's Kitchen, *Daredevil's* locale remains gritty, struggling, and under the thumb of Big Power. And Matt Murdock, despite being a lawyer, is firmly placed in the working class. (Once, he and his partner are paid in cobbler.) He defends the innocent from the accusations of ambitious

A poster promoting the Netflix web television series *Daredevil*, based on the Marvel comic. In the series Charlie Cox plays Matt Murdock, a blind, financially strapped lawyer who moonlights as the titular superhero. By depicting a badly bruised man in a suit and tie, the poster throws into sharp relief Murdock's dual lives as vigilante and litigator, and contrasts his working-class roots with his aspirational career.

prosecutors. He protects rent control clients from condo-building developers. Even as a superhero, Daredevil seems a world away from the other heroes of the Marvel Cinematic Universe he shares. The simple difference of the lighting scheme of the Avengers films as compared to the Daredevil series—bright and glossy versus dark and indeterminate—marks his environs as those of a different class. While the most powerful cinematic Avengers live literally in towers, in bunkers, and amongst the gods and fight aliens and glossy technology gone awry, Daredevil lives in a walkup and stops muggers and child molesters. He works so hard that he has to stop to catch his breath after thrashing a biker.[52]

Daredevil, in both the series and the comics, is an embodiment of the working-class man who does not necessarily want membership in what passes for the establishment, or Big Power, but merely free agency for himself and those like him, to be out from under a succession of heavy, heavy thumbs.

Notes

1. Stan Lee (writer) and Bill Everett (illustrator), "The Origin of Daredevil," *Daredevil* 1, no. 1 (1964), 2.

2. Here I depend on T.S. Eliot's construction of the objective correlative, a literary mechanism by which an accumulation of external elements—"a set of objects, a situation, a chain of events"—evokes a particular emotion. The fact that the image occurs *before* the accumulation of those elements is testament to the sophistication of the comic form. See "Hamlet and His Problems," *The Sacred Wood and Major Early Essays* (Mineola: Dover, 1998), 58.

3. Lee and Everett, "Origin of Daredevil," 8–14.

4. Ibid., 5–10.

5. Though I identify the eras with particular writers, it is important to note that a number of writers helmed the series during each period. However, Lee, Miller, and Bendis are seen as having established the tone and storytelling styles that most characterize their respective periods.

6. These distinctions—Marxist and Weberian, based on the ideas of Karl Marx and Max Weber—are simplistic descriptions of the changing academic discourse on class over the last few decades, with a third model focused on representation growing since the 1990s, but they are still generally seen as useful entryways into understanding thinking on class generally and on working-class identity more specifically. See Leszek Kolakowski, *Main Currents of Marxism: The Founders—The Golden Age—The Breakdown* (New York: Norton, 2008); also see Max Weber, "The Nature of Social Action," trans. Eric Matthews, *Selections in Translation*, ed. W. G. Runciman (New York: Cambridge University Press, 1978), 7–32.

7. The "myth of classlessness" argument has been deployed for decades to highlight the exclusion of challenging narratives of class, so much so that it has moved into the territory of scholarly cliché. However, the phrase retains its cultural power (likely because newspaper and magazine writers remain influenced by their college years, thank goodness). For recent evidence, see the

dozens of pundits and journalists who invoke the phrase in reviews of Nancy Isenberg's book *White Trash: The 400-Year Untold History of Class in America* (New York: Viking, 2016).

8. See Sherry Linkin and John Russo, "Class Confusion: American Media Discourse about Class," *Amerikastudien/American Studies* 4, no. 3 (Winter 2001): 367–69.

9. Brian Michael Bendis (writer) and Alex Maleev (artist), "Lowlife: Part 4," *Daredevil* 2, no. 44 (2003): 4–5.

10. Edwin G. Burrows and Mike Wallace, *Gotham: A History of New York City to 1898* (New York: Oxford University Press, 1999), 887–99, 1003–8.

11. Eric J. Hobsbawm, *The Age of Capital: 1848–1875* (New York: Vintage Books, 1975), 218. It should be noted that freed slaves would likely lack sympathy for white men upset about the dehumanizing changes following the end of slavery.

12. Anthony Petros Spanakos, "Hell's Kitchen's Prolonged Crisis and Would-Be Sovereigns: Daredevil, Hobbes, and Schmidt," *PS: Political Science and Politics* 47, no. 1 (2014): 95.

13. Frank Miller (writer), John Romita Jr. (penciller), and Al Williamson (inker), *Daredevil: The Man without Fear*, nos. 1–2 (1993).

14. Ibid., 4, 11.

15. "Stan Lee Interview: The Comic Book Creator on Adventures, Women, & Which Superhero Has The Highest Value to Humanity," by Lucy Blodgett, *TheHuffingtonPost.com*, April 28, 2012. http://www.huffingtonpost.com/2012/04/27/stan-lee-interview_n_145953gtml.

16. Daredevil is generally also depicted as superhumanly agile, athletic, and acrobatic. Sometimes this is vaguely associated with his heightened senses, and sometimes merely with his native athleticism and ninja training. Nevertheless, even amongst superheroes, he is generally seen as largely "human."

17. Stan Lee (writer) and Wally Wood and Bob Powell (artists), "That He May See!" *Daredevil* 1, no. 9 (1965), 7–16.

18. Wally Wood (writer and artist) and Bob Powell (artist), "While the City Sleeps!" *Daredevil* 1, no. 10 (1965); and Stan Lee (writer) and Wally Wood and Bob Powell (artists), "A Time to Unmask!" *Daredevil* 1, no. 11 (1965).

19. Highlights near the end of Lee's run on *Daredevil* include stories in which Foggy Nelson's girlfriend, an ex-con, is seen on TV protesting government inaction on poverty (#44–45) and a powerful story arc (#47–49) about Willie Lincoln, a black policeman who lost his sight fighting in Vietnam. After Lincoln is framed for corruption, Daredevil helps him by using both of his personas. Lincoln is explicitly a working-class figure and is presented as equally heroic compared to Murdock/Daredevil.

20. Roy Thomas (writer) and Gene Colan and Syd Shores (artists), "Suddenly . . . the Stunt-Master!" *Daredevil* 1, no. 64 (1970).

21. Roy Thomas (writer) and Gene Colan and Syd Shores (artists), "Phoenix and the Fighter!" 1, no. 68.

22. Roy Thomas (writer) and Gene Colan and Syd Shores (artists), "A Life on the Line," 1, no. 69: 11.

23. Roger McKenzie (writer) and Frank Miller and Klaus Janson (artists), "A Grave Mistake!" *Daredevil* 1, no. 158 (1979): 1.

24. Roger McKenzie (writer), Frank Miller (artist), and Klaus Janson (inker), "Exposé," *Daredevil* 1, no. 164 (1980): 30.

25. William DeGenaro, "'The New Deal': Burkean Identification and Working-Class Poetics," *Rhetoric Review* 26, no. 4 (2007): 385–87.

26. Frank Miller (writer and artist) and Klaus Janson (artist), "Elektra," *Daredevil* 1, no. 168 (1981).

27. Frank Miller and David Mazzucchelli (creators), "Apocalypse," *Daredevil* 1, no. 227 (1986).

28. Frank Miller (writer and artist) and Klaus Janson (artist), "Daredevil . . . Goes Berserk—," *Daredevil* 1, no. 173 (1981).

29. Frank Miller and David Mazzucchelli (creators), "God and Country," *Daredevil* 1, no. 232: 1–5.

30. Frank Miller and David Mazzucchelli (creators), "Armageddon," *Daredevil* 1, no. 233: 9.

31. Miller and Mazzucchelli, "God and Country," 17.

32. Miller and Mazzucchelli, "Armageddon," 18. Miller's mid-career writing, especially in *Daredevil* and with *The Dark Knight Returns*, seems to me to represent a kind of working man's libertarianism—part fear, part resentment and anger—that reacts against all forms of power, especially governmental, and which would metastasize into the darker turn of the Tea Party in 2008 and 2009, defining, as it did, a very narrow idea of Americanness and turning against perceived difference as inherent evidence of Big Power.

33. John Harkness (writer) and Louis Williams, Al Williamson, and Danny Bulanadi (artists), "Context!" *Daredevil* 1, no. 237 (1986): 6.

34. Ann Nocenti (writer) and Keith Pollard and Danny Bulanadi (artists), "Caviar Killer," *Daredevil* 1, no. 242 (1987).

35. Ann Nocenti (writer) and Mark Bagley (artist), "The American Nightmare," *Daredevil* 1, no. 283 (1990): 4.

36. Ibid., 15.

37. Ibid., 18.

38. Ibid., 29.

39. The multiyear story arc became more dominant in the 2000s, as the comics industry more fully embraced the changing demographics of its audience (more and more adult) and assumed the readers wanted ever-more-sophisticated plots.

40. Brian Michael Bendis (writer) and Alex Maleev (artist), "Hardcore: Part 5," *Daredevil* 2, no. 50 (2003): 23.

41. Ibid., "The King of Hell's Kitchen: Part 1," *Daredevil* 2, no. 56 (2004): 9–13.

42. Some recent examples of this discussion include Jason Dittmer, *Captain America and the Nationalist Superhero: Metaphors, Narratives, and Geopolitics* (Philadelphia: Temple University Press, 2012); Matthew Wolf-Meyer, "The World Ozymandias Made: Utopias in the Superhero Comics, Subculture, and the Conservation of Difference," *Popular Culture* 36, no. 3 (2003):

497–517; and Christian Steinmetz, "A Genealogy of Evil: Captain America vs. the Shadows of an Imagined National Community," *Captain America and the Struggle of the Superhero: Critical Essays*, ed. Robert G. Weiner (Jefferson, NC: McFarland, 2009), 190–203.

43. Brian Michael Bendis (writer) and Alex Maleev (artist), "The King of Hell's Kitchen: Part 1," *Daredevil* 2, no. 56 (2004): 13.

44. Brian Michael Bendis (writer) and Alex Maleev (artist), "The King of Hell's Kitchen: Part 2," *Daredevil* 2, no. 57 (2004): 12.

45. Brian Michael Bendis (writer) and Alex Maleev (artist), "Thou Shalt Not Kill," *Daredevil* 2, no. 75 (2005): 31–32.

46. In a bit of dark humor, Osborn created the acronym for H.A.M.M.E.R., because he thought it sounded aggressive, before having an actual name for the organization, which is never revealed. Osborn's role is never specifically defined, but he functions as a combination of director of Homeland Security, the CIA, and the FBI (though each of these exists in some form in the Marvel Universe as well). Osborn also often acts as the Iron Patriot, an explicitly nationalistic version of Iron Man that he creates after stealing many suits of Iron Man's armor.

47. Andy Diggle (writer) and Billy Tan and Matt Banning (artists), *Dark Reign: The List-Daredevil* 1 (2009): 8.

48. Ibid., 19.

49. Ibid., 21.

50. Andy Diggle (writer), Billy Tan (pencils), and Victor Olazaba (inks), *Shadowland* 1–5 (2010–2011).

51. Ibid. 16.

52. *Daredevil*. Marvel. Netflix. 2015–2016. Television.

JACK KIRBY
The Not-So-Secret Identity
of the Thing

Andrew Alan Smith

It seems self-evident that Ben "The Thing" Grimm of the Fantastic Four is now, and always has been, a working-class guy. His language, speech pattern, and lifestyle all indicate his blue-collar background, despite the vast amount of money at his disposal as a principal in Fantastic Four, Inc. But his origins go back further than his first appearance in 1961, all the way back to the childhood of his cocreator and original artist, Jack Kirby. Kirby, a working-class Jew from the slums of Lower East Side New York City in the early part of the twentieth century, patterned Grimm after himself. Even after both Kirby and cocreator Stan Lee left *Fantastic Four,* later writers would include bits of background cementing the Thing as one of Kirby's alter egos in comics.

Remembrance of Things Past

There is no question about Jack Kirby's bona fides as a working-class kid.

The man who would one day be dubbed "The King" by Marvel Comics' Stan Lee was born Jacob Kurtzberg in the tenements of the Lower East Side of Manhattan in 1917, the son of Benjamin and Rosemary Kurtzberg, who had immigrated from Austria. Kirby was born in America, joined a few years later by a brother, David. This hardscrabble family was hardly unique in the area, which was bounded roughly by East Houston on the north, Chrystie Street on the west, Canal Street on the south and East Broadway on the East.

While largely gentrified today, at the turn of the last century the tenement apartments of the Lower East Side were crammed to the rafters with immigrants—most of them Jewish, most of them from Germany, Austria, Eastern Europe, Greece, and Russia.

The Kurtzbergs endured grinding poverty, as was typical of the neighborhood. Describing his childhood, Kirby said, "My mother once wanted to give me a vacation, so she put me on a fire escape for two weeks and I was out in the open air sleeping . . . on a fire escape and having a grand time" (Howe 16).

Jakie, as he was called, was well aware of his family's need for income and pitched in where he could. He worked messenger jobs and painted signs. Hawking newspapers was a regular gig, although Kirby didn't feel particularly successful at it. "You'd have to go to this building and pick up your papers from the back of a truck. I was the shortest guy and the other boys used to run right over me" (Evanier 19).

Nevertheless, anxiety about providing for his family would remain with Kirby for the rest of his life. In the early days, according to longtime partner Joe Simon, Kirby's "$15 a week salary was the steadiest portion of the family income" (40). Throughout his life, Kirby took on as much work as he could—which, given his uncanny speed, was a lot.

That income anxiety was strong enough to push Kirby into claiming more than his due at least once, in 1982. Kirby claimed he and his former partner Joe Simon were the true creators of Spider-Man—much to Simon's surprise. When Simon asked why, Kirby said, "I had no work—I had family to support, rent to pay—what else could I do?"

Fighting for your place was something of a motif on the Lower East Side. Kirby joined the Suffolk Street Gang and scrapped with other gangs, according to Kirby's biographer, Mark Evanier. "Each street had its own gang of kids, and we'd fight all the time," Kirby said. "We'd cross over the roofs and bombard the Norfolk Street Gang with bottles and rocks and mix it up with them" (Evanier 22). It got up close and personal sometimes too: "I would wait behind a brick wall for three guys to pass and I'd beat the crap out of them and run like hell" (Howe 16).

While Kirby's rough-and-tumble existence was no doubt difficult, it turned out to be valuable, at least according to Kirby. "He later cited his experiences growing up in a rough neighborhood where good boys learned to survive by acting tough and standing up to bullies as a primary inspiration for his comic book work and his politics" (Wright 35).

Kirby carried his tough-guy persona into his first job at the Eisner-Iger Studios in 1938. The legendary Will Eisner, who was the first name in that partnership, told *Jack Kirby Collector* magazine an anecdote about Kirby challenging a rough customer who was pushing a towel service the shop no longer wanted. Eisner said that Kirby, despite being a "little fellow," seemed to think he was tough-guy actor John Garfield. "We were beginning to talk loud, and from the other room, in comes Jack Kirby. He says to me, 'Will, is he giving you a problem? I will beat him up'" (Depelley).

Later, when Kirby was working on *Captain America Comics* at Timely Comics (which would become Marvel Comics), German bundists were making threats. Bundists were members of the German American Bund, the semi-official arm of the Nazi Party in the United States, whose high point was probably a rally at Madison Square Garden on February 29, 1939. As supporters of Adolph Hitler, they were no fans of Captain America, who famously punched Der Führer in the face on the cover of his first issue.

As Evanier tells it, one time Kirby answered the phone, and a voice said three men were waiting in the lobby for the guy who "does this disgusting comic book" to show him what real Nazis would do to the Sentinel of Liberty. "To the horror of others in the office, Kirby rolled up his sleeves and headed downstairs" (Evanier 55). Fortunately, the callers were no longer there.

And when Simon and Kirby were trying to create a backlog of material during the draft for World War II, the tough guy that was Kirby said their goal was "to get enough work backlogged that I could go into the Army, kill Hitler, and get back before the readers missed us" (Evanier 66).

The war was another element in Kirby's psychological makeup, and an important one. Kirby not only served but saw combat with Company F of 11th Infantry under Gen. George Patton. His outfit battled at Bastogne during the infamous Battle of the Bulge, fighting not just the Nazis but also the weather. Pvt. Kirby nearly lost both feet to frostbite but recovered.

The Big One stuck with Kirby, who was certainly patriotic—he had changed his name from Jacob Kurtzberg to Jack Kirby because "I wanted to be an American" (Wright 35). But his experiences weighed on him, at least according to Raphael and Spurgeon: "Kirby draws a world haunted by memories and echoes of war, a world of men and supermen who shuffle from gray building to gray building in heavy overcoats" (92).

Kirby himself was unprepossessing in the 1960s, somewhat reflecting the quote above. Nat Freedland of the *New York Herald Tribune* said of Kirby that "if you stood next to him on the subway, you'd peg him for the assistant foreman of a girdle factory" (Howe 64).

That was the makeup and mind-set of a man who, with Stan Lee, created perhaps the greatest working-class character of all.

The Shape of Things to Come

If anyone was surprised at Kirby putting himself in *Fantastic Four*, they shouldn't have been. Because it wasn't the first time he had figuratively thrown himself into his work.

When Simon and Kirby launched kid gangs in comics with *Young Allies* in 1941, it was something, Evanier joked, that Kirby "had been dabbling in ... since his childhood" (61). And, unsurprisingly, Kirby drew on his Lower East Side experience for inspiration.

"Every teen gang Joe and Jack did had one member who resembled Kirby," Evanier said (62). In *Young Allies* it was a tough kid from New York named Knuckles. In *Newsboy Legion*, it was a tough kid from New York named Scrapper. And in *Boy Commandos*, it was a tough kid from New York named Brooklyn. (I guess naming a kid "Lower East Side" was too much of a mouthful.)

But the tough kids from New York were just Kirby's warm-up. The main attraction was a tough grown-up from New York, Benjamin Jacob Grimm— Benjamin for Kirby's father, Jacob for Kirby himself.

Grimm is, metaphorically, Kirby's street kids grown up, as is Kirby himself. Although some didn't see the Thing as much of a grown-up.

Physically he was much larger than the street kids, of course, initially a lumpy monster with reptilian skin and enormous strength that wasn't much of a stretch from the many monsters Kirby had been drawing for Atlas Comics (which also would become Marvel Comics). That look evolved eventually into the bricklike exterior familiar today, albeit not before Johnny Storm memorably described it as "a clump of peach pits" (Ivie 11).

Les Daniels, who wrote the official Marvel Comics history, began his discussion of Ben Grimm as most do, describing him as "the [Richards] family's gruff but lovable uncle, one who came from a distinctly less privileged background." But he followed that up, interestingly, with the observation that the Thing's "emotional responses and frequent tantrums suggested he might really be the baby of the household. The others sported spiffy uniforms, he wore a big blue diaper" (86).

While that intriguing idea will no doubt become a master's thesis someday, most academics and critics describe the Thing in more adult terms:

"Ben Grimm is the cantankerous, but ultimately lovable, uncle or grandfather who sits grousing in his armchair" (Knowles 173).

"Reading the words alone, Lee's Thing seemed less educated and generally angrier than Mr. Fantastic" (Raphael 94).

"I tried to have Ben talk like a real tough, surly, angry guy," said Lee, "but yet the reader had to know he had a heart of gold underneath" (McLaughlin 94).

Not just angry, but also working-class. Lee sprinkled Grimm's patter with a number of expressions associated with, as Daniels phrased it above, "a distinctly less privileged background." For example, one of Grimm's favorite expressions is "Wotta revoltin' development this is!" which is generally attributed to the lead character in the TV show *Life of Riley*, a blue-collar worker played by William Bendix.[1] Other Thing-isms include "We wuz robbed!" and "I shoulda stood in bed," which *Los Angeles Times* columnist Jack Smith and dictionary.com attribute to various sports personalities. And if the ironic "idol o' millions" isn't part of a Catskills comedian's routine, it surely should be.

But while the creation of the Thing may have taken elements from various popular personalities and a clump of peach pits in 1961, Evanier says at heart the Thing's personality reflected that of his cocreator. "The character had his lineage in the monster comics that Jack was still drawing at the time, but Jack saw another point of origin: himself" (114).

"If you'll notice the way the Thing talks and acts, you'll find that the Thing is really Jack Kirby," Kirby said. "He had my manners, he has my manner of speech, and he thinks the way I do. He's excitable, and you'll find that he's very, very active among people, and he can muscle his way through a crowd. I find I'm that sort of person" (122).

The Once and Future Thing

Throughout Ben Grimm's adventures in comic books—those considered canon,[2] anyway—the many writers working on the character's diverse titles have fleshed out the facets of his personality and background. Some identify the character more strongly with Kirby, some simply position the character more strongly with the working class, and many do both.

But it took a while to fill in that background. Stan Lee and Jack Kirby, the cocreators of the first 101 issues of *Fantastic Four* and first six *Fantastic Four Annuals*, didn't give us much insight. But they did provide some clues that later writers embellished.

It Started on Yancy Street

Beginning with *Fantastic Four* no. 6 (1962), Grimm has been constantly needled by a street gang on Yancy Street—which it doesn't take a Reed Richards to figure out was a stand-in for Delancey Street on New York's Lower East Side, near where Kirby grew up. For years the antagonism of the mysterious Yancy Street

Gang—their names and faces weren't revealed until long after Lee and Kirby left the title—were simply an inexplicable, but accepted, part of the mythology. The Gang wrote nasty letters, sent exploding packages,[3] and spray-painted graffiti on Grimm's vehicles. In *Fantastic Four* no. 29 (1964), they taunted the whole team, dropping a garbage can on Grimm, throwing a bucket of water on the Human Torch, clouting Mr. Fantastic with a vegetable, and dosing the Invisible Girl with sneezing powder. "This is ridiculous!" laments Richards. "The world's most famous, fighting foursome being pelted by a head of lettuce!" ("Yancy," Lee 1).

But for all that, the Yancy Street Gang never seemed malevolent, merely obnoxious—and eventually it became something of an ally. In both *Marvel Two-In-One* no. 47 (1979) and *Marvel Two-In-One* no. 70 (1980), the Gang rides to Grimm's rescue—while still tagging Grimm's truck and taunting him from rooftops and alleyways.

Over time it became obvious that Grimm had grown up on Yancy Street, even referring to it on more than one occasion as "the old neighborhood." In *Marvel Two-In-One* no. 6, he responds to a call from an old woman named Mrs. Cooper on the Lower East Side, whom he refers to as "almost a second mother to me. If not fer the way she looked after me as a kid—whut with both my folks workin' ta keep us eatin'—heck, I'd prob'ly spent my life shootin' pool an' brawlin' in the streets, 'stead o' goin' to college an' gettin' ejjicated!" (Gerber 11).[4]

So why the antagonism?

All was explained in *The Thing* no. 1 in 1983. Once again responding to a call for help from "the old neighborhood," Grimm lectures the new leader of the Yancy Street Gang (visible for a change) about not getting trapped in the slums. To his surprise, the kid calls him a traitor! "You heard me, Blue Eyes," the kid says. "Yer a traitor, you an' all them fancy-pants do-gooders that quit Yancy Street—that betrayed the code" (Byrne 10).

The story was written by John Byrne, who was born three decades after Lee and Kirby and grew up in Britain and Canada, not the pregentrification slums of the Lower East Side of New York. Whether that was the original intent of the Thing's cocreators, it at least explained those years of antagonism—and tied Grimm much more tightly to Kirby.

In his lecture, Grimm explains his origins, which include running with the Yancy Street Gang, much like Jack Kirby did with the Suffolk Street Gang. Grimm also spoke of an older brother, Daniel, who died in a gang fight—again mirroring Kirby, whose younger brother David preceded him to the grave.

Another Yancy Street story cemented the deal: *Fantastic Four* (third series) no. 56 (2002) revealed that Grimm, like both of his cocreators, is Jewish! In the course of the story, Grimm even recites the Jewish prayer Kaddish over an injured Jewish man named Sheckerberg he'd known from his youth. Once again, this non-Lee/Kirby story (it was written by Karl Kesel) links Grimm to Kirby, who reportedly kept a drawing he'd made of the Thing wrapped in his own ritual Jewish skullcap and prayer shawl (Packer 169).

One may wonder why it took forty-one years to reveal Grimm's religion. In the story, Sheckerberg asks if Grimm's ashamed of being a Jew. "Nah, that ain't it," the Thing responds. "Anyone on the Internet can find out, if they want. It's just . . . I don't talk it up, is all. Figure there's enough trouble in this world without people thinkin' Jews are all monsters like me" (Kesel 28). However, the real-world reason probably has more to do with the usual conventions of comics until roughly the 1990s, where religion, politics, and other controversial topics were studiously avoided.

Regardless, it all started on Yancy Street. As Evanier says, "Ben 'The Thing' Grimm—an obvious Kirby self-caricature—would fight a running battle with a mob called the Yancy Street Gang. The references to Jack's childhood—and skirmishes with the gangs of his childhood—would be unmistakable" (22).

Smarter Than He Looks

Despite his rough exterior—verbally, as well as physically—Ben Grimm is a pretty smart guy. Hints as to his intelligence go back as far as *Fantastic Four* no. 1, where Grimm points out that the rocket Reed Richards wants to use to go to the moon has inadequate shielding—something only someone well versed in a variety of disciplines would know.

Later, in *Fantastic Four* no. 11 (1963), Lee and Kirby established that Richards and Grimm were roommates at "State U" (where Richards mentioned that Grimm was from "the wrong side of the tracks"). In *Fantastic Four Annual* no. 2 (Summer 1964) and *Fantastic Four* no. 35 (1965), we learn that Grimm not only attended State University—now amended to "Empire State University"—but met Victor Von Doom there, as well as Richards. While all these stories established that Grimm was on a football scholarship, he nevertheless graduated, which indicates a greater intelligence than his working-class speech patterns might indicate (to the more "classist" readers of the comic book).

Lee corroborates this a few years later in *Fantastic Four* no. 37, when Reed Richards is delivering a typically long-winded explanation, this time about subspace, and Grimm complains, "Boy! Give you a piece o' chalk and a blackboard, and there's no stoppin' ya!" But Richards responds, "Ben, you old phony, as an ex-test pilot, you probably know more about all this than any of us do!" (Lee, "Star" 5). As if to underscore the point, in the following issue Grimm recognizes a "Q-Bomb" at first glance.

In *Fantastic Four* (vol. 3) #56 (August 2002), writer Karl Kesel revealed that Ben Grimm was Jewish, like cocreators Jack Kirby and Stan Lee. Written by Karl Kesel. Art by Stuart Immonen.

Later writers have mentioned Grimm's intelligence, but it was Tom DeFalco who spelled it out, in *Fantastic Four* no. 367 (1992). "You do not fool me, Grimm!" says one of the Thing's antagonists. "I know that you are nowhere near as ignorant as you attempt to appear! You hold many advanced degrees in engineering!" (DeFalco, "Betrayed" 9).

And yet, Grimm holds on to his blue-collar speech pattern, as well as pretending he doesn't understand Richards's technobabble. It just goes to show that you can take the boy out of Yancy Street, but you can't take Yancy Street out of the boy.

Life during Wartime

Like his cocreators, Ben Grimm served in World War II. *Fantastic Four* no. 11 established that Grimm and Richards both served, the former as a fighter pilot in the Pacific theater and the latter with the Office of Strategic Services (which became today's CIA) in occupied France. Marvel even treated readers to a wartime adventure with Grimm, when he was rescued from a POW camp in the pages of *Capt. Savage and His Leatherneck Raiders* (a short-run *Sgt. Fury and His Howling Commandos* clone). It was Grimm's wartime experience and postwar years as a test pilot that made him Richards's first choice to fly the spaceship in *Fantastic Four* no. 1.

All of this was eminently plausible when *Fantastic Four* debuted in 1961, as Richards and Grimm would be in their late thirties or early forties—still vital men. But as the years passed, the age problem grew increasingly acute for not only Grimm and Richards, but all Marvel characters associated with specific wars.

Various means were found to explain longevity, or to simply untether characters from specific dates. Nick Fury was given an "Infinity Formula" to stay perpetually young. Iron Man was created in Vietnam, but eventually Marvel started referring to Tony Stark building his exoskeleton "in the last war." And World War II references were quietly dropped in comics featuring Ben Grimm and Reed Richards.

But not as quickly as you'd imagine. *Marvel Two-In-One* no. 77 featured a scene where Grimm recalls meeting the Howling Commandos during the war—a book that appeared in 1981. Even if Grimm was only eighteen when the United States entered the war, he'd have been pushing sixty! One can only assume some reluctance to let the war disappear from Grimm's background; that would separate him a bit from his creator.

But there was no question about the war being part of Grimm's character in the early days of *Fantastic Four*. If nothing else, Spurgeon's remark about Kirby's art—"a world haunted by memories and echoes of war, a world of men and supermen who shuffle from gray building to gray building in heavy overcoats"—perfectly describes the Thing himself when out in public. During Kirby's tenure on *Fantastic Four*, Grimm would adopt a hat and heavy trench coat so as not to terrify New York pedestrians as he moved among them. It was a disguise, sure, but a very morose one. The war echoed on.

Working for the Weekend

Saving the world isn't a full-time job. Readers have been treated to numerous instances of Grimm enjoying his downtime. And while it is unknown if Kirby shared all of Grimm's interests, they are certainly blue-collar in reputation, if not in fact.

Wrestling: When choosing an occupation outside the Fantastic Four in 1963, Grimm's first choice was to become a wrestler (*Fantastic Four* no. 15). He did so again for several issues in 1985 by joining "Unlimited Class Wrestling," a league featuring super-strong wrestlers.

Poker: There have been innumerable scenes of cigar-smoking, tough-guy poker games in the Marvel Universe, usually featuring (but not limited to) Grimm, Nick Fury, and Logan (Wolverine). The cigars are long gone—no heroes smoke in Marvel Comics any more—but Grimm still plays cards with other heroes, notably the "first-ever superhero poker tournament" following Grimm's bar mitzvah in *The Thing* (second series) no. 8 in 2006, with dozens of heroes and villains in attendance (yes, that happened).

Beer: Grimm has been depicted nursing a cold one both at the Baxter Building and in various neighborhood bars (presumably near Yancy Street). On one occasion in 1982, he's called by a bartender who says he has the supervillain Flint "Sandman" Marko "cornered in my bar" (DeFalco, "Time" 6). Grimm doesn't believe him but goes anyway to drink a few brews and maybe "catch a ballgame on the tube." It turns out Sandman is in the bar, and Grimm drinks with him as Marko tells his life story—which, it turns out, is very similar to Grimm's, beginning with football. "I never realized how much I had in common with Sandy. Football was my ticket out of the slums, too! Without it, I never would have gone to college—or met Reed Richards—or ended up with the Fantastic Four" (9). After sharing a beer with a fellow survivor of the slums, Grimm lets Sandman go.

Marvel Two-In-One

Jack Kirby and Ben Grimm share a lot of characteristics: a love of cigars, a gruff temperament, a history in street gangs and World War II. They are both

In *The Thing* (vol. 2) #8 (August 2006), Ben Grimm showed his working-class stripes with a poker tournament, and his Jewish heritage by getting his bar mitzvah. Written by Dan Slott. Art by Kieron Dwyer.

In *Fantastic Four* (vol. 3) #511 (May 2004), on page 15 the Quantum Quartet discovers that God looks an awful lot like Jack Kirby, who cocreated them all. Written by Mark Waid. Art by Mike Wieringo.

working-class men who rose far but never forgot their roots. And it's clear from all evidence that Kirby put a lot of himself in Ben Grimm, who is an avatar of sorts for the King of Comics in his favored medium.

But Kirby is more than a blueprint for the Thing—he's his cocreator. And that, too, has been recognized in the comics.

In 2004 Ben Grimm died. Ever the explorers, his teammates ventured into heaven (never named, but clearly that's what it was) to fight for his return. And there, behind a huge door, they met the Creator—and it was Jack Kirby.

Again, no names. But who else would it be? Who else could it be?

"What you see is what I am to you," says the Kirby lookalike at the drawing table. "Don't worry. It's a compliment, not an insult. That is why my creations do. They find the humanity in God." (Waid, "Hereafter" 16).

And it was this God that put the humanity in Ben Grimm—his own.

Notes

1. Bendix gets a reference in *Fantastic Four* no. 196, thanks to writer Marv Wolfman. As John Wayne makes a cameo, Grimm says, "Right next'a Willie Bendix, he's my one an' only idol!"

2. Comic book characters aren't always consistent. Some appear differently in other media than they do in the comics, and some comics stories involve dreams, doppelgangers from alternate dimensions, hoaxes, imaginary stories, "what ifs," and the like. Given the multiple iterations of a given character available at any given time, comics editors, writers, and fans have a usually unspoken agreement on which stories "count" for a given character, and which don't. The stories that count are referred to as "canon."

3. It should be noted that *Fantastic Four* no. 61 (third series) established that all the packages sent to the Fantastic Four's Baxter Building headquarters by the Yancy Street Gang were actually pranks by Johnny Storm—presumably to explain how booby-trapped packages could make it through the FF's security. That remains the official story, but many fans (including this one) prefer to believe that all those stink bombs and such were the product of Yancy Street.

4. This version of Grimm's youth was amended in *The Thing* no. 1 to indicate that his father was a drunk who rarely worked, and that both of his parents died before Grimm hit the age of majority.

Bibliography

Byrne, John. "Lifelines!" *The Thing* no. 1 [July 1983].

Carlin, Mike. "In This Corner!" *The Thing* no. 28 [October 1985].

Daniels, Les. *Marvel: Five Fabulous Decades of the World's Greatest Comics.* New York: Henry N. Abrams, 1991.

DeFalco, Tom. "By Reed . . . Betrayed!" *Fantastic Four* no. 367 [August 1992].

———. "Only the Swamp Survives!" *Marvel Two-In-One* no. 77 [July 1981].

———. "Time Runs Like Sand!" *Marvel Two-In-One* no. 86 [April 1982].

Depelley, Jean. "Will Eisner Speaks!" *Jack Kirby Collector* no. 16 [June 1997]. http://twomorrows
.com/kirby/articles/16eisner.html [accessed August 11, 2015].

Evanier, Mark. *Kirby: King of Comics.* New York: Harry N. Abrams, 2002.

Gerber, Steve. "Death-Song of Destiny!" *Marvel Two-In-One* no. 6 [November 1974].

Goodwin, Archie. "Objective: Ben Grimm!" *Capt. Savage and His Leatherneck Raiders* no. 7.
October 1968.

Gruenwald, Mark, and Ralph Macchio. "A Moving Experience!" *Marvel Two-In-One* no. 70.
December 1980.

Howe, Sean. *Marvel Comics: The Untold Story.* New York: Harper Perennial, 2013.

Ivie, Larry. "The Sinister Space Trap," *Strange Tales* no. 132 [May 1965].

"A Jewish Tour to New York's Lower East Side," *New York* online [Aug. 7, 2013]. http://nymag.
com/visitorsguide/neighborhoods/jewishles.htm [accessed Nov. 25, 2015].

Jordan, Raphael, and Tom Spurgeon. *Stan Lee and the Rise and Fall of the American Comic Book.*
Chicago: Chicago Review Press, 2003.

Kesel, Karl. "Remembrance of Things Past!" *Fantastic Four* (third series) no. 56 [August 2002].

Knowles, Christopher. *Our Gods Wear Spandex: The Secret History of Comic Book Heroes.* San
Francisco: Weiser Books, 2007.

Lee, Stan. "Behold! A Distant Star!" *Fantastic Four* no. 37 [April 1965].

———. "Calamity on the Campus!" *Fantastic Four* no. 35 [February 1965].

———. "Captives of the Deadly Duo!" *Fantastic Four* no. 6 [September 1962].

———. "The Fantastic Four Battle the Mad Thinker and His Awesome Android!" *Fantastic Four*
no. 15 [June 1963].

———. "It Started on Yancy Street!" *Fantastic Four* no. 29 [August 1964].

———. "Origin of Doctor Doom!" *Fantastic Four Annual* no. 2 [Summer 1964].

———. "A Visit with the Fantastic Four!" *Fantastic Four* no. 11 [February 1963].

Lee, Stan, and George Mair. *Excelsior: The Amazing Life of Stan Lee.* New York: Simon & Schuster,
2002.

Mantlo, Bill. "Happy Deathday, Mr. Grimm!" *Marvel Two-In-One* no. 47 [January 1979].

McLaughlin, Jeff, ed. *Stan Lee Conversations.* Jackson: University Press of Mississippi, 2007.

Packer, Sharon. *Superheroes and Superegos: Analyzing the Minds Behind the Masks.* Santa Barbara:
Praeger, 2010.

Simon, Joe, and Jim Simon. *The Comic Book Makers.* Lebanon, NJ: Vanguard, 2003.

Slott, Dan. "Last Hand." *The Thing* (second series) no. 8 [August 2006].

Smith, Jack. "Who Said It First and How Did He Really Say It?" *Los Angeles Times* online [Nov.
9, 1989]. http://articles.latimes.com/1989-11-09/news/vw-1199_1_joe-jacobs [accessed
Nov. 25, 2015].

Waid, Mark. "24 Blocks and One Blockhead." *Fantastic Four* (third series) no. 61 [November 2002].

Waid, Mark. "Hereafter." *Fantastic Four* (third series), no. 511. May 2004.

Wolfman, Marv. "Who in the World Is the Invincible Man?" *Fantastic Four*, no. 196 [July 1978].

Wright, Bradford W. *Comic Book Nation: The Transformation of Youth Culture in America.* Baltimore: Johns Hopkins University Press, 2001.

MARVEL'S SHAMROCK
Haunted Heroine, Working Woman, Guardian of the Galaxy

Christina M. Knopf

Guardians of the Galaxy #3 proclaimed Shamrock "one of the most fascinating super heroes of the late 20th century!"[1] This was a startling statement to make given that the Irish superheroine had thus appeared in only seven Marvel issues, and was an integral part of the story in just three (excluding parodic appearances as "Sham-Luck," a member of The Obscurity Legion in Marvel's humor title *What The . . . ?*[2]). Though she never achieved stardom within the Marvel Universe, she has had a variety of recurring cameos throughout assorted Marvel titles between 1982 and 2014, including appearances as an injured hairdresser, a New York bartender, a zombie, and an agent of S.H.I.E.L.D. This may not make her the most fascinating superhero, but it does make her a notable and intriguing character. This essay considers the three most prominent elements of Shamrock's character: her gender, her powers, and her non-superhero identity. To do this, we must begin with her story.... After all, storytelling is a grand Irish tradition.

Shamrock's Troubles

When Molly Fitzgerald was three years old, her father "an embittered Irish Republican" took her and her older brother to the North Ireland Mountainside near their house and asked the heavens to grant his child "the power to strike down thine enemies!" For years it seemed the prayer had gone unanswered until Molly was in college and discovered that she had been blessed with a protective aura that caused random probabilities to manifest in her favor whenever attacked. With these "good luck powers," she became Ireland's seldom-seen superheroine, Shamrock. But that ended when she became a first-grade teacher in Dublin.[3] Shamrock first appeared during the Contest of Champions, in which heroes from around the globe were used as pawns in a game with Death.[4] She celebrated with the Avengers when Dr. Banner/Hulk was pardoned for his past destruction[5] and assisted them in a doomsday fight against the Wraiths,[6] and she advised Alpha Flight during their world tour.[7] She was reportedly even one of Earth's heroes taken to the planet Battleworld for the "Secret Wars."[8]

Estranged from her family, Molly returned home following the death of her brother, who was killed by a terrorist's bomb. Molly's father sought retribution for his son's death, but Molly refused to use her powers to fight, arguing that the war had already claimed enough lives and that she served Ireland better by teaching "the young people of this country that there's a world outside of these war-torn hills." Angry that his prayers were wasted on such "spineless daydreams,"[9] he drugged his daughter, giving her to the evil genius Arnim Zola to analyze, in hopes that Molly's powers could be duplicated in militants. But the attempt backfired. Zola discovered that Molly's body was a repository for the tortured souls of innocent war victims, and these poltergeists were the source of her powers. The spirits would manifest themselves to protect Molly, causing the improbable events attributed to her Irish luck. The poltergeists destroyed first Zola and then Molly's father, causing his gun to explode when he tried to kill her. Standing at his grave, Molly swore that her superhero days were behind her forever.[10]

During the thirty-first century of the Marvel Universe's alternative timeline known as Earth-691, Martians invaded Earth, the staggering death toll stirred Molly's subconscious mind, and, "unable to ignore the overpowering input, Shamrock was reborn!"[11] She distinguished herself fighting alongside Earth's mightiest superheroes, but when it became clear America was lost, she returned home, certain that Europe would be next. A psychic summons led her to the Giant's Causeway, where Doctor Druid told her that Celtic War Goddesses foresaw the triumph of the Martians and the eventual renewal of the spirit of mankind. They had preserved and updated the ancient Book of Kells to ensure the record of the past was not destroyed and then entrusted it to Molly for centuries' keeping. For this task, the poltergeists within her granted her eternal life, and Doctor Druid provided a companion in the form of the legendary ancient warrior Cuchulain—the Irish Wolfhound. Eventually, the Guardians came to retrieve the Book, but the God Samhain and his army of Blue Banshees interfered. After Shamrock defeated Samhain she gave the Book to the Guardians, returning it to mankind. Invited to join the Guardians of the Galaxy, Molly and Cuchulain instead chose to "follow in the footsteps of their Celtic ancestors" to discover what remained of Europe and to reintroduce civilization.[12]

In these efforts, they settled in an international shantytown of survivors, where Molly resumed work as a schoolteacher. It is here the Celts again encountered the Guardians of the Galaxy. Fearing an extraterrestrial attack, Molly donned the mantle of Shamrock to protect the children. The Guardians wanted to enlist the help of the Celtic warriors to recover a lost teammate, but Shamrock refused, "I gave up super heroics back in the late twentieth century! [. . .] Teaching's always been my true calling! I'm not about to abandon the children here in Dochals to go adventuring again." But she told Cuchulain to go if he wished, knowing that he longed for action and combat.[13]

In the primary Marvel Universe continuity timeline of Earth-616, however, Molly did not become an immortal guarding the Book of Kells and instead spent her post-superhero days as a highly sought-after hairdresser in Dublin, giving haircuts to Wolfsbane and Shadowcat of the X-Men, while sporting a cast and crutches because her "Irish luck ran out."[14] Despite retirement, Molly's poltergeists stayed with her, pushing her to remember Shamrock—but, older and heavier, she only felt like a "sham." As her salon filled with superhero-ines such as the Invisible Woman, Molly admitted that she only worked with superhero hair because it did not require any talent to make it look good. Yet Molly soon rediscovered her worth when, through a series of mishaps, she boosted the self-esteem, and the hair, of Black Cat's non-super teenage niece.[15] (Meanwhile, as part of the Marvel Zombies Universe/Earth-2149 in *Deadpool Merc with a Mouth*, Molly was infected with a bioweapon that afflicted the globe and battled with the uninfected Deadpool, who talked his way around her luck and killed her.[16])

Molly was next seen behind a bar bearing her superheroine visage at the "Luck o' the Irish Pub" in New York City. After listening to a group of male superheroes lamenting the problems of dating female superheroes, Molly informed them that they were "a right bunch of moaners" who "don't think a girl can handle this super hero business without a big heap of man to hug them close when @#$% hits the fan!"[17] And recently, she appears to have come out of retirement to join S.H.I.E.L.D. as Agent Molly Fitzgerald.[18]

It is important to place Shamrock's complicated yet brief history against the backdrop of European politics, as they are the basis for her character. Shamrock was introduced in 1982, a year marked by several bombings connected to branches of the Irish Republicans, including the Hyde Park, Regent's Park, and Droppin Well bombings. Such Irish-British hostilities are noted by distrust between Shamrock and Captain Britain in the Contest of Champions. Shamrock's character receives her full origin story in 1993—a year that saw even more violence in the Troubles, with 26 killed and 99 injured in a series of bomb attacks and shootings, including the Greysteel Massacre, which took place during a Halloween party at a bar. Ironically, Shamrock had fought and defeated *Samhain*, Gaelic for "Halloween," just two months earlier. Marvel transformed Shamrock into a retired superhero and hairdresser in 1997, midway through the peace talks that led to the Belfast Agreement, with Shamrock's departure from fighting paralleling the eventual ceasefire in the Irish conflict. Shamrock's gender is likewise of importance, particularly because she has no male predecessor or counterpart in the Marvel Universe—unlike Spider-Woman to Spider-Man, Lady Deadpool to Deadpool, She-Hulk to Hulk, etc. Therefore, a feminist reading of her story will examine how gender interacts with Molly's proximity to war, her connection to poltergeists, and her work as a teacher, hairdresser, and bartender, making Shamrock symbolically significant though seldom seen.

Women and War

Women were long viewed as a reason to fight, as symbols of the home and hearth to be defended, kept safely away from the violence.[19] Western tradition "assumes an affinity between women and peace, men and war,"[20] and feminism has more often been tied to efforts for peace than to shows of force, as with demilitarization movements fueled by feminist ideas about masculinized politics and sexualized violence.[21] Such ideas are reinforced throughout gender depictions in pop culture, which tend to emphasize men as more powerful and aggressive than women, and women as more sexualized than, and dependent on, men.[22]

In the context of the Troubles of Northern Ireland, masculine ideologies of Irish Nationalism/Republicanism have prevailed over the war experiences of women,[23] reflecting deep gendered inequalities of Northern Ireland's society.[24] Though women have historically been warriors around the world, they have not historically been remembered as such, just as female superheroes who "can be heroes . . . are very rarely obligated to be heroes."[25] Shamrock's costuming represents women's subordinate, overlooked, and forgotten place in Irish history and society.[26] Whereas many superheroines—particularly from Marvel in the 1980s to 1990s—sport a "lingerie-as-costume look,"[27] outfitted in thongs with spike-heeled, thigh-high boots,[28] Shamrock's costume covers her from head to toe. Showing no skin except for the lower part of her face, Shamrock wears a light green short-sleeved leotard over darker green tights and long sleeves, with light green gauntlet gloves and flat-footed, calf-high boots. Her original costume included a cowl that disguised her face and covered her hair, while later versions used a mask that allowed her long, red hair to flow freely. Her chest and forehead both bear a dark green shamrock emblem. The overall effect of this attire is to reflect the devotion of the Northern Irish to Ireland, while hiding Molly and camouflaging Shamrock, rendering both identities invisible. This subordinate status is further reinforced by Shamrock's background role in the Marvel Universe. In eight issues of the nineteen in which she has a recorded presence,[29] she is seen only in part, usually situated behind other heroes, and is given little to no dialogue.

Despite the low visibility of women in the war, feminists acknowledge that the Troubles were integral to women's place in Irish society—with some arguing that liberating Ireland was part of liberating women, and others claiming that the status of women needed to improve before Ireland could be helped—with both sides hinging on the divisions and interactions of the public (war) and private (domestic) realms.[30] The fact that Molly's father put his politics and militaristic goals ahead of his own daughter has precedent in reality for members of the Irish Republican Army. A woman from Limerick recounts that though her father loved his family, he loved Ireland more, and it made her mother angry that he prioritized the people of the North over his own family.[31] The resigned position of Irish women to war is also seen when Molly sends Cuchulain to do combat alongside the Guardians and promises to be waiting when he returns—taking the traditional female role in war of the keeper of the hearth.

Girls and Ghosts

The Modern American Spiritualist movement that began in 1848, which attracted thousands of people searching for truth in a changing world, was strongly connected with women. Spiritualists most closely associated the ability to speak to the spirit world with young women, and many women used the idea of ghostly communication to imagine social and political possibilities beyond the confines of their present world. Spiritualism's popularity was due, in part, to its use in providing politically subordinate women with a voice.[32] It is no coincidence that a "distinctive women's tradition of ghost story writing" appeared in 1850 as a means of challenging the mainstream patriarchy,[33] wherein ghosts served as dead representations of women's lived experiences—considered irrational, unseen ,and unheard by many, trapped within the house with only limited agency, and yet trying to find power in their powerlessness.

Just as the séances of the nineteenth century offered an acceptable, alternate, public venue for women to speak, Molly's poltergeists empower her to speak against the politics of her father. And the idea of giving voice to the voiceless is reified through the souls of innocent war victims gaining agency through

This scene is typical of many of Shamrock's appearances—one of a group of heroes, silent and unobtrusive in her concealing green costume. (From *ROM* #65. "Doomsday." Bill Manto, story. Steve Ditko and P. Craig Russell, art. April 1985. Marvel Comics.)

Molly. The fact that Molly's supernatural encounter involves poltergeists, in particular, is of further interest. *Poltergeist* means "playful spirit" in German and denotes the fact that phenomena related to such spirits are often mischievous. But *poltergeist* also means "noisy mind," which points to the idea that these phenomena also most often occur around particular individuals and are thought related to recurrent spontaneous psychokinesis in which the individual "supposedly discharges tensions, provoked by relationships," that cause the occurrences attributed to spirits.[34] With her unhappy family, war-torn society, feelings of guilt for the dead, and mostly solitary existence, Molly seems a likely candidate for a "noisy mind"—as manifested through the poltergeists who pester her into her retirement.

Ladies and Labor

A key element of the superhero story is the alter-ego. The secret identity of the superheroes not only allows for readers to fantasize about their own hidden potentials[35] but also "acknowledges the schizophrenic splitting of identity into divided subjectivities in modern society"[36]—including the powerful masculine and weak feminine,[37] the selfless and the selfish,[38] the public and private, and the heroic and economic. Selfless superheroism is not regular or paying work, and so it comes as no surprise that most superheroes living double lives are professionals with scheduling freedom and financial stability.[39] Since the Marvel revolution of the 1960s that introduced more complex and troubled characters,[40] superheroes have struggled with secret identities in efforts to pursue full-time non-superhero roles.[41] This seems to be especially true for female

Shown as part of her origin story, this image demonstrates the source and nature of Shamrock's power—the tortured souls of innocent casualties of war, housed within the body of Molly Fitzgerald. It also illustrates the "noisy mind" definition of *poltergeist*. (From *Guardians of the Galaxy* 64 Page Annual #3: "There Is No Future—Only the Past Happening Again and Again." Michael Gallagher, writer. Colleen Doran, penciller. 1993. Marvel Comics.)

characters—such as versions of Diana Prince/Wonder Woman, She-Hulk/Jennifer Walters, and Wasp/Janet Van Dyne—who traditionally are much more likely to quell not only their identity but also their powers to the greater good, especially for loved ones, in a maternal role of nurturance and protectiveness.[42]

Working-class women in pop culture are often depicted as more admirable and capable than working-class men,[43] and the cultural ideal of the modern working mother is that of a "supermom"—a moniker symbolically dependent on the idea of the superhero successfully straddling the public and private spheres.[44] And yet in debates regarding class, the labor market is largely considered "male" territory,[45] with men and women historically competing in separate labor markets wherein occupations such as teacher, hairdresser, and waiter have been considered "female" jobs.[46] Again, Shamrock's concealing costume is significant, reflecting the invisibility of the working class in the public sphere,[47] and of the historical invisibility of working-class women.[48] As Marc DiPaolo noted in the introduction to this volume, wealthy superheroes such as Batman and Green Arrow or Iron Man and Black Panther are among the most recognized and well known; these millionaire superheroes are also predominantly male.

Though feminized labor is often marked as inferior,[49] each of these occupations requires special skill sets for success. Superheroes with day jobs frequently demonstrate that similar skills are needed as both superhero and successful professional: time-management and task assignments, putting the group ahead of the self, managing power, and using available resources to resolve problems.[50] Schoolteachers, bartenders, and salespersons are all considered high-communication occupations,[51] which is perhaps fitting for Molly's heritage, as conversation is central to Irish culture.[52] And Molly's ability to remake herself from hero to laborer, as needed, reflects the very real need of modern women who are alert to "the stressors associated with enacting multiple life roles"[53] in economic and personal circumstances that shape career patterns.

Bartenders possess autonomy and exclusivity over their work and uniquely act as cultural intermediaries between production and consumption using their own skills and personalities to add value to the service interaction.[54] Similarly, superheroes act as intermediaries between the citizenry and official/government-sponsored heroes.[55] Up-scale hairdressers must exercise personal task discretion as artists, while also adhering to managerial control and customer demand as salespersons,[56] just as the superhero negotiates between collective and individual needs.[57] Good teachers are thought to be inspirational models of behavior, with competencies in instruction and coaching,[58] much like superheroes represent civic virtues, modeling "right" action.[59]

While each of these occupations allowed Molly to heroically and modestly serve others, she spoke passionately only about her work as a teacher. For many working-class persons, especially women, education and child nurturance are supported as means for economic advancement and a better life.[60] Moreover, poverty among women in Ireland, and women's ability to balance paid work with child care, have been notable problems in Irish society.[61] It is therefore fitting that Molly related her call to teaching with her powers, which she believed sacred and entrusted to her for a reason by spirits who sought to end war, not perpetuate it. So, though Molly is uncomfortable with her powers, she chooses not to use them as a superhero as being the best way to fulfill their purpose of ending war. (Indeed, even as Shamrock she is rarely seen fighting unless protecting her given charges and boasts of her combatant skills only when she is a zombie.) Molly, too, believes education is the key to building a better life—an idea that is reinforced when she is entrusted with the Book of Kells so that future generations can learn of, and from, the past.

Females and Fatigue

Shamrock was put into retirement just a short fifteen years after her powers were debuted in the Contest of Champions, compared to the now seventy-five-year career of her opponent, Captain America. Given the nature of Shamrock's powers, and her non-super vocations, her early retirement could be seen as emblematic of "compassion fatigue"—the secondary traumatic stress, resulting in emotional and physical exhaustion, caused through the chronic use of empathy by those who work in trauma and caregiving professions.[62] As Blair Davis notes (in this volume), Marvel's concern for working-class politics was demonstrated through the published adventures of the empath Man-Thing. Molly Fitzgerald, through her sensitivity to poltergeists and the interpersonal skills used in her various jobs, also makes connections with empathy, victimization, and the working class, but whereas Man-Thing offered aid in behalf of his own existence, Molly offered aid at the expense of her own existence.

As a superhero, Shamrock could be classified as an emergency/trauma responder; additionally, her powers are the manifestation of tortured souls who surround her. The trauma of war, including care for its casualties, may lead to the phenomenon of compassion fatigue.[63] Shamrock's, or rather Molly's, other jobs—teacher, hairdresser, and bartender—are also part of various caregiving professions that have been linked to the experience or symptoms of compassion fatigue and professional burnout[64] that may lead to a dereliction of work responsibilities[65] and to the decision to leave a caregiving profession.[66] Emotional or spiritual fatigue is exhibited by Molly in the "Good to Be Lucky" story of *Girl Comics* #2, which takes place in her post-superhero days. As she attempts to try on her now-too-small Shamrock costume, Molly expresses depression and disillusionment regarding the direction of her life and what she perceives to be the deterioration of both her physical appearance and her social value. She refers to herself as a "sham" rather than as Shamrock, saying that her luck ran out years ago.[67] Individuals with a history of stressful lives—such as Molly's family trauma in war-torn Ireland—prior to becoming caregivers are particularly susceptible to experiencing secondary stress.[68]

Teachers must value children to make connections and thereby be effective.[69] This often involves providing care for children with emotional or behavioral disabilities.[70] The combination of life stressors, such as work, family, and relationships, with the particular demands of teaching, including the support of troubled students, compromises the health and well-being of teachers, resulting in burnout—emotional exhaustion, depersonalization, and demoralization.[71] Social support can help mitigate burnout in teachers,[72] but with her father's resentment and then the lack of resources following the Martian invasion, it is doubtful that Molly had many sources for support.

The emotional work of hairdressers is well established in research,[73] with reports suggesting that hairdressers spend an average of twenty-three hours per week conversing with fifty-five clients, often providing support for their personal problems, such as health concerns, marital discord, depression, and anxiety. Not only do clients anticipate that hairdressers will listen, offer sympathy, and suggest alternative courses of action,[74] but the community mental health movement has also sought to engage the service of hairdressers as nonprofessional caregivers.[75] Hairdressers tend to enjoy the conversational aspect of their job but are often perplexed by the problems their clients discuss,[76] which can cause in them feelings of sympathy, worry,[77] discomfort, and even helplessness.[78]

Bartenders, likewise, serve as informal helpers for their customers and are also looked to as gatekeepers and assistants in community mental health initiatives,[79] particularly in regard to preventing alcohol abuse[80] and interventions with military veterans suffering from mental health problems, such as depression and posttraumatic stress disorder.[81] Neighborhood bartenders, in particular, see the care of their customers' social and emotional needs as the most important part of their service.[82] And, as with hairdressers, serving in these informal counseling roles can make bartenders feel depressed.[83] Chronic exposure to populations that are vulnerable or suffering can cause physical, emotional, psychological, and spiritual exhaustion.[84]

For working-class women, family ideology is more important than work enjoyment, and both working- and middle-class women often make significant changes to work in order to provide care for their families.[85] We see this in Shamrock's story: When Molly's brother is killed, she leaves her teaching job in Dublin to return to her father in Dunshaughlin. With the death of her father, she takes care of the only families she has remaining. In the Earth-691 timeline, this includes forsaking adventure in favor of the children in her care as a teacher. In the Earth-616 timeline, through both her hairdressing and her bartending, she provides nurturance for her superhero friends. These various job changes reflect not only the familial ties of working-class women but also the economic realities of working-class women. Though the young Molly studied to be a teacher, her retirement from being a superhero found her working as a hairdresser and as a bartender. This is consistent with the experience of other working-class women who need to return to the workforce after retirement to supplement their income. This is particularly the case for women who have worked in low-paying jobs traditionally segregated by sex,[86] such as that of hairdresser, which is a female–dominated profession[87] often considered lowly.[88] Perhaps, then, Molly Fitzgerald returned to the superhero industry in 2014 as a S.H.I.E.L.D. agent for better pay and more respect? Moreover, her move from one caregiving role to another points to the complications caregivers have in simply abandoning that role when it becomes too difficult.[89]

Conclusion

Molly "Shamrock" Fitzgerald is one of the most fascinating superheroines to appear in the Marvel Universe. Psychically connected to a war she disavows, she stays modestly in the background when possible and takes up a feminine stance against fighting, and a maternal role of caregiving. Yet Shamrock is no wilting flower, and Molly is no "woman in a refrigerator."[90] Her character was not based on an earlier male character, and both her super and ordinary identities often succeed without the assistance or companionship of a man; even her male partner, Cuchulain, has but a belated and brief role as a sidekick before she sends him away. The interplay of Shamrock's gender, nationality, powers, and vocations is intricately revealing about the place of woman in history, modern society, international affairs, and economies of work. Though Molly does not want her powers, she accepts the responsibility of them and uses them to speak on behalf of those who have no voice—women, laborers, children, and the dead—even at the cost of her own emotional well-being. She does what must be done to help others, however great or small the task—proving that "a girl can handle this super hero business" even if she is reLUCKtant to do so.

Notes

1. Michael Gallagher, "There Is No Future—Only the Past Happening Again and Again," *Guardians of the Galaxy* #3 (New York: Marvel, 1993), 31.

2. Scott Lobdell, "The Obscurity Legion! In Second Guesses," *What The . . . ?* #9 (New York: Marvel, 1990), 25–32; Scott Lobdell, "Auld Lang Syne," *What The . . . ?* #11 (New York: Marvel, 1991), 25–32.

3. Scott Lobdell, "Shamrock in I Haven't Got Time for the Pain," *Marvel Comics Presents* #24 (New York: Marvel, 1989).

4. Mark Gruenwald, Bill Mantlo, and Steven Grant, "A Gathering of Heroes," *Marvel Super Hero Contest of Champions* #1 (New York: Marvel, 1982); Mark Gruenwald, Bill Mantlo, and Steven Grant, "Siege in the City of the Dead," *Marvel Super Hero Contest of Champions* #3 (New York: Marvel, 1982).

5. Bill Mantlo, "Everybody Loves a Parade," *Incredible Hulk* #279 (New York: Marvel, 1983).

6. Bill Mantlo, "Doomsday," *ROM* #65 (New York: Marvel, 1995).

7. Scott Lobdell, "The Global Village," *Alpha Flight* #108 (New York: Marvel, 1992).

8. Cullen Bunn, *Deadpool's Secret Wars* #1 (New York: Marvel, 2015).

9. Lobdell, "Shamrock," 19.

10. Ibid., 22.

11. Gallagher, "There Is No Future," 38.

12. Ibid.

13. Michael Gallagher, "He Who Loses Hope, May Then Part with Anything," *Guardians of the Galaxy* #51 (New York: Marvel, 1994).

14. Ben Raab, "The Old Ways," *Excalibur* #108 (New York: Marvel, 1997).

15. Kathryn Immonen, "Good to Be Lucky," *Girl Comics* #2 (New York: Marvel, 2010).

16. Victor Gischler, "Turn the Page to Find Out," *Deadpool Merc with a Mouth* #8 (New York: Marvel, 2010).

17. Cullen Bunn, *The Fearless Defenders* #9 (New York: Marvel, 2013).

18. Joe Keatinge, "Transform," *Marvel Knights Hulk* #4 (New York: Marvel, 2014).

19. Ex.: Lorraine Dowler, "'And They Think I'm Just a Nice Old Lady' Women and War in Belfast, Northern Ireland," *Gender, Place and Culture* 5, no. 2 (1998): 159–76; Jean Bethke Elshtain, *Women and War* (Chicago: University of Chicago Press, 1995); Robert B. Westbrook, "'I Want a Girl, Just Like the Girl That Married Harry James': American Women and the Problem of Political Obligation in World War II," *American Quarterly* 42, no. 4 (1990): 587–614.

20. Elshtain, *Women and War*, 4.

21. Cynthia Enloe, *Bananas, Beaches and Bases: Making Feminist Sense of International Politics* (Berkeley: University of California Press, 2014), Kindle e-book.

22. Karen E. Dill and Kathryn P. Thill, "Video Game Characters and Socialization of Gender Roles: Young People's Perceptions Mirror Sexist Media Depictions," *Sex Roles* 57 (2007): 851–64; Michael R. Lavin, "Women in Comic Books," *Serials Review* 24, no. 2 (1998): 93–100; Mike Madrid, *The Supergirls: Fashion, Feminism, Fantasy and the History of Comic Book Heroines* (n.p.: Exterminating Angel Press, 2009); Karen McGrath, "Gender, Race, and Latina Identity: An Examination of Marvel Comics' *Amazing Fantasy* & *Araña*," *Atlantic Journal of Communication* 15 (2007): 268–83; H. Leslie Steeves and Marilyn Crafton Smith, "Class and Gender in Prime-Time Television Entertainment: Observations from a Socialist Feminist Perspective," *Journal of Communication Inquiry* 11, no. 1 (1987): 43–63; Douglas Wolk, *Reading Comics: How Graphic Novels Work and What They Mean* (Cambridge: Da Capo Press, 2007).

23. Sara McDowell, "Commemorating Dead 'Men': Gendering the Past and Present in Post-Conflict Northern Ireland," *Gender, Place and Culture* 15, no. 4 (2008): 335–54.

24. Fidelma Ashe, "Gendering War and Peace: Militarized Masculinities in Northern Ireland," *Men and Masculinities* 15, no. 3 (2012): 230–48.

25. Noah Berlatsky, *Wonder Woman: Bondage and Feminism in the Marston/Peter Comics, 1941–1948* (New Brunswick: Rutgers University Press, 2015), Kindle e-book, loc. 1371–72.

26. See Pat O'Connor, "Private Troubles, Public Issues: The Irish Sociological Imagination," *Journal of Sociology* 15, no. 2 (2006): 5–22; McDowell, "Commemorating Dead 'Men.'"

27. Lavin, "Women in Comic Books."

28. Trina Robbins, *From Girls to Grrrlz: A History of ♀ Comics from Teens to Zines* (San Francisco: Chronicle Books, 1999).

29. See her entry at ComicVine.com.

30. Dowler, "And They Think."

31. Ibid.

32. Jeffrey Sconce, *Haunted Media: Electronic Presence from Telegraphy to Television*. (Durham: Duke University Press, 2000).

33. Lynnette Carpenter and Wendy K. Kolmar, "Introduction," in *Haunting the House of Fiction: Feminist Perspectives on Ghost Stories by American Women*, ed. Lynnette Carpenter and Wendy K. Kolmar (Knoxville: University of Tennessee Press, 1991), 10.

34. Fátima Regina Machado, "A New Look at Haunting and Poltergeist Phenomena: Analyzing Experiences from a Semiotic Perspective," in *Hauntings and Poltergeists: Multidisciplinary Perspectives*, ed. James Houran and Rense Lange (Jefferson, NC: McFarland, 2001), 228.

35. Danny Fingeroth, *Superman on the Couch: What Superheroes Really Tell Us about Ourselves and Our Society* (New York: Continuum, 2004).

36. Greg M. Smith, "The Superhero as Labor: The Corporate Secret Identity," in *The Contemporary Comic Book Superhero*, ed. Angela Ndalianis (New York: Routledge, 2009), 126.

37. Jeffrey A. Brown, *Black Superheroes, Milestone Comics, and Their Fans* (Jackson: University Press of Mississippi, 2001).

38. G. C. Bunn, "The Lie Detector, Wonder Woman, and Liberty: The Life and Works of William Moulton Marston," *History of Human Sciences* 10, no. 1 (1997): 91–119.

39. Smith, "Superhero as Labor."

40. Gerard Jones and Will Jacobs, *The Great Comic Book Heroes* (Rocklin, CA: Prima Publishing, 1997).

41. Smith, "Superhero as Labor."

42. Bunn, "Lie Detector"; Laura Mattoon D'Amore, "The Accidental Supermom: Superheroine and Maternal Performativity, 1963–1980," *Journal of Popular Culture* 45, no. 6 (2012): 1226–1248; Peter W. Lee, "Not Quite Mod: The New Diana Prince 1968–1973," in *The Ages of Wonder Woman: Essays on the Amazon Princess in Changing Times*, ed. Joseph J. Darowski (Jefferson, NC: McFarland, 2012), Kindle e-book, loc. 1930–2247; Christina M. Knopf and Christine M. Doran, "PTXD: Gendered Narratives of Combat, Trauma, and the Civil-Military Divide," in *The X-Men Films: A Cultural Analysis*, ed. Claudia Bucciferro (Lanham: Rowman & Littlefield, 2016), 61–73.

43. Richard Butsch, "Class and Gender in Four Decades of Television Situation Comedy: Plus ça change . . ." *Critical Studies in Mass Communication* 9 (1992): 387–99.

44. D'Amore, "Accidental Supermom."

45. Dianne Reay, "Rethinking Social Class: Qualitative Perspectives on Class and Gender," *Sociology* 32, no. 2 (1998): 259–75.

46. Valerie Kincade Oppenheimer, "The Sex-Labeling of Jobs," *Industrial Relations: A Journal of Economy and Society* 7, no. 3 (1968): 219–34.

47. See, for example, Loïc Wacquant, "Relocating Gentrification: The Working Class, Science and the State in Recent Urban Research," *International Journal of Urban and Regional Research* 32, no. 1 (2008): 198–205.

48. See, for example, Joan W. Scott, "On Language, Gender, and Working-Class History," *International Labor and Working-Class History* 31 (1987): 1–13; June Purvis, *Hard Lessons: Lives*

and Education of Working Class Women in Nineteenth Century England (Cambridge: Polity Press, 1989).

49. Butsch, "Class and Gender."

50. Smith, "Superhero as Labor."

51. John A. Daly and James C. McCroskey, "Occupational Desirability and Choice as a Function of Communication Apprehension," *Journal of Counseling Psychology* 22, no. 4 (1975): 309–313.

52. Tadhg Hayes, *Gift of the Gab* (Dublin: O'Brien Press, 2012).

53. Susan D. Phillips and Anne R. Imhoff, "Women and Career Development: A Decade of Research," *Annual Review of Psychology* 48, no. 1 (1997): 31–59.

54. Richard E. Ocejo, "At Your Service: The Meanings and Practices of Contemporary Bartenders," *European Journal of Culture* 15, no. 5 (2012): 642–58.

55. Smith, "Superhero as Labor."

56. Tracey Yeardon-Lee, Nick Jewson, Alan Felstead, Alison Fuller, and Lorna Unwin, "Bringing in the Customers: Regulation, Discretion and Customer Service Narratives in Upmarket Hair Salons," *International Journal of Interdisciplinary Social Sciences* 6, no. 3 (2011): 101–114.

57. Smith, "Superhero as Labor."

58. Fred A. J. Korthagen, "In Search of the Essence of a Good Teacher: Towards a More Holistic Approach in Teacher Education," *Teaching and Teacher Education* 20, no. 1 (2004): 77–97.

59. Jason Dittmer, *Captain America and the Nationalist Superhero* (Philadelphia: Temple University Press, 2013); Rebecca Wanzo, "The Superhero: Meditations on Surveillance, Salvation, and Desire," *Communication and Critical/Cultural Studies* 6, no. 1 (2009): 93–97.

60. Reay, "Rethinking Social Class."

61. Pat O'Connor, "Private Troubles, Public Issues: The Irish Sociological Imagination," *Journal of Sociology* 15, no. 2 (2006): 5–22.

62. Charles R. Figley, *Compassion Fatigue: Coping with Secondary Traumatic Stress Disorder in Those Who Treat the Traumatized* (Levittown, PA: Brunner/Mazel, 1995); Claire Sorenson, Beth Bolick, Karen Wright, and Rebekah Hamilton, "Understanding Compassion Fatigue in Healthcare Providers: A Review of Current Literature," *Journal of Nursing Scholarship* 48, no. 5 (2016): 456–65.

63. Della W. Stewart, "Casualties of War: Compassion Fatigue and Health Care Providers," *MEDSURG Nursing* 18, no. 2 (2009): 91–94.

64. Jason M. Newell and Gordon A. MacNeil, "Professional Burnout, Vicarious Trauma, Secondary Traumatic Stress, and Compassion Fatigue: A Review of Theoretical Terms, Risk Factors, and Preventative Methods for Clinicians and Researchers," *Best Practices in Mental Health* 6, no. 2 (2010): 57–68.

65. Michàl E. Mor Barak, Jan A. Nissly, and Amy Levin, "Antecedents to Retention and Turnover among Child Welfare, Social Work, and Other Human Service Employees: What Can We Learn from the Past Research? A Review and Metanalysis," *Social Service Review* 75, no. 4 (2001): 625–61.

66. J. Louis Spencer, Bruce E. Winston, and Mihai C. Bocarnea, "Predicting the Level of Pastors' Risk of Termination/Exit from the Church," *Pastoral Psychology* 61 (2012): 85–98.

67. Immonen, "Good to Be Lucky."

68. Sean Collins and A. Long, "Working with the Psychological Effects of Trauma: Consequences for Mental Health-Care Workers—A Literature Review," *Journal of Psychiatric and Mental Health Nursing* 10 (2013): 417–24.

69. Judith A. Deiro, *Teaching with Heart: Making Healthy Connections with Students* (Thousand Oaks, CA: Corwin Press, 1996); James G. Henderson, "Two Stories of Caring in Teaching," in *Caregiving: Readings in Knowledge, Practice, Ethics, and Politics*, ed. Suzanne Gordon, Patricia Benner, and Nel Noddings (Philadelphia: University of Pennsylvania Press, 1996), 189–202.

70. Catherine Medina and Gaye Luna, "Teacher as Caregiver: Making Meaning with Students with Emotional/Behavioral Disabilities," *Teacher Development* 3, no. 3 (1999): 449–65.

71. See discussion in Jennifer L. Fleming, Mary Mackrain, and Paul A. LeBuffe, "Caring for the Caregiver: Promoting the Resilience of Teachers," in *Handbook of Resilience in Children*, ed. Sam Goldstein and Robert B. Brooks (New York: Springer, 2013), 387–97.

72. Sandra M. Starnaman and Katherine I. Miller, "A Test of a Causal Model of Communication Burnout in the Teaching Profession," *Communication Education* 41 (1992): 40–53.

73. See the argument in Helen Holmes, "Transient Craft: Reclaiming the Contemporary Craft Worker," *Work Employment and Society* 29, no. 3 (2014): 479–95.

74. Emory L. Cowen, Ellis L. Gesten, Mary Boike, Pennie Norton, and Alice B. Wilson, "Hairdressers as Caregivers. I. A Descriptive Profile of Interpersonal Help-Giving Involvements," *American Journal of Community Psychology* 7, no. 6 (1979): 633–48.

75. Alan R. Wiesenfeld and Herbert M. Weis, "Hairdressers and Helping: Influencing the Behavior of Informal Caregivers," *Professional Psychology* 10, no. 6 (1979): 786–92.

76. Cowen et al., "Hairdressers as Caregivers."

77. Krystal M. Sattler and Frank P. Dean, "Hairdressers' Preparedness to Be Informal Helpers for Their Clients," *Journal of Community Psychology* 44, no. 6 (2016): 687–94.

78. Emory L. Cowen, Ellis L. Gesten, Edward Davidson, and Alice B. Wilson, "Hairdressers as Caregivers II: Relationships between Helper Characteristics and Helping Behaviors and Feelings," *Journal of Prevention* 1, no. 4 (1981): 225–39.

79. Raymond Bissonette, "The Bartender as a Mental Health Service Gatekeeper: A Role Analysis," *Community Mental Health Journal* 13, no. 1 (1977): 92–99.

80. Mary L. Waring and Inez Sperr, "Bartenders: An Untapped Resource for the Prevention of Alcohol Abuse?" *International Journal of the Addictions* 17, no. 5 (1982): 859–68.

81. Keith A. Anderson, Jeffrey J. Maile, and Lynette G. Fisher, "The Healing Tonic: A Pilot Study of the Perceived Ability and Potential of Bartenders," *Journal of Military and Veterans' Health* 18, no. 4 (2010): 17–24.

82. Ocejo, "At Your Service."

83. Mary L. Waring and Inez Sperr, "Female Bartenders: Their Perspectives on Bartending and Alcohol Use," *International Journal of the Addictions* 18, no. 4 (1983): 455–64.

84. Ayala Malakh-Pines and Elliot Aronson, *Career Burnout: Causes and Cures* (New York: Free Press, 1988).

85. Deborah M. Merrill, Caring for Elderly Parents: Juggling Work, Family, and Caregiving in Middle and Working Class Families (Westport, CT: Greenwood, 1997).

86. Kathleen Perkins, "Working-Class Women and Retirement," *Journal of Gerontological Work* 20, no. 3–4 (1994): 129–46.

87. Holmes, "Transient Craft."

88. Don Herzog, "The Trouble with Hairdressers," *Representations* 53 (1996): 21–43.

89. See Suzanne Gordon, "Ella," in *Caregiving: Readings in Knowledge, Practice, Ethics, and Politics*, ed. Suzanne Gordon, Patricia Benner, and Nel Noddings (Philadelphia: University of Pennsylvania Press, 1996), 173–88.

90. "Women in refrigerators" is a term used, particularly in geek feminism, in reference to women's dependence on men and the violence perpetrated against them to advance a male protagonist's storyline.

Bibliography

Anderson, Keith A., Jeffrey J. Maile, and Lynette G. Fisher. "The Healing Tonic: A Pilot Study of the Perceived Ability and Potential of Bartenders." *Journal of Military and Veterans' Health* 18, no. 4 (2010): 17–24.

Ashe, Fidelma. "Gendering War and Peace: Militarized Masculinities in Northern Ireland." *Men and Masculinities* 15, no. 3 (2012): 230–48.

Berlatsky, Noah. *Wonder Woman: Bondage and Feminism in the Marston/Peter Comics, 1941–1948*. New Brunswick: Rutgers University Press, 2015, Kindle e-book.

Bissonette, Raymond. "The Bartender as a Mental Health Service Gatekeeper: A Role Analysis." *Community Mental Health Journal* 13, no. 1 (1977): 92–99.

Brown, Jeffrey A. *Black Superheroes, Milestone Comics, and Their Fans*. University Press of Mississippi, 2001.

Bunn, G. C. "The Lie Detector, Wonder Woman, and Liberty: The Life and Works of William Moulton Marston." *History of Human Sciences* 10, no. 1 (1997): 91–119.

Butsch, Richard. "Class and Gender in Four Decades of Television Situation Comedy: Plus ça change . . ." *Critical Studies in Mass Communication* 9 (1992): 387–399.

Carpenter, Lynnette, and Wendy K. Kolmar, "Introduction." In *Haunting the House of Fiction: Feminist Perspectives on Ghost Stories by American Women*, edited by Lynnette Carpenter and Wendy K. Kolmar, 1–25. Knoxville: University of Tennessee Press, 1991.

Collins, S., and A. Long. "Working with the Psychological Effects of Trauma: Consequences for Mental Health-Care Workers—A Literature Review." *Journal of Psychiatric and Mental Health Nursing* 10 (2013): 417–24.

Cowen, Emory L., Ellis L. Gesten, Mary Boike, Pennie Norton, and Alice B. Wilson. "Hairdressers as Caregivers. I. A Descriptive Profile of Interpersonal Help-Giving Involvements." *American Journal of Community Psychology* 7, no. 6 (1979): 633–48.

Cowen, Emory L., Ellis L. Gesten, Edward Davidson, and Alice B. Wilson. "Hairdressers as Caregivers II: Relationships Between Helper Characteristics and Helping Behaviors and Feelings." *Journal of Prevention* 1, no. 4 (1981): 225–39.

Daly, John A., and James C. McCroskey, "Occupational Desirability and Choice as a Function of Communication Apprehension." *Journal of Counseling Psychology* 22, no. 4 (1975): 309–13.

D'Amore, Laura Mattoon. "The Accidental Supermom: Superheroine and Maternal Performativity, 1963–1980," *Journal of Popular Culture* 45, no. 6: 1226–48.

Deiro, Judith A. *Teaching with Heart: Making Healthy Connections with Students.* Thousand Oaks, CA: Corwin Press, 1996.

Dill, Karen E., and Kathryn P. Thill. "Video Game Characters and Socialization of Gender Roles: Young People's Perceptions Mirror Sexist Media Depictions." *Sex Roles* 57 (2007): 851–64.

Dittmer, Jason. *Captain America and the Nationalist Superhero.* Philadelphia: Temple University Press, 2013.

Dowler, Lorraine. "'And They Think I'm Just a Nice Old Lady': Women and War in Belfast, Northern Ireland." *Gender, Place and Culture* 5, no. 2 (1998): 159–76.

Elshtain, Jean Bethke. *Women and War.* Chicago: University of Chicago Press, 1995.

Enloe, Cynthia. *Bananas, Beaches and Bases: Making Feminist Sense of International Politics.* Berkeley: University of California Press, 2014. Kindle e-book.

Figley, Charles R. *Compassion Fatigue: Coping with Secondary Traumatic Stress Disorder in Those Who Treat the Traumatized.* Levittown, PA: Brunner/Mazel, 1995.

Fingeroth, Danny. *Superman on the Couch: What Superheroes Really Tell Us about Ourselves and Our Society.* New York: Continuum, 2004.

Fleming, Jennifer L., Mary Mackrain, and Paul A. LeBuffe. "Caring for the Caregiver: Promoting the Resilience of Teachers." In *Handbook of Resilience in Children,* edited by Sam Goldstein and Robert B. Brooks, 387–97. New York: Springer, 2013.

Gordon, Suzanne. "Ella." In *Caregiving: Readings in Knowledge, Practice, Ethics, and Politics,* edited by Suzanne Gordon, Patricia Benner, and Nel Noddings, 173–88. Philadelphia: University of Pennsylvania Press, 1996.

Hayes, Tadhg. *Gift of the Gab.* Dublin: O'Brien Press, 2012.

Henderson, James G. "Two Stories of Caring in Teaching." In *Caregiving: Readings in Knowledge, Practice, Ethics, and Politics,* edited by Suzanne Gordon, Patricia Benner, and Nel Noddings, 189–202. Philadelphia: University of Pennsylvania Press, 1996.

Herzog, Don. "The Trouble with Hairdressers." *Representations* 53 (1996): 21–43.

Holmes, Helen. "Transient Craft: Reclaiming the Contemporary Craft Worker." *Work Employment and Society* 29, no. 3 (2014): 479–95.

Jones, Gerard, and Will Jacobs. *The Great Comic Book Heroes.* Rocklin, CA: Prima, 1997.

Knopf, Christina M., and Christine M. Doran. "PTXD: Gendered Narratives of Combat, Trauma, and the Civil-Military Divide." In *The X-Men Films: A Cultural Analysis,* edited by Claudia Bucciferro. (Lanham: Rowman & Littlefield, 2016), 61-73Korthagen, Fred A. J. "In Search of

the Essence of a Good Teacher: Towards a More Holistic Approach in Teacher Education."
Teaching and Teacher Education 20, no. 1 (2004): 77–97.

Lavin, Michael R. "Women in Comic Books." *Serials Review* 24, no. 2 (1998): 93–100.

Lee, Peter W. "Not Quite Mod: The New Diana Prince 1968–1973." In *The Ages of Wonder Woman: Essays on the Amazon Princess in Changing Times.* edited by Joseph J. Darowski, loc. 1930–2247. Jefferson, NC: McFarland, 2012. Kindle e-book.

Machado, Fátima Regina. "A New Look at Haunting and Poltergeist Phenomena: Analyzing Experiences from a Semiotic Perspective." In *Hauntings and Poltergeists: Multidisciplinary Perspectives,* edited by James Houran and Rense Lange, 227–247. Jefferson, NC: McFarland, 2001.

Madrid, Mike. *The Supergirls: Fashion, Feminism, Fantasy and the History of Comic Book Heroines.* NP: Exterminating Angel Press, 2009.

Malakh-Pines, Ayala and Elliot Aronson, *Career Burnout: Causes and Cures.* New York: Free Press, 1988.

McDowell, Sara. "Commemorating Dead 'Men': Gendering the Past and Present in Post-Conflict Northern Ireland." *Gender, Place and Culture* 15, no. 4 (2008): 335–354.

McGrath, Karen. "Gender, Race, and Latina Identity: An Examination of Marvel Comics' *Amazing Fantasy* & *Araña.*" *Atlantic Journal of Communication* 15 (2007): 268–83.

Medina, Catherine, and Gaye Luna. "Teacher as Caregiver: Making Meaning with Students with Emotional/Behavioral Disabilities." *Teacher Development* 3, no. 3 (1999): 449–65.

Merrill, Deborah M. *Caring for Elderly Parents: Juggling Work, Family, and Caregiving in Middle and Working Class Families.* Westport: Greenwood, 1997.

Mor Barak, Michàl E., Jan A. Nissly, and Amy Levin. "Antecedents to Retention and Turnover among Child Welfare, Social Work, and Other Human Service Employees: What Can We Learn from the Past Research? A Review and Metanalysis." *Social Service Review* 75, no. 4 (2001): 625–61.

Newell, Jason M., and Gordon A. MacNeil. "Professional Burnout, Vicarious Trauma, Secondary Traumatic Stress, and Compassion Fatigue: A Review of Theoretical Terms, Risk Factors, and Preventative Methods for Clinicians and Researchers." *Best Practices in Mental Health* 6, no. 2 (2010): 57–68.

Ocejo, Richard E. "At Your Service: The Meanings and Practices of Contemporary Bartenders." *European Journal of Culture* 15, no. 5 (2012): 642–58.

O'Connor, Pat. "Private Troubles, Public Issues: The Irish Sociological Imagination." *Journal of Sociology* 15, no. 2 (2006): 5–22.

Oppenheimer, Valerie Kincade. "The Sex-Labeling of Jobs." *Industrial Relations: A Journal of Economy and Society* 7, no. 3 (1968): 219–234.

Perkins, Kathleen. "Working-Class Women and Retirement." *Journal of Gerontological Work* 20, no. 3–4 (1994): 129–46.

Phillips, Susan D., and Anne R. Imhoff. "Women and Career Development: A Decade of Research." *Annual Review of Psychology* 48, no. 1 (1997): 31–59.

Purvis, June. *Hard Lessons: Lives and Education of Working Class Women in Nineteenth Century England*. Cambridge: Polity Press, 1989.

Reay, Dianne. "Rethinking Social Class: Qualitative Perspectives on Class and Gender." *Sociology* 32, no. 2 (1998): 259–75.

Robbins, Trina. *From Girls to Grrrlz: A History of ♀ Comics from Teens to Zines*. San Francisco: Chronicle Books, 1999.

Sattler, Krystal M., and Frank P. Dean. "Hairdressers' Preparedness to be Informal Helpers for Their Clients." *Journal of Community Psychology* 44, no. 6 (2016): 687–94.

Sconce, Jeffrey. *Haunted Media: Electronic Presence from Telegraphy to Television*. Durham: Duke University Press, 2000.

Scott, Joan W. "On Language, Gender, and Working-Class History." *International Labor and Working-Class History* 31 (1987): 1–13.

Smith, Greg M. "The Superhero as Labor: The Corporate Secret Identity." In *The Contemporary Comic Book Superhero*, edited by Angela Ndalianis, 26–143. New York: Routledge, 2009.

Sorenson, Claire, Beth Bolick, Karen Wright, and Rebekah Hamilton. "Understanding Compassion Fatigue in Healthcare Providers: A Review of Current Literature." *Journal of Nursing Scholarship* 48, no. 5 (2016): 456–65.

Spencer, J. Louis, Bruce E. Winston, and Mihai C. Bocarnea. "Predicting the Level of Pastors' Risk of Termination/Exit from the Church." *Pastoral Psychology* 61 (2012): 85–98.

Starnaman. Sandra M. and Katherine I. Miller. "A Test of a Causal Model of Communication Burnout in the Teaching Profession." *Communication Education* 41 (1992): 40–53.

Steeves, H. Leslie & Marilyn Crafton Smith. "Class and Gender in Prime-Time Television Entertainment: Observations from a Socialist Feminist Perspective." *Journal of Communication Inquiry* 11, no. 1 (1987): 43–63.

Stewart, Della W. "Casualties of War: Compassion Fatigue and Health Care Providers." *MEDSURG Nursing* 18, no. 2 (2009): 91–94.

Wacquant, Loïc. "Relocating Gentrification: The Working Class, Science and the State in Recent Urban Research." *International Journal of Urban and Regional Research* 32, no. 1 (2008): 198–205.

Wanzo, Rebecca. "The Superhero: Meditations on Surveillance, Salvation, and Desire." *Communication and Critical/Cultural Studies* 6, no.1 (2009): 93–7.

Waring, Mary L. and Inez Sperr. "Bartenders: An Untapped Resource for the Prevention of Alcohol Abuse?" *The International Journal of the Addictions* 17, no. 5 (1982): 859–68.

Waring, Mary L., and Inez Sperr. "Female Bartenders: Their Perspectives on Bartending and Alcohol Use." *The International Journal of the Addictions* 18, no. 4 (1983): 455–64.

Westbrook, Robert B. "'I Want a Girl, Just Like the Girl that Married Harry James': American Women and the Problem of Political Obligation in World War II." *American Quarterly* 42, no. 4 (1990): 587–614.

Wiesenfeld, Alan R. and Herbert M. Weis. "Hairdressers and Helping: Influencing the Behavior of Informal Caregivers." *Professional Psychology* 10, no. 6 (1979): 786–92.

Wolk, Douglas. *Reading Comics: How Graphic Novels Work and What They Mean.* Cambridge: Da Capo Press, 2007.

Yeardon-Lee, Tracey, Nick Jewson, Alan Felstead, Alison Fuller, and Lorna Unwin. "Bringing in the Customers: Regulation, Discretion and Customer Service Narratives in Upmarket Hair Salons." *International Journal of Interdisciplinary Social Sciences* 6, no. 3 (2011): 101–114.

THE WORKING CLASS PI (AKA JESSICA JONES)
Alias as a Narrative of Quiet Desperation

Terrence R. Wandtke

When *Alias* was first published (introducing Marvel's MAX imprint in 2001), Jessica Jones's debut in the Marvel superhero universe was notable for several reasons. She is a private investigator who is struggling to make ends meet, and even though she has superpowers, Jones chooses to no longer use them as a superhero. In addition, her superheroic past (wholly invented for the series) is known and shared by many of the major players in the Marvel superhero universe—or at least many of the major players as they exist in the R-rated version of the Marvel superhero universe presented within the various MAX series. With this description in place, the general complexity and metatextual slipperiness of *Alias*, written by Brian Michael Bendis and illustrated by Michael Gaydos, should be apparent. And quite notably, this retcon of Marvel through a supposedly preexistent character in a more obscene version of their superhero world was readily welcomed by the publisher, critics, and reading audience. One possible explanation for its success is that Jones's story is simultaneously made a familiar and an unfamiliar experience by forcefully reinstituting the working-class origins of Marvel superheroes; Bendis and Gaydos rework the superhero crime story by situating a woman in the working-class role and rejecting typical means of coping with trauma within the grim and gritty superhero power fantasy. After reviewing the working-class origins of Marvel superheroes, this essay examines the way that the working class are represented as second-class citizens metaphorically through the life of Jessica Jones, a character invented as a former member of the superhero B-list. Then it shows how Jones's depiction as a woman exposes the typical limitations in content and in form of the currently gentrified genres of superhero stories and crime fiction. And ultimately, this discussion leads to a critique of the Netflix series *Jessica Jones*, which fails to realize the working-class narrative of quiet desperation so well depicted in *Alias*.

Jessica Jones as a Working-Class Superhero Antihero

In American history, working-class literature (loosely defined as "writing by and about America's working people"[1]) has existed for hundreds of years. However, this type of literature has often been known only by a limited few, held in low regard by purveyors of high culture, and even suppressed by political powers that find such stories threatening.[2] Due to the workers' movements of the 1930s, this literature was recovered, produced, and consumed to a much greater extent; concomitantly, more affordable means of producing literary entertainment led to pulp fiction magazines and comic books tailored for an increasingly literate working-class population. In 1938 Superman would make an indelible impact on the comic book world (and the rest of the media world) as a costumed superhuman crime fighter whose alter ego was a mild-mannered reporter. While Superman certainly represented a wish fulfillment of many stuck in their working-class roles,[3] he had autonomy even as Clark Kent that many in the working class didn't enjoy. And the publishing company later known as DC, and its superhero titles, didn't demonstrate a consistent interest in the particular state of the working class.[4] But due to the social changes and political movements of the 1960s, working-class literature would again have a notable presence[5] and would gain a more forceful voice in the superhero world through the superheroes of Marvel comic books. From the Fantastic Four failing to pay the rent on the Baxter Building to Peter Parker selling photos to the reprehensible J. Jonah Jameson to help his aunt make ends meet,[6] Stan Lee's liberal leanings caused him to consistently deal with working-class issues.[7] This would continue within Marvel comics over the years with Archie Goodwin's Luke Cage as a "hero for hire" in the 1970s and Frank Miller's Daredevil as a superhero fighting a system distorted by the rich and powerful in the 1980s. In many ways, *Alias* is part of this focus seen often in the Marvel superhero universe.

Before coming to Marvel and making a splash with his work on *Ultimate Spider-Man* in 2000, Brian Michael Bendis was known for titles such as *AKA Goldfish* and *Jinx*, put out by the small publisher Caliber Comics. Stories of a small-time con artist and a bounty hunter, respectively, they made the financial desperation of the characters central to dialogue-heavy, character-driven drama. After spending a year at Marvel, Bendis pitched a story idea for a B-list superhero to Bill Jemas in the form of a play with profanity characteristic of Bendis's independent comics. To Bendis's surprise, Jemas liked the gritty honesty of the script and developed the idea of the MAX line (an adult imprint taking place in the Marvel superhero universe but featuring language, violence, and sexual content consistent with an R-rating in film).[8] And Bendis's *Alias* would be the flagship title for the MAX line, inaugurating this new orientation to content with the word "Fuck!" yelled by one of Jessica Jones's clients in the first panel.[9] The opening sequence represents Jones as a private investigator and part of the working class dealing with the problems of delivering bad news to her client. And the series as a whole represents the struggles of working-class life in a complex superhero/crime story synthesis with content likely considered profane by readers who have the luxury to be part of high culture.

In contrast with superhero traditions where the openness of a cityscape is presented at the start, the Alias Investigations office is claustrophobic and dingy. In contrast with crime story traditions where the private investigator offers evidence against a cheating wife, Jones tells her client that his wife is a mutant. The husband angrily complains, "How can a person marry another person and live a life like us and—and—and—and not say something?" Jones snuffs out her cigarette and says plainly, "We live in complicated times."[10] When he tries to deal with his frustration by attacking Jones, she easily throws him through the window of her office door (indicating to the reader that she may be more than just a private detective in the Marvel Universe). Rendered realistically by Michael Gaydos, the sequence is colored by Matt Hollingsworth almost entirely in browns and greys, in contrast the primary colors associated with superheroes before the late twentieth century. However, when the police arrive, they notice photos on the wall (showcased in individual panels) depicting Jones's past as the superhero called Jewel. They feature her with members of the Avengers and are rendered in a traditionally vibrant comic book color scheme in stark contrast with Jones's office and world. With Jones's past completely invented for *Alias*, the series begins with not only her past but the Marvel Universe's past as something real only in ways enabled by a nostalgic imagination. In other words, even the working-class past of the Silver Age Marvel Universe is rose-colored in comparison to the working-class present of Jones.

The "reality" of her working class is articulated by Jones in her conversation with the police, who wonder why she'd leave behind her life as a superhero (as if her life as a superhero was viable as a career choice). One officer says, "But you do this shit instead?" she replies, "Girl's gotta eat,"[11] reflecting a material reality often neglected in a standard superhero narrative. The use of profanity, frank presentation of sex, and graphic depiction of violence not only disassociate *Alias* from Comics Code superhero comic books safe for the public

The bleaker color palette of the world depicted in *Alias* works in contrast to a photograph that comically represents Jessica Jones's past as a superhero. Brian Michael Bendis and Michael Gaydos, *Alias* (New York: Marvel Comics, 2003), 6.

but also suggest a harsher, more realistic sense of life in the working class. And Jones's life has many traditional markers of working-class life drawn from other media depictions of limited means, including rumpled clothes, modest accommodations, and limited financial resources that mean taking seedy cases she doesn't want. Those unwanted cases notably include various types of surveillance, including a case where she tracks a husband attempting to meet with gay men via Internet chat rooms. Since a "girl's gotta eat," Jones doesn't seem to have the luxury of choosing a more noble route in life, as superheroes regularly do with little thought of the financial implications.[12] The psychological consequences of these limited opportunities are represented in Jones's excessive drinking and her impulsive sexual behavior (in fact, the back cover of the first trade paperback in the *Alias* series describes her as "a chain-smoking, self-destructive alcoholic with a mean inferiority complex").[13] After getting drunk in Luke Cage's bar, she sleeps with the "hero for hire" with the sole goal of escaping a life that seems to deaden her to everything she would like to be: "I don't care what he feels like. I just want to feel something. It doesn't matter what. Pain. Humility. Anger."[14]

Jones knows that Cage is also Power Man and remains connected to the superhero world (Carol Danvers a.k.a. Ms. Marvel is Jones's best friend, and Scott Lang a.k.a. Ant Man becomes her boyfriend). It becomes apparent that Jones chooses her exile from the superhero world for reasons that remain undisclosed for much of the series. However, while almost no one understands her rejection of a career as a costumed crime fighter, other cases make that rejection understandable to the reader. Whether accidentally or purposefully determined by the cases she takes, Jones regularly works in the darkest corners of the Marvel Universe, where superheroes are exploited as celebrities, humans are persecuted as mutants, and super-powered people exchange their super-powered blood for drugs. Clearly, the lack of autonomy that Jones feels is a regular part of the superhero's cultural landscape, especially within the MAX version of the Marvel Universe. Moreover, Jones's attitude toward her life as a superhero is most directly represented by her conversation with Steve Rogers a.k.a. Captain America; he says, "Why don't you do it anymore? . . . I never met anyone who—I just really want to know," and she responds, "Because it became very clear I could never be you."[15] In this way, the stratification of the superhero world becomes more apparent, and her identity as a B-list superhero serves as a metaphor for her pronounced second-tier, working-class status.[16]

When Jones takes a job from a girl desperate to find Rick Jones (a non-powered sidekick to the Hulk, Captain America, and the Avengers), she reads his bargain-bin biography. She deeply identifies with his bystander life of commenting on others who actually have the power to change things, and she tells him so when she finds him. However, despite the fact that the quiet desperation created by her second-tier experience is common, it is a shame that cannot be eased in this sharing; the Rick Jones she was employed to find turns out to be a pretender, someone who aspires to be famous even if only by false association. The final story arc of the series accentuates her second-tier status and portrays her as previously having a crush on her high school classmate Peter Parker. Of course, Parker is subject to scorn from his high school peers and initially decides to use his super-powers to make money; however, he later becomes an A-list superhero and member of the Avengers.

Jessica Jones as a Hard-Boiled Antihero in a Man's World

As noted, *Alias* owes almost as much to crime story pulps as it does to super-hero comics (and accentuates and subverts their traditions as well). Roughly coinciding with the rise of superhero comics, the hard-boiled detective story worked with a similar audience. With pulps like *Black Mask*, writers like Dashiell Hammett had the opportunity to rework the genteel tradition of the parlor room murder mystery.[17] Plucked from his comfortable position of often undefined economic independence, a detective like Sherlock Holmes became the private investigator who had to take cases regardless of his moral leanings. And with a private investigator like Sam Spade working against corrupt police to solve mysteries for corrupt clients, the hard-boiled detective represented the rejection of Enlightenment hope for orderly society. Instead, hard-boiled detective fiction represents the cynical fears of a post-Depression era through a private investigator who had no faith in the American dream.[18] While myster-ies might be solved, the hard-boiled detective merely keeps the chaos at bay, a loner in the mass of humankind longing for power to change things in the face of an oppressive world.[19] This pulp sensibility can be clearly seen in superhero comics with Batman, debuting in *Detective Comics*, a non-powered superhero fighting against a corrupt world of both gangsters and supernatural threats. Before Frank Miller would fully restore Batman's hard-boiled ethos, undone by WWII patriotism and the Comics Code, he would bring the crime story worldview to Marvel Comics through his work on *Daredevil* in the early 1980s. Understood as doing pioneering work in the grim and gritty superhero trend, Miller brought the works of Raymond Chandler and Mickey Spillane to bear on superhero comics.[20] As a costumed crime fighter, Daredevil was somewhat like the hard-boiled detective, ignoring the laws he pledged to obey in his other life as lawyer Matt Murdock, fighting a corrupt system on the fringes, but never reaching the Kingpin, the crime lord behind it all.

Bendis would write *Daredevil* at the same time he wrote *Alias*, but of course Bendis would take the superhero/crime story synthesis a step further in *Alias*;[21] rather than *be like* the hard-boiled detective, Jessica Jones would leave behind her superheroism and *be* the hard-boiled detective. Taking his lead from Marvel tropes that feature J. Jonah Jameson persecuting Spider-Man and human beings ready to hunt mutants at a moment's notice, Bendis fills the world of *Alias* with questionable authority figures and a general populace often unaware of the consequences of their own self-interests. Contempt for authority is an integral part of Jones's character, set at odds with the police from the very first scene. When subsequently interrogated by the police regarding the murder of a woman she was hired to follow, she is not so subtly accused of the murder on a flimsy pretext; she replies with belligerent indignation: "Is that what you're accusing me of, you asshole man? Is that your theory? Why? Because I don't like wearing a God damn costume . . . Well, fuck you directly then." While she is often forced by her economic situation to take on work that is disagreeable, her suspicion of the moral authority of the powerful who sometimes hire her works against her economic advantage. When hired to track the woman who is later murdered, she first tracks her to the home of Steve Rogers, whom she inadvertently photographs changing into his costumed identity as Captain America. Determining that the case was meant to lead her to that discovery, she refuses to sell Captain America's identity as the politician behind it all hopes. With a hard-boiled mix of morality and resentment for the powers that be, Jones fulfills the expectations placed on the detective who regularly inspires contemporary superhero and crime comics. As Frank Miller states, "The noir hero is a knight in blood caked armor. He's dirty and he does his best to deny the fact that he's a hero the whole time."[22]

Of course, Miller's statement highlights the male identity of the noir hero by calling the noir hero a knight and repeatedly using masculine pronouns. This orientation toward the noir hero as a man developed at the inception of hard-boiled detective fiction and its cinematic counterpart, film noir. When the post-Depression culture lost faith in the hopeful future of the American dream, concerns about individualism made their way to the forefront, and this general anxiety is organized in patriarchal terms in the 1930s and '40s. Erin Smith states, "The rise of consumer capitalism, the erosion of all-male work and leisure spaces, and disappearance of skilled, autonomous work forced white, working-class men to renegotiate the sources of their gender, class, and professional identities."[23] Since the standard method for the noir hero to order the disorder is to resist a sense of powerlessness before monolithic social systems, resistance means that he must insist on some sort of individual identity: male identity defined relative to women. Women who aid in this male quest are the relatively powerless and loyal secretary, girlfriend, or wife; and women who thwart this quest are the relatively powerful and seductive temptress, better known as the *femme fatale*. As described by Mary Ann Doane, "The *femme fatale* is an articulation of fears surrounding the loss of stability and centrality of the self, the 'I.'"[24] This dichotomy has existed in literature within many patriarchal cultural contexts, including comics featuring the good girl and the *femme fatale* with characters like Batman (Julie Madison versus Selina Kyle as Catwoman) and Spider-Man (Gwen Stacey versus Felicia Hardy as the Black Cat). Within the superhero world, the femme fatale's duplicity is regularly represented by the costume worn by the other woman in a superhero's life. This approach to a working-class story limits its applicability to the working class in significant ways.

In addition to taking on the occupation of private eye (reserved for men in classic hard-boiled detective fiction), Jones doesn't simply assume a male role and perform the same type of noir story like a character in drag.[25] In particular regard to her sexuality, *Alias* reverses the expectations placed on the story, undermines the contemporary nostalgia for crime fiction, and causes this crime story to be more broadly subversive. *Alias* exposes the connection between mainstream understandings of the working class and understandings of gender and sexuality; as asserted by Nicholas Coles and Janet Zandy, "class as a shaping force is inseparable from other markers of identity: gender, sexuality, race, region, and ethnicity."[26] In terms of Jones's visual presentation, *Alias* resists what Laura Mulvey describes as the "to-be-looked-at-ness" of women in films of the 1930s, '40s, and beyond.[27] Both the good girl and the femme fatale of film noir have a glamour that separates them from the economic limitations that leave the hard-boiled detective in a rumpled trench coat. Moreover, the femme fatale encourages the male gaze that objectifies her, because she uses her body in order to seduce men. While this may subvert the power of the gaze to some extent, the femme fatale is almost always punished for the power she gains by manipulating patriarchal desire.

Similarly, the supposedly powerful female crime fighters of superhero comics not only are subjected to a leering male gaze but become a semipornographic male fantasy through their impractical costumes. Jones resists the expectations placed on women as objects in both hard-boiled detective and superhero stories. Throughout the series, her fashion choices remain consistently unglamorous and do not reveal her body; she is seen most often in baggy clothes and flat shoes that reinforce the practical necessities of her work. Splash pages are typically used to present a woman's to-be-looked-at-ness but in *Alias* have contrary goals. For instance, Jones covers herself up with some regret after her night with Luke Cage, and if any figure on that splash page is sexualized, it is Cage. Later, as Jones mulls over the details of a case, a splash page features her with her pants down, but not sexually, as she sits on the toilet. When she dresses in more typically revealing attire for women, to enter a club, she mutters, "God forgive me for what I'm about to do," and spends part of her time in the club complaining about the club culture that encourages women to dress that way. And, of course, she has left her skin-tight superhero costume behind long before the series begins.

Further, by taking control of her sex life, Jones demonstrates the potential of her character to rewrite the dichotomous model typically applied to women. Jones is sexually active and initiates sexual encounters with the men in her life, like Luke Cage and Scott Lang. In this way, she has the same power that is often limited to men within hard-boiled detective and superhero stories. While she is sometimes drunk when doing so, she moves beyond the stereotype of the slut, because the story is hers and her character is sympathetic. The extensive first-person narration typical in hard-boiled detective fiction not only prevents her from becoming an object but clearly establishes her control over the story of *Alias*. And when there are scenes of Jones in the bedroom, they are vehicles to further explore her character. When she first sleeps with Luke Cage, the focus remains on her face and the narration that represents her thoughts. And her pleasure is not a certain end result of every sexual liaison with a man, as represented one particular time with Scott Lang. When in bed together, she interrupts their physical encounter because she is distracted by other things that took place that day. This leads to a conversation that stretches over the course of two issues and culminates in a moment that reminds her of a traumatic moment in her life. When she says she doesn't want to talk about it, Lang ventures, "Were you raped?" She yells, "No!! Why would you ask that? ... Such a guy thing to say!! A girl has a secret in her past—she must have been raped!"[28] Lang tries to put a woman who has been victimized into a specific role as a sexual victim, and Jones asserts that female experience (including the experience of trauma) is much more multifaceted than he suggests.

The most important way that *Alias* rewrites hard-boiled detective fiction with a woman as a private investigator is that Jones becomes pregnant and decides to keep the child. With plans to keep the child and share in the responsibilities of raising it with the father, Luke Cage, she moves further beyond the roles of hard-boiled detective, good girlfriend, and femme fatale. The role she develops for herself is crucially important, as her choice serves as a central part of her coping with the trauma that has shaped her life and something that makes the typical superhero power fantasy less relevant. An illegitimate pregnancy, stereotypically a shameful class-lowering fall from grace reserved for women, serves as an opportunity and a reorientation within her life. This radical rewriting of the hard-boiled detective story comes not from simply

Depictions of Jessica Jones generally defy the typical expectations for splash-page presentations of women in superhero comic books. Brian Michael Bendis and Michael Gaydos, *Alias* (New York: Marvel Comics, 2003), 136.

blending crime fiction with the superhero story but from the transformation of expectations placed upon a woman. Classic crime fiction and superhero stories once available in pulp magazines and comic books have become something quite different in an era when classic fiction is bound in respectable hardcover editions and superhero stories printed on high-quality paper and collected as graphic novels. Pulp fiction no longer serves a social function for the working class, as classic crime stories have now become enshrined as great literature.[29] Now the vigilante outsiders of these stories are respected as significant literary figures and regarded with excessive nostalgia with its sexism enshrined in contemporary forms such as Frank Miller's *Sin City*. The rewriting of the private eye as a profane ex-superhero who keeps her "illegitimate" child keeps the sexist clichés of crime fiction and superhero stories from becoming rarified truth of literature that has stood the test of time.

Jessica Jones in and out of a Postmodern Comic Book World

If part of the project of *Alias* is to self-consciously question class and gender limitations of the superhero story, placing Jones in the role of a female ex-superhero in the Marvel Universe offers great opportunities for parody. For instance, in the first panel of a conversation with Carol Danvers, Jones makes comments that evoke common knowledge about Spider-Man (endowed with spider powers): "So I said to him, I said, well, if that's true shouldn't you shoot the webs out of your ass?"[30] Later in the series, she takes a meeting that goes beyond Jones poking fun at the Marvel Universe. The meeting is with Lord Kevin Plunder, better known as Ka-Zar, jungle warrior of the Savage Land, in need of her services because Zabu, his saber-toothed tiger, has gone missing. She rejects the job in no uncertain terms: "Dude, no offense, but I don't even go over the Queensborough Bridge because I'm scared that Green Goblin might drop someone on me. So there's, basically, no way in hell I am going into the jungle to fight dinosaurs because you lost your cat."[31] Even though Jones avoids the case, its absurdity threatens the gritty realism her occupation has brought to the Marvel Universe. However, this is hardly unprecedented, and that has been the enduring problem with Stan Lee's working-class heroes in frequent science-fiction scenarios that threaten the entire world. Archie Goodwin's Luke Cage would further Lee's working-class concerns as a hero for hire, but, as a character drawn from the limitations of Blaxploitation films and placed into a world of Marvel supervillains, his stories quickly veer from the harsh realities of life as a black man in the 1970s with Steve Englehart. In issues #8 and #9 of the series' original run, none other than Dr. Doom hires Cage and fails to pay for services rendered; consequently, Cage borrows rocket transportation from Mr. Fantastic to travel to Latveria to collect.

Alias doesn't walk a careful line between realism and absurdity but systematically exposes the Marvel Universe's absurdity for the reader. From the start, Jones's heavy narration acknowledges another frame of reference by presenting her story for the sake of an audience: "I know. You're thinking what was the point of that little interaction? Well, listen, in my travels through this steaming shitworld I have found . . ."[32] In the very first scene, the picture of herself on the wall with the Avengers not only presents a brightly colored world in contrast with Michael Gaydos's film noir style: it depicts Jewel surrounded by A-list male superheroes who have their heads cut off by the photographer in order to center the much shorter Jones: an intentionally humorous depiction of her second-class status. And less than halfway through the series, Jones has a dream of herself as Jewel rendered in an artistic style that departs from *Alias*'s bleak realism with images colorful, sleek, and in line with a style typical in 1990s superhero comics (drawn by Mark Bagley).[33] This contrast sets off the final story arc of the series, "The Secret Origins of Jessica Jones," poking holes in the pretense of the reality seemingly rendered by the crime fiction edge of this superhero series. Jones's origin story begins "fifteen years ago" with the famous splash page image from the first page of the *Amazing Fantasy* Spider-Man origin story in the brighter colors of Silver Age comics and blending Steve Ditko's style with that of Michael Gaydos. Shifting from Peter Parker's ridicule on the first page to Jones's moon-eyed love for him on the next, Jones makes plans to profess her love for Parker at the science exhibit. Unfortunately, his weak-kneed reaction to a radioactive spider bite prevents her from doing so, and as she leaves she is narrowly saved from being hit by a truck labeled "Ajax-Atomic Radio-Active Materials: Danger." After using over-the-top humor to expose the workings of the origin story in which an unlikely hero is endowed with powers by a technological accident, Jones's story continues in a way tonally more consistent with the gritty realism of the series as a whole. Her younger brother catches her masturbating with a poster of Johnny Storm and teases her the next day as the family drives down the highway. When her father tries to stop their argument, he careens into an army truck (carrying "hazardous experimental material," of course), and everyone in the family except for Jones dies in the horrible car crash.

However, as important to her identity as this initial trauma might be, the subsequent part of life as a superhero that she shares with Luke Cage is more important as a rejection of the notion that the superhero's life is a means to overcome the trauma of one's origin. Instead, her life as a superhero led to a greater trauma. During her time as the superhero Jewel, she was mentally controlled by Killgrave, the Purple Man, and served his whims for eight months. However, with wild oscillation between dramatic character development and parody, the flashback to these harrowing events is again drawn by Mark Bagley in a 1990s style (and written with the exaggerated prose of an earlier time). On a splash page that enthusiastically recaps her origin in a short paragraph for a story titled, "Purple Haze," a smiling pink-haired Jewel flies through the skies and says: "I tell ya, thank goodness for flying! It gives me a minute to stop thinking about looking for a job or the fact that I just can't find a boyfriend. What's a girl got to do in this town to find a decent guy?"[34] And when the family of Killgrave victims contacts Jones to help determine the ultimate fate of their loved ones, Jones's story is kept from being an embrace of comic book tropes (including those in *Alias*) by clearly exposing them. Killgrave greets her from his prison cell as his "favorite comic book character of all time"[35] and describes the time they share in terms of the way that it's being presented: "So, this is Jessica's comic book. Subtle yet expressive artwork. Mainstream with just a touch of indy. Powerful color palette. (Interesting.) Seen worse. Been in worse. . . . You're annoying me already and it's only page one."[36] Pushing the reader out of the story is a curious practice for a series that grounds Jones with relatively realistic personal and economic struggles. Of course, "relatively realistic" is a key phrase, as Bendis's aesthetically fragmented, postmodern approach demonstrates the absurdity of a working-class female ex-superhero who happens to now be a private investigator in the Marvel Universe.

However, as Linda Hutcheon argues in characterization of parody in a postmodern era, parody need not be a cynical end in itself that completely rejects the world portrayed.[37] Instead, parody can be a systematic questioning of all ideologies, including those that represent the struggles of a working-class woman in a world of privileged (super)men, in order to acknowledge 1) limitations of the source material and 2) limitations of reboots that co-opt that source material. And while this may question the absolute reality of the situation, parody gives some integrity to a story willing to acknowledge its own problems. If *Alias* worked with the male power fantasy that drives most superhero comic books, her secondary trauma should be rectified by a call back to action. When Killgrave escapes from prison, it plays into expectations for the power fantasy in which the superhero is restored through the use of violence to punish the wrongdoer. However, since the full exposure of comic book conventions makes it so clearly expected, Jones's big punch that brings to an end Killgrave's new reign of terror seems less significant than her realization that she doesn't need to let external forces (like this man's mind control) shape her. The series itself is less a search for justice and/or revenge and more a picaresque journey on which Jones makes or breaks relationships in the Marvel Universe. This adds significance to an ending far beyond the conventions of the superhero story

When Jessica Jones relates the significant trauma of her life as a superhero, the flashback is represented in notably different narrative and artistic styles. Brian Michael Bendis and Mark Bagley, *Alias: The Secret Origins of Jessica Jones* (New York: Marvel Comics, 2004), 78.

and crime fiction, where Jones sits on the stoop of an apartment building and tells Cage she wants to keep their baby. And he acknowledges the integrity of this moment by using a phrase that acknowledges their constructed sense of themselves: "Okay then. New chapter."[38] The "secret origins" of the arc's title is used rather than "secret origin" because more than one trauma is presented, and because her story is presented in more than one way in terms of narrative and artistic styles. However, more significant is the fact that the arc presents the secret origins of Jessica Jones, rather than the secret origins of Jewel, as the goal is to understand this working-class woman as fully as the comic book will allow.

Jessica Jones out of a Comic Book and under Another Alias

In a letter that accompanies the last issue of *Alias*, Bendis explains that he will pursue other projects but also continue Jessica Jones's story in a main-stream Marvel title involving the Daily Bugle Staff called *The Pulse*: "I like say-ing 'fuck' a lot (some say too fucking much); the big eff word was stifling a couple of things I wanted to do with Jessica—like using Spider-Man and some other big name Marvel guest stars."[39] Bendis's choice to pursue work with A-list Marvel superheroes is a bit ironic, considering the focus of *Alias*. And unfortunately, the clean-mouthed Jones in the ensemble cast is at best a middle ground between *Alias* and more conventional superhero fare.[40] The co-opting of Jones by the mainstream Marvel Universe becomes complete in the first *New Avengers* annual as Jones (drawn with big-breasted glamour) dons a white dress and marries Luke Cage in a wedding attended by an array of superhero guests.[41] Nevertheless, fans of *Alias* were hopeful with the 2010 announcement of a television series called *AKA Jessica Jones* to be developed for ABC (mak-ing her the first superhero created after the 1970s and the first female to have a solo showcase in the Marvel Cinematic Universe). Although ultimately not produced for ABC, Jessica Jones became one of four superheroes to have their own television series in Marvel's venture with Netflix. Adding to the previous hopes, *Daredevil*, the first of those Netflix series featuring a Marvel character, is more character-driven, notably darker in theme and explicit in content than anything else in Marvel's lineup (a film equivalent to the MAX imprint). *Jessica Jones* doesn't shy away from content such as sex, violence, and profanity (even though it doesn't use one of Bendis's favorite words in any way). Taking place in a New York City whose crime wave was enabled by the Avengers' battle to save the world, Jones's story begins with a scene in which she throws an angry client through her office window. In addition to this literal correspondence, Jones is quite clearly a working-class private eye, living in low-rent surroundings, broken by her experiences, and drinking far too much.

However, her experiences don't remain in the past, as her very next case brings Killgrave back into her life, and the remainder of the first season is dominated by her search for Killgrave in order to save his latest mind control victim from a life in prison. Despite her seeming lack of resources, she works only infrequently and seems to have the financial means to embark on this heroic quest. And the first season ends with her killing Killgrave, a much more conventional superhero road to redemption for this sour but generally heroic character. Consequently, the series makes overtures to her identity as a working-class woman but quickly leaves this behind and fails to approach the radical ideas of the comic book. Since the television series is shaped by the realism of the relatively young Marvel Cinematic Universe, it doesn't emulate Bendis's postmodern approach (incorporating different narrative and artistic styles for parodic effect). Concomitantly, it remains within a relatively affirming plot structure driven by the need to stop a sinister villain (albeit with some significant detours to spend time with Killgrave's surviving victims).[42] *Alias* spends most of its time with cases unrelated to Killgrave but still important to Jones's character development. This previously mentioned narrative meandering is seen to some extent in hard-boiled detective fiction: clues for one case are discovered when working another case, real cases develop from false leads, and minor details are never resolved. Serving as a working-class critique of the American Dream in which everything is purposeful and leads to a grand resolution, these stories offer a narrative full of quiet desperation drawn from a look at the life of a hard-boiled detective. While Jones seems desperate at a superficial level in *Jessica Jones*, her story is one of heroism that results in the greater good of a world without Killgrave (and a world in which Jones is famous and the phone at Alias Investigations rings off the hook).

Since the situation of the current Marvel Cinematic Universe is quite different than that in the comic books, it may be unfair to judge *Jessica Jones* too harshly. In addition to the smaller number of characters in play (and their community being much less open), the Marvel comic book universe has been around for over fifty years and in that time has gone through many reboots and seen much work done with retroactive continuity. Consequently, Bill Jemas may understand his long-term readers as being much more open to narrative experiments than Kevin Feige (president of Marvel Studios) may understand his newly acquired viewers to be, especially in a very high-stakes market. Regardless, the narrative and artistic experimentation of *Alias* creates a space where the story of a working-class woman is not co-opted by conventional expectations. Through the layering of the stories about the superhero, hard-boiled detective, and working-class woman, the reader is encouraged to be self-conscious about tropes of familiar stories about independent men who live beyond material concerns; in turn, the reader is encouraged to be interested in something rarely seen, such as Jessica Jones on a city stoop declaring, "I'm pregnant. And . . . [I want it.] Very, very, very much."[43]

Notes

1. Nicholas Coles and Janet Zandy, "Introduction," *American Working Class Literature: An Anthology*, ed. Nicholas Coles and Janet Zandy (New York: Oxford University Press, 2007), xv.

2. Ibid., xix.

3. Bradford W. Wright, *Comic Book Nation: The Transformation of Youth Culture in America* (Baltimore: Johns Hopkins University Press, 2001), 10.

4. Ibid., 61.

5. Coles and Zandy, "Introduction," xix.

6. Wright, *Comic Book Nation*, 211.

7. Also see Salvatore Mondello, "Spider-Man: Superhero in the Liberal Tradition," *Journal of Popular Culture* 10 (Summer 1976): 232–38.

8. The development of *Alias* is recounted by Bendis in his interview by Arnold Blumberg, "AKA Bendis," *Jinxworld*, last modified September 4, 2001, http://www.jinxworld.com/interviews /cinescape/cinescape08-04-01.htm. . In John Parker's retrospective review of *Alias*, he adds that Bendis's original intention was to use Spider-Woman as the main character ("'Alias' Jessica Jones: A Critical Look Back at Marvel's Mature Readers Hero and New Netflix Star," *Comics Alliance*, last modified November 5, 2014, http://comicsalliance.com/alias-omnibus-review/).

9. Although part of a work-for-hire corporation that owned all of his artistic work, this situation placed Bendis in this liminal space between being a worker subject to company demands and an artist able to influence his world.

10. Brian Michael Bendis and Michael Gaydos, *Alias* (New York: Marvel Comics, 2003), 3.

11. Ibid., 6–7.

12. Blumberg acknowledges the material needs of her life as an ex-superhero in a negative way in Blumberg, "AKA Bendis": "[H]er life took a downward turn that found her resorting to work as a private investigator to pay the bills."

13. Bendis and Gaydos, *Alias*, back cover.

14. Ibid., 12. Controversy over this scene's supposed portrayal of anal sex led Marvel to seek a different printer, as noted in "AKA Bendis." In addition, criticism that this scene implied that Jones wanted to dehumanize herself by having sex with a black man was redeployed in Paul Morton, "An Interview with Brian Michael Bendis," *Bookslut*, last modified February 2009, http: //www.bookslut.com/features/2009_02_014023.php.

15. Bendis Gaydos, *Alias*, 107–8.

16. Bendis states, "I guess what I'm more fascinated with, in the case of Jessica, is someone deciding that she could never be A-list. That decision and what that world is. It's fun to watch Cap, but what about the person who could never be Captain America?" (Michael Dean, "The Brian Michael Bendis Interview," *Comics Journal* 266 (Feb./Mar. 2005): 113.)

17., Erin A. Smith, *Hard-Boiled: Working Class Readers and Pulp Magazines* (Philadelphia: Temple University Press, 2000), 37–38.

18. Coles and Zandy note, "America . . . is often viewed in 'exceptionalist' terms as a land of possibility. Work hard and you will succeed. While it is true that America has produced some rags-to-riches success stories . . . , the larger historical picture is more complicated and less sanguine" ("Introduction," xxi).

19. Alain Silver and Elizabeth Ward, *Film Noir* (New York: Overlook, 1992), 2.

20. Milo George, *Frank Miller: The Interviews: 1981–2003* (Seattle: Fantagraphics, 2003), 83.

21. *Daredevil* was then part of the "Marvel Knights" lineup of titles, in content somewhere between the mainstream Marvel Universe and the MAX Marvel Universe (all three overlapping in a strange way).

22. George, *Frank Miller*, 111.

23. Smith, *Hard-Boiled*, 12.

24. Mary Ann Doane, *Femmes Fatales* (New York: Routledge, 1991), 2.

25. Beginning in the 1980s, contemporary crime fiction features women more often as private investigators in stories with hard-boiled trappings like those of Sara Paretsky (with V. I. Warshawski) and Sue Grafton (with Kinsey Millhone).

26. Coles and Zandy, "Introduction," xx.

27. Laura Mulvey, "Visual Pleasure and Narrative Cinema," *Feminism and Film Theory*, ed. Constance Penley (New York: Routledge, 1988).

28. Brian Michael Bendis and Michael Gaydos, *Alias: The Underneath* (New York: Marvel Comics, 2003), 66–67.

29. Smith, *Hard-Boiled*, 2.

30. Bendis and Gaydos, *Alias*, 110.

31. Brian Michael Bendis and Michael Gaydos, *Alias: The Secret Origins of Jessica Jones* (New York: Marvel Comics, 2004), 51.

32. Bendis and Gaydos, *Alias*, 81.

33. Although Bendis gives the readers twelve issues to settle into the relative realism of Gaydos's noir style, the overlapping of artistic styles is already suggested in a subtle way with mixed-media covers by David Mack.

34. Bendis and Gaydos, *Alias: The Secret Origins* , 78.

35. Ibid., 117.

36. Ibid., 143.

37. Linda Hutcheon, *The Politics of Postmodernism* (New York: Routledge, 1989), 101.

38. Bendis and Gaydos, *Alias: The Secret Origins*, 167.

39. Brian Michael Bendis, "A Few Words from Bendis . . ." *Alias* 28, Marvel (January 2004), 30.

40. John Parker makes this argument about the *Pulse* in his retrospective review of *Alias*: "The adults only world is where she truly belonged . . . [L]osing the ability to curse shaves off some of that reality—not to mention the ability to smoke, drink, and do other things that pregnant women should probably avoid. But it turns out that in the case of Jessica Jones, all that stuff actually mattered. *Alias* is dark, grimy, and damaged, and that's absolutely integral to its impact" ("'Alias' Jessica Jones").

41. Bendis and Gaydos produced another *Alias* story for *Marvel's 75th Anniversary Celebration*, but the case she works is a surprisingly nostalgic exploration of Marvel's superhero past (Brian Michael Bendis and Michael Gaydos, "Alias," *Marvel 75th Anniversary Celebration* 1, Marvel (December 2014): 27–35). More recently Bendis and Mack produced *Marvel's Jessica Jones*, an "exclusive preview" to Netflix's *Jessica Jones*, that served as a fairly simple advertisement for both *Daredevil* and *Jessica Jones* (Brian Michael Bendis and David Mack, *Marvel's Jessica Jones* 1, *Marvel Unlimited*, last modified September 14, 2015, http://read.marvel.com/#/book/40226).

42. Along these lines, the relationship she has with Luke Cage is tied to the larger plot and simplified. Cage's wife had information sought by Killgrave, and Killgrave ordered Jones to kill Cage's wife. Consequently, the primary conflict in their relationship became what Killgrave ordered her to do.

43. Bendis and Gaydos, *Alias: The Secret Origins*, 166–67.

Bibliography

Bendis, Brian Michael. "A Few Words from Bendis . . ." *Alias* #28. Marvel. January 2004: 30.
———. *Goldfish*. Orange, CA: Image Comics, 2001.
———. *Jinx*. Orange, CA: Image Comics, 2001.
Bendis, Brian Michael, and Oliver Coipel. "Happily Ever After." *New Avengers Annual* 1. *The Pulse: Fear*. 95–134. New York: Marvel Comics, 2006.
Bendis, Brian Michael, and Michael Gaydos. *Alias*. New York: Marvel Comics, 2003.
———. "Alias." *Marvel 75th Anniversary Celebration* 1. Marvel. December 2014: 27–35.
———. *Alias: Come Home*. New York: Marvel Comics, 2004.
———. *Alias: The Secret Origins of Jessica Jones*. New York: Marvel Comics, 2004.
———. *Alias: The Underneath*. New York: Marvel Comics, 2003.
Bendis, Brian Michael, and David Mack. *Marvel's Jessica Jones*. *Marvel Unlimited*. Last modified September 14, 2015. http://read.marvel.com/#/book/40226.
Blumberg, Arnold T. "AKA Bendis," interview with Brian Bendis, *Jinxworld*. Last modified September 4, 2001. http://www.jinxworld.com/interviews/cinescape/cinescape08-04-01.htm.
Coles, Nicholas, and Janet Zandy. "Introduction." *American Working Class Literature: An Anthology*, edited by Nicholas Coles and Janet Zandy, xix–xxix. New York: Oxford University Press, 2007.

Dean, Michael. "The Brian Michael Bendis Interview." *Comics Journal* 266 (Feb./Mar. 2005): 95–134.

Doane, Mary Ann. *Femmes Fatales*. New York: Routledge, 1991.

Englehart, Steve, and George Tuska. "Crescendo!" *Luke Cage, Hero for Hire 8*. *Luke Cage, Power Man: Essentials, Vol. 1*, 154–174. New York: Marvel Comics, 2005.

———. "Where Angels Fear to Tread!" *Luke Cage, Hero for Hire 9*. *Luke Cage, Power Man: Essentials, Vol. 1*, 175–195. New York: Marvel Comics, 2005.

George, Milo. *Frank Miller: The Interviews: 1981–2003*. Seattle: Fantagraphics, 2003.

Hutcheon, Linda. *The Politics of Postmodernism*. New York: Routledge, 1989.

Jessica Jones. Netflix, November 15, 2015.

Miller, Frank. *Daredevil: Visionaries, Vol. 2*. New York: Marvel Comics, 2002.

Mondello, Salvatore. "Spider-Man: Superhero in the Liberal Tradition." *Journal of Popular Culture* 10 (Summer 1976): 232–38.

Morton, Paul. "An Interview with Brian Michael Bendis." *Bookslut*. Last modified February 2009. http://www.bookslut.com/features/2009_02_014023.php.

Mulvey, Laura. "Visual Pleasures and Narrative Cinema." *Feminism and Film Theory*, edited by Constance Penley, 57–68. New York: Routledge, 1988.

Parker, John. "'Alias' Jessica Jones: A Critical Look Back at Marvel's Mature Readers Hero and New Netflix Star." *Comics Alliance*. Last modified November 5, 2014. http://comicsalliance.com/alias-omnibus-review/.

Silver, Alain, and Elizabeth Ward. *Film Noir*. New York: Overlook, 1992.

Smith, Erin A. *Hard-Boiled: Working Class Readers and Pulp Magazines*. Philadelphia: Temple University Press, 2000.

Wright, Bradford W. *Comic Book Nation: The Transformation of Youth Culture in America*. Baltimore: Johns Hopkins University Press, 2001.

ABOUT THE CONTRIBUTORS

Phil Bevin is an independent scholar specializing in narrative in popular culture. He has a PhD in Film and Television Studies from Kingston University, London, and his publications include *Superman and Comic Book Brand Continuity* (2018) and contributions to anthologies *The Many More Lives of the Batman* (2015) and *Web-Spinning Heroics: Critical Essays on the History and Meaning of Spider-Man* (2012). He has also contributed to the comics studies website *Sequart*.

Blair Davis is an Associate Professor of Media and Cinema Studies in the College of Communication at DePaul University in Chicago. A Member at Large of the Comics Studies Society editorial board, his books include *The Battle for the Bs: 1950s Hollywood and the Rebirth of Low-Budget Cinema* (2012) and *Movie Comics: Page to Screen/Screen to Page* (2017), and he has essays included in numerous anthologies, most recently the Eisner Award–winning anthology *The Blacker the Ink: African Americans and Comic Books, Graphic Novels and Sequential Art* (2015). He is Co-chair of the Comics Studies Scholarly Interest Group with the Society for Cinema and Media Studies, and the editor of an "In Focus" section for a 2017 issue of *Cinema Journal* on the graphic novel *Watchmen*, and moderator of a roundtable on comics and methodology for the debut issue of the journal *Inks: The Journal of the Comics Studies Society*.

Michele Fazio is Associate Professor of English at the University of North Carolina at Pembroke and teaches courses on American literature, contemporary US ethnic literature, service-learning, and working-class studies. She was awarded a Massachusetts Historical Society Fellowship to conduct research on her book project examining the cultural legacy of Sacco and Vanzetti and is coediting *The Routledge International Handbook of Working-Class Studies* (forthcoming). Her documentary film, *Voices of the Lumbee*, received the Studs Terkel Award for Media and Journalism and the North Carolina Folklore

Society Brown-Hudson Award. She received her PhD in English from Stony Brook University and currently serves as president of the Working-Class Studies Association.

James Gifford is Associate Professor of English and Director of the University Core at Fairleigh Dickinson University. His book *Personal Modernisms* recuperated Late Modernist anarchist literary networks of the 1940s, and he publishes widely on Modernism and Postcolonial literatures. He edited *The Henry Miller–Herbert Read Letters: 1935–58*, three editions of Lawrence Durrell's work, Oscar Wilde's 1890 *Picture of Dorian Gray*, and the special issue *Archives & Networks of Modernism*.

Kelly Kanayama is a comics scholar and critic born and raised in Hawaii but now living in Scotland. She is pursuing a PhD in comics studies at the University of Dundee and is currently writing a book on the comics of Garth Ennis. Her work has been published in the Eisner Award–nominated anthology of comics criticism *Critical Chips* and by *Nerdist, Independent, Bitch Media, Media Diversified*, and the Eisner-nominated site *Women Write about Comics*, among others.

Orion Ussner Kidder teaches at Columbia College in Vancouver, Canada. His work combines cultural studies and formalism to locate comics within artistic and social conditions. His most recent published work, "Everybody's Here": Radical Reflexivity in the Metafiction of *The Sandman* examines a singular moment in which fiction and reality collapse in Neil Gaiman's most famous work.

Christina M. Knopf is Assistant Professor in the Communication Studies Department at SUNY Cortland. She is the author of *The Comic Art of War: A Critical Study of Military Cartoons, 1805–2014, with a Guide to Artists* (2015). She also has articles appearing in several journals and anthologies, including *The 10 Cent War: Comic Books, Propaganda, and World War II* (2017), *The Laughing Dead: The Comedy-Horror Film from* Bride of Frankenstein *to* Zombieland (2016), *The X-Men Films: A Cultural Analysis* (2016), and *Horrors of War: The Undead on the Battlefield* (2015). She has a PhD in communication and sociology from the University at Albany, SUNY.

Kevin Michael Scott is associate professor of English at Albany State University. His research covers nineteenth-century literature and culture and American popular culture. His coauthored book, *The Porning of America*, was published by Beacon Press in 2008, and he has an edited anthology dedicated to the Marvel Comics event, *Civil War*, forthcoming from McFarland Publishing.

Andrew Alan Smith learned to read from his older brother's *Fantastic Four* comics in the early 1960s and, like Ben Grimm, never forgot where he came from. A thirty-three-year newspaper veteran, Smith has also toiled in the vineyards of comics journalism and commentary as a syndicated newspaper columnist on comics, Webmaster of *Captain Comics Round Table*, Contributing Editor at *Comics Buyer's Guide* magazine, and a contributor to such books as *Web-Spinning Heroics* (McFarland & Co., 2012) and *What Is a Superhero?* (Oxford University Press, 2013).

Terrence R. Wandtke is Director of the Film & Media program at Judson University, where he also directs the Imago Film Festival. As a professor, he teaches literature, film, and graphic novels, making connections between old media and new. And as a scholar, he writes about comic books and movies, examining the way culture is shaped by the intersection of word and image. His books include *The Dark Night Returns: The Contemporary Resurgence of Crime Comics* (RIT, 2015) and *The Meaning of Superhero Comics* (McFarland, 2012), and his edited collections include *Ed Brubaker: Conversations* (University Press of Mississippi, 2016) and *The Amazing Transforming Superhero: Essays on the Revision of Character in Comic Books, Film, and Television* (McFarland, 2007). His articles have appeared in several anthologies and journals, most recently in *Critical Insights: The Graphic Novel* (Salem, 2014).

INDEX

Printed in Great Britain
by Amazon